17: PERSPECTIVES IN CRITICISM

PERSPECTIVES IN CRITICISM

1: *Elements of Critical Theory*

2: *The Disinherited of Art*

3: *Stream of Consciousness in the Modern Novel*

4: *The Poet in the Poem*

5: *Arthurian Triptych*

6: *The Brazilian Othello of Machado de Assis*

7: *The World of Jean Anouilh*

8: *A New Approach to Joyce*

9: *The Idea of Coleridge's Criticism*

10: *Introduction to the Psychoanalysis of Mallarmé*

11: *This Dark Estate: A Reading of Pope*

12: *The Confucian Odes of Ezra Pound*

13: *The Religious Sonnets of Dylan Thomas*

14: *Interpretations in Shakespeare's Sonnets*

15: *Tennyson's* Maud: *The Biographical Genesis*

16: *Joyce's Benefictions*

17: *James Thomson (B.V.): Beyond "The City"*

17:

WILLIAM DAVID SCHAEFER

James Thomson (B.V.): Beyond "The City"

UNIVERSITY OF CALIFORNIA PRESS
Berkeley and Los Angeles
1965

University of California Press
Berkeley and Los Angeles, California
Cambridge University Press
London, England

LIBRARY OF CONGRESS CATALOG CARD NO. 65-23462
Printed in the United States of America

Preface

IN THE GENERAL CATALOGUE at the British Museum, the troublesome problem of distinguishing between the eighteenth- and nineteenth-century James Thomsons has been solved by referring to the former as "James Thomson, the poet," and to the latter as "James Thomson, author of The City of Dreadful Night." The distinction is significant, for, although "The City of Dreadful Night" is a famous poem, one that has received and continues to receive a considerable amount of critical attention, there are probably very few scholars who, at least today, could discuss, or perhaps even mention, a second work by its author. In recent years, moreover, as much and as often as reference is made to "The City," remarkably few critics pretend that Thomson's masterpiece, much less his other verse, is, as poetry, worth serious consideration. R. A. Foakes, for instance, although he devotes an entire chapter to the poem in his 1958 study, *The Romantic Assertion,* and feels that Thomson's "vision" was "more true and valuable than that of the other poets of his time," considers the poem itself to be an uneven work, of great power only because the crude rhetoric is sustained by the themes and the imagery. Hoxie N. Fairchild, likewise devoting a chapter to Thomson in his 1957 volume of *Religious Trends in English Poetry,* also notes that the poem is "powerful," but adds that it is "lengthy, repetitive, and awkwardly constructed." John Heath-Stubbs's 1950 *The Darkling Plain* seems to contain the strongest praise, but even here the critic is noticeably cautious, for he says only that the poem "approaches, in my opinion, near to being great poetry." It would seem, then, that the poem lives today (and James Thomson with it), not as great poetry, but as something else—a document in ideas, perhaps, the classic statement of a pessimist's creed, a convenient touchstone for gaining insight into an intellectual trend of the Victorian Age. And yet, in spite of this, no attempt has been made to go beyond "The City," to consider Thomson as an intellectual, or to trace the development of the ideas that led to the pessimism of his acknowledged masterpiece. His prose writings, which greatly exceed his poetry in volume (and possibly in quality also), are virtually unknown. Although recognized as a minor, if a not particularly good, poet, he is almost completely ignored as a journalist, a reviewer, an essayist, a translator, a scholar, and a literary critic. Most students of Victorian literature recall that he was an alcoholic who supposedly drank himself into an early grave while grieving over the death of his young love, but few realize that when "Whitman" was a dirty word to most Englishmen, Thomson was writing vigorous essays in his defense; that at a time when Meredith's novels were ignored or ridiculed, Thomson was publishing reviews that acclaimed him "the Robert Browning of our novelists." "The City of Dreadful Night" has been discussed in terms of Leopardi, Heine, Shelley, and Blake, but Thomson's translations of Leopardi and Heine are seldom read, the laborious notes he made on Shelley remain hidden, and forgotten, in the footnotes of William Michael Rossetti's early editions, and his essay in praise of Blake, published a year before Swinburne's study, does not even appear in most Blake bibliographies. Historians of the period recall that he was a close friend of the atheist reformer, Charles

Bradlaugh, but only a handful are aware that Thomson wrote a weekly column commenting on reform, education, the government, the international situation, and, to be sure, religion. His blasphemous anti-Christian satires are, in fact, the only part of his prose writings of which most scholars are aware, and few realize that when Arnold first initiated his attacks against the Philistines, Thomson was publishing a series of essays containing equally outraged assaults against the middle classes. Although he is remembered as a pessimistic atheist, his position as an intellectual moralist, which, to Thomson at least, was far more significant, is almost completely unknown today.

This study, then, is an attempt to come to terms with the mind of the man who has been called, with questionable validity, "the English Leopardi." I have traced Thomson's intellectual development under three main headings. First, I have treated his ideas on religion, for his intellectual castles, whatever strange shapes they might have taken, were largely based upon his views on the relationship between man and God. Second, I have treated his ideas on social, economic, and political problems, his views on man in relation to his fellowman. Finally, I have traced the development of his attitude toward poetry and literary criticism, for it was, of course, as poet and critic that he attempted to propagate his ideas on God and man. For the most part, the Thomson who emerges from this study is radically different from the Thomson portrayed in earlier biographical and critical studies, for, in addition to the obvious primary and secondary sources, I have drawn upon a good deal of material that has not been utilized in the past. In searching through more than a thousand issues of the "disreputable" (and now extremely rare) secularist periodicals, I have been fortunate in discovering a good many articles on and by Thomson which have not been previously noted, including several important essays that were apparently unknown to even his literary executor and bibliographer. Equally important, I have worked closely with the unpublished and largely unexplored manuscript material in Oxford and London, which has enabled me not only to shed new light on his intellectual position and his life, but, as Thomson carefully dated virtually every word he wrote, to present my analysis chronologically with stronger conviction than one can usually bring to such a "development" study.

Although numerous critics have seen fit to comment on Thomson's life and work, it is worth asking why such an approach has never been taken, why his intellectual development has never been considered worthy of close examination. The answer, I believe, lies in what might be described as the biographical trap, a seemingly unavoidable propensity on the part of his critics to intermingle, and thus thoroughly confuse, his personal unhappiness with his intellectual position as an atheist and a pessimist. No one who has yet written about Thomson seems to have escaped unharmed on this point, for inevitably his intellectual position is explained, in large part if not entirely, not by analyzing his ideas, but by piecing together a few sordid fragments from his biography, or, even worse, from his poetry, and thus concluding that his pessimism was mainly the result of a lifelong gloom. Although it should be obvious that an extremely unhappy man can evolve an optimistic philosophy, and that a man whose personal life is filled with good fortune can still believe that life is meaningless, progress impossible, and the prognosis for mankind's future bleak, Thomson's unhappiness has so often been blindly cited as the cause of his pessimism that I am convinced that if he is to be seriously considered, not as a case history, but as an intellectual whose philosophy was evolved through an honest evaluation of God and man, it is essential that my analysis begin with a clarification of the nature and the degree of his unhappiness. My first chapter, therefore, attempts to clear the ground for a study of Thomson's intellectual development by adjusting the focus on our presently blurred image of "The Man."

I should like to acknowledge my indebtedness to the Fulbright Commission for a grant that enabled me to complete this study in England. I am grateful for the cooperation of the staffs at the Pierpont Morgan, Newberry, Bodleian, and British Museum libraries, and to the library staffs at the University of Wisconsin and the University of London. I am particularly indebted to Mr. R. J. Dobell, grandson of Thomson's close friend, Bertram Dobell, for his advice and assistance in helping me to locate manuscript material, and to Mr. Hector Hawton, managing director of the Rationalist Press Association, Ltd., for permission to examine manuscript material in his possession and to use the invaluable facilities of the RPA library in London. Finally, I should like to express my sincere appreciation for advice and encouragement given generously by Alvin Whitley of the University of Wisconsin, by Carl Woodring of Columbia University, and, especially, by Kathleen Tillotson and her colleagues at London's Bedford College.

W. D. S.

Contents

Chronological Table of James Thomson's Life

1834	Born November 23 at Port Glasgow, Scotland, first child of James Thomson and Sarah Kennedy Thomson; father a sailor in the merchant service; mother a devoutly religious woman, a follower of Edward Irving.
1840	Father suffers a paralytic stroke while at sea.
1842	Family living in East London. A second son, John, born February 4. Thomson admitted to Royal Caledonian Asylum, a school for children of poor Scottish soldiers and sailors. Mother dies in December; Thomson's infant brother sent to Glasgow in care of his aunt.
1842–1850	Thomson in school at Royal Caledonian Asylum. Spends holidays in London with the William Gray family, growing up with the two daughters, Helen and Agnes.
1850	Enters Royal Military Asylum, Chelsea, on August 2 to train as an army schoolmaster. Meets George Duncan, lifelong friend and correspondent. Continues visits to the Grays during holidays.

1851–1852 Completes first phase of his training and on August 5 is sent to Ballincollig, Ireland, for eighteen months of training as a teacher's assistant. Lives with the garrison schoolmaster and his wife, Joseph and Alice Barnes. Meets Charles Bradlaugh, then serving as a private in the army. Meets Matilda Weller, the 12- or 13-year-old daughter of the regiment's armourer-sergeant. Earliest extant poems in 1852.

1853 Leaves Ballincollig, returning to Royal Military Asylum in Chelsea to complete formal training. Father dies; Matilda Weller, age 14–15, dies in Ireland.

1854–1855 Enlists as an army schoolmaster on August 7. Sent to Plymouth with the South Devon Militia Regiment. In 1855 transferred to Aldershot with the Rifle Brigade. Continues friendship with the Grays and the Duncans; corresponds with Bradlaugh.

1856–1860 Transferred to Ireland; attached to the 55th Foot in Dublin and Curragh Camp. Meets John Grant, another army schoolmaster, lifelong friend. Writes numerous poems. Earliest publications in *Tait's Edinburgh Magazine* and *London Investigator*. First uses pseudonym "B.V." Earliest tendencies toward alcoholism.

1860–1861 Transferred from Ireland to Aldershot, later to Jersey. Continues to write and publish. First contribution to Bradlaugh's *National Reformer.*

1862 Regiment sent to Portsmouth in May. From September 18 to 28 Thomson is placed in confinement at Portsmouth, then is reduced to schoolmaster 4th class. Discharged from army on October 30, probably because of alcoholism. In November

	moves to London, living with the Bradlaughs. Contributes eight pieces to *National Reformer.*
1863	Through Bradlaugh (with whom he continues to live), Thomson is employed as secretary of the Polish Committee. Alcoholism makes him an unreliable employee.
1864–1865	Moves with the Bradlaughs to their new home in Tottenham. Publishes two pieces in *Daily Telegraph.* Begins working for Naples Colour Company, a paint company in which Bradlaugh had an interest, probably Thomson's main source of income for next five years. Begins to write poetry again, including "Vane's Story," "Sunday up the River," and "Sunday at Hampstead."
1866–1868	Moves out of Bradlaugh's home, taking the first of many rooms in the Pimlico district. Frequent contributor to *National Reformer* —poems, essays, and translations. Writes "In the Room"; begins "Weddah and Om-el-Bonain."
1869	Completes "Weddah" and unsuccessfully attempts to publish it in the "respectable journals." "Sunday up the River" appears in *Fraser's Magazine;* has breakfast with Froude. Publications in *National Reformer* limited to translations and a biography of Leopardi. On November 4, shortly before his thirty-fifth birthday, burns most of his papers, manuscripts, and letters.
1870–1871	Bradlaugh gives up the paint business; Thomson works as secretary for three different companies. Again publishes frequently in *National Reformer*, including "Weddah." Writes half of "The City of Dreadful Night."

1872	William Michael Rossetti writes Thomson, praising "Weddah"; correspondence begins. On April 27 leaves London for America, as secretary of the Champion Gold and Silver Mines Company. From May 15 through December 28 in Central City, Colorado. When mining venture fails, is recalled to London.
1873	Arrives in London in January, again taking a room in Pimlico. Through Bradlaugh's aid is hired by the *New York World* to cover the Carlist Revolution in Spain. In Spain July 22 through September 23. Before departure for Spain, begins work again on "The City of Dreadful Night." Completes "The City" in October, immediately after his return to London.
1874	Working full time as a staff writer on *National Reformer*. "The City" published in *National Reformer* (March 22 through May 17), receiving a favorable notice in the *Academy*, a hostile review in the *Spectator*. Sends copies of "The City" to Carlyle and George Eliot, receiving an encouraging reply from the latter. Friendship begins with Bertram Dobell.
1875	Between January and June, publishes eleven essays in *National Reformer*. In June argues with Bradlaugh and the friendship is broken. Thomson never again publishes in *National Reformer*. Publishes first essay in *Cope's Tobacco Plant*, his main source of income for next five years.
1876–1880	Publishes in almost every issue of *Cope's*. Work also appears in secularist periodicals, the *Liberal* and the *Secularist*. Friendship with G. W. Foote and Phillip Bourke Mars-

ton, the blind poet. Begins correspondence with George Meredith.

1880 In April, largely through the persistent endeavors of Bertram Dobell, Thomson's first volume of poetry appears, *The City of Dreadful Night and Other Poems.* Reviews generally favorable; Thomson has first meeting with Meredith on April 29. In October a second volume of poems is published, *Vane's Story, Weddah and Om-el-Bonain, and Other Poems.*

1881 Continues friendship with secularists, particularly John Barrs. Becomes romantically attached to Barrs's sister, Harriet, spending two happy months with them in their country home, Forest Edge, near Leicester. Alcoholism increasing. Writes a few new poems, revises and completes old poems in an attempt to bring out a third volume of poetry. In April publishes *Essays and Phantasies.* Work appears in *Fortnightly Review, Gentleman's Magazine,* and *Athenaeum.* Furnivall asks him to become a charter member of the Browning Society.

1882 Poems published in *Weekly Dispatch, Cornhill Magazine.* Spends February through April at Forest Edge with the Barrs, ending with Thomson insanely drunk. Alcohol craving almost constant. Spends two weeks in jail in May. On June 1 collapses in home of Phillip Marston. Dies from intestinal hemorrhage in the hospital at University College on June 3. Buried in grave of Austin Holyoake at Highgate Cemetery on June 8.

1

The Man

THOMSON has not suffered from want of willing biographers. The first of many memoirs written by his friends appeared within three weeks of his death; seven years later the first full-length biography was published; in the past half century, in addition to numerous shorter articles, at least five other long studies, mainly biographical in nature, have been written by scholars on both sides of the Atlantic. Thomson's life, in fact, has received considerably more attention than his poetry, which may or may not reflect on the quality of his verse, but certainly attests to the fact that his biography is an intriguing one. John Addington Symonds seems to have summed up the attraction for many later critics when he wrote that "there is something incalculable, sphinx-like, daemonic in Thomson, to one who never heard his voice or touched his hand," and there is indeed, sphinxes and demons notwithstanding, an element of mystery in Thomson's life. The mystery, however, has largely been manufactured, and Thomson would probably have reacted to Symonds' statement as he did when, in a "saintly passion," he once accused himself of being the chief of sinners:

> Then stooped my guardian angel
> And whispered from behind,
> "Vanity, my little man,
> You're nothing of the kind."

It has generally been assumed that the author of "The

City of Dreadful Night" was, by nature, a gloomy man, and that his lifelong gloom was responsible for, or at least significantly contributed to, his pessimistic philosophy. Because of this unfortunate impression, it seems best to begin a clarification of the "mystery" in Thomson's life by noting that his most intimate friends were unanimous in describing him, not as gloomy, but as charming, pleasant, merry, witty, and thoroughly agreeable. The headmaster during his school days reported that he was one of the cleverest and most amiable of companions; a close friend of his boyhood and early years recalled him as being "of a lovable and genial disposition, anything but pessimistic," one who laughed "at 'old Schopenhauer' and was the merriest companion possible"; Hypatia Bradlaugh, who knew him best in his middle years, 1860–1870, described him as a "genial, merry friend and companion"; his sister-in-law thought him "genial and happy and funny"; the wife of his close friend, George Duncan, regarded him as a man with a "great fund of humour who could say witty things." William Michael Rossetti, Thomson's friend and correspondent during the last decade of his life, reported that he "never saw him out of temper, vehement, or noticeably gloomy," and G. W. Foote, who knew Thomson intimately during the same period, wrote that "he was little of a cynic and less of a misanthrope," that his pessimism, which was "not a mood, but a philosophy," could not be inferred from his ordinary conversation. Even Bertram Dobell, his friend and publisher and author of one of the gloomiest of all the many gloomy portraits of Thomson, admitted that "a man could hardly wish for a better companion; while as regards women there was a charm about him which invariably made them his friends and admirers." One such woman, Harriet Barrs, recalled his extraordinary charm of manner, his vivacity, wealth of conversation, and perfect ease in society, while her brother, who was perhaps Thomson's closest friend in the last year of his life, questioned "if any friend ever knew him in any mood representing the City of Dreadful Night":

> Whatever has been said or written of his charm of manner and conversation has not and cannot give a just representation of them. Few men have known so delightful a friend, and his hilarity could equal his sombreness when in congenial company —one could hardly say more to anyone who knows "The City."

Finally, Henry S. Salt, who, without personally knowing Thomson, wrote the earliest full-length biography, had to conclude after interviewing Thomson's friends that he had

> impressed all those who knew him intimately, and many who only knew him in part, as not only the most brilliantly gifted, but the noblest, gentlest, most lovable man with whom they had ever come in contact. The charm of his manner and conversation is attested by the united record of many independent witnesses—there was a grace, a glamour, an attractiveness about his personality which has been possessed in equal measure by few poets of his century.[1]

This was the Thomson his friends actually knew—noble, gentle, lovable; and yet some of the same friends who most emphatically admitted that this was the "real" Thomson are chiefly responsible for perpetuating an image of him as an incurable melancholic. Foote, for instance, who asserted that his pessimism was not a mood but a philosophy, also claimed that the "secret of Thomson's life-tragedy" was that he "suffered from constitutional melancholia," and Dobell, who admitted that a man could hardly wish for a better companion, repeatedly insisted that his life had been "hopeless and joyless," that "his was rather a death-in-life than a healthy and natural existence." [2] In attempting to solve this dilemma, Salt, when writing his influential biography, apparently decided to shrug off everything "that may seem incongruous and contradictory" in Thomson's life by suggesting that "his nature was a compound of two diverse and warring elements—a light-hearted gaiety and rich sensuous capacity for enjoyment being set side by side with a constitutional and ever-deepening melancholia." [3] This solution, is, however, an absurd one, for, although we have abundant testimony to Thomson's "light-hearted gaiety," no one who knew him was able to report a significant instance of his "ever-deepening melancholy." Obviously Thomson had, like all men, his unhappy moments, and indeed, more than most men, he had a good deal to be unhappy about, but, although suffering was definitely a part of his experience, "melancholia," no matter what psychiatric twists we care to give the word, was simply not a part of his nature. To suggest, then, that the man described in the above quotations had a "hopeless and joyless" existence or suffered from "constitutional melancholia" is to ignore overwhelming evidence to the contrary and assume that because he was, at the end of his life, a pessimist, because he had great cause for unhappiness, and—most damning of all—because he wrote some of the gloomiest poetry in the English language, he must necessarily have been a gloomy man.

Poems like "The City of Dreadful Night," "In the Room," and "Insomnia" are, no doubt, largely responsible for the belief that Thomson suffered from lifelong gloom, and, after first reading such poems, it is admittedly tempting to conclude that their author could not have been the most cheerful of men. Although we may legitimately, if not always profitably, examine a man's poetry for internal evidence in support of a biographical fact previously established, or at least strongly suggested, by external evidence, we are, however, on dangerous ground when we reverse the process and assume biography solely on our reading of a man's poetry, particularly when the external evidence negates the implications in that poetry. Thomson's poems may, and at times undoubtedly do, reflect certain experiences and moods in his life, but it does not follow that the poems reveal the "real" James Thomson. Fortunately, no one has ever suggested that his "happy" poems reflect his true nature, or reveal lifelong jollity, although roughly half of his work consists of joyous outbursts in line with his plea to

> Let my voice ring out and over the earth,
> Through all the grief and strife,
> With a golden joy in a silver mirth:
> Thank God for Life! [4]

Yet for almost a century, critics, who would ridicule the idea that such a passage be considered a thermometer with which to measure the degree of happiness in Thomson's life, have misunderstood the nature and extent of his unhappiness through assuming that the gloomy passages in his poetry are chapters in his autobiography, expressions of the innermost reality of his thoroughly miserable being.

Unfortunately, Thomson himself did little to discourage this misunderstanding, for he took great delight in expressing what he once called "the nightside of nature." Indeed, at one time he held the theory that "genuine, thoughtful, and earnest literature, literature as an end in and for itself," was the refuge of the unhappy artist, and for this reason he felt that "the nightside of nature has been the theme of literature more often than the dayside." [5] He also shrewdly realized that, although half of his work was written at high noon, his best poems were "nightside," for he felt, as he expressed it in a sonnet written while still in his twenties, that while striving to "sing glad songs" he attained only "wild discords":

> My mirth can laugh and talk, but can-
> not sing;
> My grief finds harmonies in everything.

He wrote, moreover, some half-dozen poems, several unpublished, which certainly appear to be autobiographical from beginning to end, and seem to demand explanation in terms of biography. "The City of Dreadful Night" can, no doubt, be profitably discussed without recourse to his life, but it is not easy to come to terms with a poem like the unpublished "I Had a Love"—particularly when the manuscript copy contains the notation "more truth than poetry"—without reading it as autobiographical. Perhaps, then, biographers who have read Thomson's works before writing his life—and what biographer would do otherwise?—can be forgiven for approaching their subject with the preconceived notion that he was unhappy. One is less sympathetic with biographers when they perpetuate such notions without investigating the nature and extent of his unhappiness, or assume that such unhappiness was necessarily the cause of his pessimistic philosophy.

Admitting, then, that the "constitutional melancholia" theories are, at best, extremely unlikely, one is still forced to come to terms with several other "unhappiness" explanations for Thomson's intellectual position, explanations proposed not only by those who wish to deny any philosophical basis for religious beliefs they find repugnant, but also by those who, although basically in agreement with Thomson's conclusions that the universe is godless, do not believe that atheism must lead to pessimism, and prefer that this uncomforting aspect of Thomson's thought be blamed on emotional instability. Perhaps the least satisfactory of these explanations, one that caused a minor flurry of excitement among critics and reviewers shortly after Thomson's death, is the idea that his pessimism resulted from failure to attain success as a poet. Thomson did desire fame, or at least recognition, fully as much as any writer, and, although his secularist friends were willing to publish anything submitted to them by "B.V.," until the last years of his life he struggled in vain to publish his poetry in what he called the "respectable" periodicals. The notations he carefully recorded at the bottom of his manuscript copy of the long narrative poem, "Weddah and Om-el-Bonain," tell their own story.[6]

Sent to Fortnightly Review (with stamps for return if rejected)	—	Tuesday	6/ 7/69
returned	—	Thursday	8/ 7/69
Sent to St. Paul's Magazine	—	Friday	9/ 7/69
returned	—	Monday	26/ 7/69
Sent to Macmillan's	—	Monday	2/ 8/69
returned, after 3 letters for it	—		14/12/69
Sent to Fraser's	—		15/12/69
returned	—		21/12/69
Sent to Cornhill	—	Thursday	14/ 4/70
returned	—	Saturday	7/ 5/70

Finally, scrawled in the margin is the simple notation:

N.R. Nov. Dec. Jany. 1871–2

As a last resort Thomson had again been forced to publish his poem in Bradlaugh's *National Reformer,* the free-thought periodical whose readers, he felt, "care little or nothing for poetry or any other art; care, in fact, nothing for literature as literature, but only as a club to hit parsons and lords on the head with." [7]

Probably, as Thomson suggested, most *National Reformer* readers did care little or nothing for poetry or any other art, but, unlike a good many far greater poets we might name, Thomson found a ready and willing market in the secularist periodicals for any scrap he might choose to publish. Moreover, through publication in such journals, he did manage to obtain considerable recognition as a poet, not just from those few *National Reformer* readers, such as Bertram Dobell, who considered poetry to be something more than a parson-hitting club, but from literary giants such as George Eliot, the Rossettis, Swinburne, and Meredith. Nor was recognition confined to "The City"; Swinburne read the now-forgotten "Weddah and Om-el-Bonain" in the "same breathless way one reads in early boyhood, and with the same sense of passionate absorption," writing at once to Rossetti that the then anonymous poet "beats us hollow all round at forthright, tragic narrative." Meredith was even more emphatic; he called "Weddah" simply "the finest narrative poem we have," a not surprising comment when we note his remarks after reading the first volume of Thomson's collected poetry:

> I have gone through your volume, and partly a second time, and I have not found the line I would propose to recast. I have found many pages that no other English poet could have written. Nowhere is the verse feeble, nowhere is the expression insufficient; the majesty of the line has always its full colouring, and marches under a banner. And you accomplish this effect with the utmost sobriety, with absolute self-mastery.[8]

Thomson's two volumes of poetry received, in fact, surprisingly good notices, and when we consider that for the last ten years of his life his living was earned entirely through his writing, we cannot explain either his unhappiness or his pessimism, especially as expressed in late poems like "Insomnia," by asking "what porridge had James Thomson?" In the last years of his life his poetry was appearing in the *Cornhill* and the *Fortnightly;* his Shelley study had been published in the *Athenaeum;* his article on Browning's "The Ring and the Book" had come out in the *Gentleman's Magazine;* Furnivall had made him a charter member of the Browning Society and had invited him to deliver one of the first papers; and, at the same time, the fourth volume of his works to be published within an eighteen-month span was in preparation. It seems most unlikely, then, that literary failure seriously contributed either to his misery or to his pessimism, and we are forced to look elsewhere for the source of Thomson's unhappiness; in so doing, we need not look far before coming face to face with Matilda Weller and the idea that Thomson's disenchantment resulted from the death of his only love.

A recent and widely used anthology of Victorian

poetry succinctly states the case as it is known today: "During his army service in Ireland he fell tragically in love with a young girl named Matilda Weller, whose early death shadowed his whole philosophy." [9] When compared with other statements on the importance of the affair, this brief summary is really rather conservative; although it is undeniable that the death of this girl was an event of some interest in Thomson's life, it has proved of far greater interest to his biographers than it ever did to Thomson. I see nothing to gain by compiling a list of twentieth-century contributions to the Matilda Weller legend (the most recent being a suggestion that her death provided him with "a medium for the release of hitherto unfocused neurotic feelings," and that he used her "as a loveless way of being in love"),[10] but I might note that even the best of Thomson's biographers [11] became so obsessed with the legend that he suggested a relationship between the year of Matilda Weller's death, 1853, and the number of stanzas in "The City"—188 stanzas, if one ignores the proem and includes the stanza in Section XIV which Thomson added years after the poem was first published. It is nonsense such as this which justifies a close examination of the legend, for no one factor in Thomson's life has caused so much attention, and, I believe, done so much harm in distorting the truth about his unhappiness, as the stories about his grief over the girl who died so young.

The legend can best be understood by tracing its development step by step as it appears in the early biographical sketches. Indeed, the published memoirs written by Thomson's friends within the first decade after his death are really all we have to go on, for Thomson himself made no direct reference to this romance in any of his letters, diaries, journals, and notebooks, nor, for that matter, in conversation with his closest friends. The earliest record appears, therefore, almost thirty years after Matilda's death in a brief but extremely important memoir written, just three weeks after Thomson died, by his close friend, G. G. Flaws.[12] Flaws claimed that when Thomson was still a young man, his faith in Christianity had faded and was slowly being replaced by the "life-giving influence of love":

> . . . then came the dread stroke that so smote his heart as to send it reeling to the grave through all the twenty and more years that prolonged his grief. The girl he loved with a wondrous love died, and the light of his life went out for ever. Died? No, let me rather say she henceforth became the one animating influence, the sole companion, the living shadow of the poor heart that agonised for the desolation it knew. It knew, but no other outside creature was ever to share the knowledge as a thing of common talk. His future life was one great loneliness, relieved by communings with the now idealised object when in the sacred solitude in which he allowed himself the relief of committing his thought to paper. The falling of this crowning calamity when it did, at about his twenty-third year, . . . can well be taken as the turning point of his mind's life.

Flaws had not met Thomson until at least twenty years after Matilda Weller's death, and there is no indication in his memoir that he even knew the girl's name, but perhaps the most interesting aspect of his comment is the implication that Thomson had never discussed the affair with him or, so far as he knew, with anyone else. It would appear, then, that Flaw's information about this "crowning calamity" was obtained primarily, if not entirely, from a reading of Thomson's poetry, particularly the unpublished poems, "I Had a Love" and "Twenty-third Birthday." The latter poem makes no reference or allusion to Matilda Weller, or to any girl, but the title alone probably led Flaws to assign Matilda's death to Thomson's twenty-third year when, in reality, her death had occurred when Thomson was only eighteen.

In any event, it was not until the second memoir was published eighteen months later by Bertram Dobell, who was undoubtedly influenced by Flaws's comments, from which he quoted, that detailed information about the romance was revealed. Dobell, for the first time, explained that Thomson had met the girl while stationed in Ireland, training to be an army schoolmaster. During his eighteen-month tour of duty, Thomson had lived at the home of the schoolmaster, Joseph Barnes, and had become a great favorite with both Barnes and his wife, to whom, almost ten years later, he had written six sonnets which recalled his happy months with them. Dobell, who like Flaws had access to Thomson's manuscript books, quoted the following passage from one of these 1862 sonnets:

> . . . there my own Good Angel took my hand,
> And filled my soul with glory of her eyes,
> And led me through the love-lit Faërie Land
> Which joins our common world to Paradise.
> How soon, how soon, God called her from my side,
> Back to her own celestial sphere of day!
> And ever since she ceased to be my Guide,
> I reel and stumble on life's solemn way;
> Ah, ever since her eyes withdrew their light,
> I wander lost in blackest stormy night.

This passage, Dobell asserted,

> sums up in brief the sad story of his life. It tells the tale of his first meeting with his "Good Angel"; of his intense and overmastering affection for her; of her untimely death, and of his life-long misery and despair. Few words are needed to tell the story; but what a world of suffering is summed up in them!

Dobell also explained that the young girl was the daughter of the armourer-sergeant of a regiment in the garrison, and that it was certain "she was a creature of uncommon loveliness, both of person and of mind." He was, unfortunately, unable to give a description of this lovely creature, but, relating how Mrs. Barnes had once described her as Evangeline St. Clair in *Uncle Tom's Cabin,* he quoted a description of Little Eva which, in combination with a description of the blond girl in Thomson's satiric poem, "Vane's Story," he felt could hardly be doubted as "an essentially true picture of her." Apparently somewhat embarrassed by his inability to furnish a more accurate description, he did, in fact, apologize for the Little Eva quotation, but only because it described a very young girl, "a slight degree of alteration" being necessary "to make it apply to one much older." He then related that Thomson's love was fully reciprocated, and that the young couple's happiness "was perfect and unalloyed whilst it lasted," although it was, of course, brief in duration, for, after returning to London to complete his training, Thomson received the news of her death.

> Words cannot picture his grief and sorrow for her. For three days after receiving the news of her death, no food passed his lips, and it can hardly be doubted that he intended to starve himself to death. Had he done so the world would have lost much; but he himself would have lost nothing that he cared for, and would have been spared long dreary years of suffering and despair. Thenceforth Regret and Sorrow were his inseparable companions, and without hope and almost without object, his was rather a death-in-life than a healthy and natural existence.

The final conclusion was that "there cannot be a doubt that the death of his 'only love' was the root of his misery."

Like Flaws, then, Dobell was unable to give Matilda's name and was extremely vague about her age, for he too had met Thomson more than twenty years after her death and had admitted it was "not from Thomson himself" he had heard about the death of the "young woman." [13] His information, however, was not obtained just from reading Thomson's poetry, but had come mainly from John Grant, a close friend of Thomson's since 1856, when they were both serving as army schoolmasters. Yet even Grant had obtained his information secondhand, for he had not met Thomson until three years after Matilda's death and had heard about the affair only through the Barneses. Moreover, although Grant was intimate with Thomson for many years, he admitted that Thomson had never so much as mentioned Matilda's name.[14]

Dobell's memoir was prefixed to his edition of a posthumous collection of Thomson's verse, *A Voice from the Nile and Other Poems,* and within a few weeks of its publication in the spring of 1884, a third close friend of Thomson's later years, G. W. Foote, published a two-part essay in *Progress* ostensibly reviewing Dobell's edition but actually correcting the memoir, which, although "written with loving care," had "deficiencies." Foote insisted that we look at the facts:

> It is perfectly true that Thomson lost his first and only love when she was a girl and he was little more than a boy. It is perfectly true that he loved her with all the intensity of his nature, that her loss was a terrible blow, that her memory emerges in all his sombre work, and that he directly refers to her as ever-present in his thoughts in some very affecting verses written a year or two before his own death.

And yet, Foote continued, all this proves nothing, for Thomson was a poet who "naturally invested the objects of his affection with the hues of his imagination," and "would probably have recognized the illusion of his dreams" even had the girl lived and become his wife. Foote's conclusion, then, was that Thomson's bereavement was "only the peg on which he hung his garment of sorrow; and if it had not occurred, some other event would have served the same purpose."

The article obviously had nothing new to add to the previously published memoirs, but it is significant because in it, although no one as yet knew the name or the age of the girl, the debate as to her importance in causing Thomson's lifelong gloom was already under way. The comment about Matilda being the peg on which Thomson had hung his garment of sorrow has, in fact, been quoted in biographies ever since, and Foote himself considered it worth repeating in his preface to *Satires and Profanities*, a collection of Thomson's prose writing which he published a few months later. It was this preface that evoked the fourth significant statement on the Matilda Weller romance, a statement by Charles Bradlaugh which, incredible as it may seem, has never been repeated since, although it is the first and the only report of the affair made by someone who was in Ireland at the time, had actually known Matilda, and was intimate with Thomson during the entire period of the supposed romance. Referring to Foote's statements about Thomson's relations with his "only love," Bradlaugh wrote:

> The armourer-sergeant's daughter (of the 7th Dragoon Guards), who died in Ireland about 1852, was only a little child, playing with children's toys—a very pretty child, and it was not till long after her death, and in his morbid times, that Thomson, little by little, built the poetical romance about her memory.[15]

Foote, who had apparently received all his information on Matilda through reading Flaws and Dobell, was obviously embarrassed and wrote to Bradlaugh immediately, his letter being printed in the *National Reformer* for the following week:

> What you say as to Thomson's lost love being a "child" is doubtless true enough, but the term is

> rather elastic. Besides, large allowances must be made for men of poetic temperament. Beatrice was only a "child" when she swam like a star into Dante's heaven, and excited the passionate love which immortalised her.

Five years later, however, when reviewing Salt's biography, Foote asserted that the Matilda romance was greatly exaggerated: "That Thomson thought it wrecked his life is not proof. . . . There are indications that at one time he was not absolutely inconsolable." [16] We do not, unfortunately, know Flaws's reaction to Bradlaugh's statement; perhaps he never saw it. In any event, he never published another word on Thomson. Dobell also had no comment to make, but he undoubtedly read Bradlaugh's statement; it is amusing to trace his gradual withdrawal on the importance of Matilda Weller. In 1884, we recall, he had insisted "there cannot be a doubt that the death of his 'only love' was the root of his misery," but when the memoir was rewritten for inclusion in the 1895 *Poetical Works of James Thomson,* his convictions had changed considerably: "It might be a mistake to assert positively . . . she was the cause of his pessimism." And when, in 1910, the essay was again rewritten and published separately as *The Laureate of Pessimism,* the statement read: "I only say her influence *might* have saved him from his life-long melancholy."

The damage, however, had been done. The Matilda Weller legend had been firmly founded, and no serious attempt has since been made to question it. The depressing fact seems to be that biographers like the legend; that it makes better biographical material than anything else in Thomson's life; and that it provides critics, particularly those who deal in psychological interpretations, endless ground for discussion as to its influence on Thomson's life and works. I am not, of course, suggesting that Matilda Weller was herself a myth; she was very real, and there is no doubt that she played an important, if somewhat minor, role in Thomson's verse;

but there is simply no evidence to support the idea that she was either Thomson's sorrow or the peg on which he hung it. Nor is there any reason to suspect that we are missing important documents on the affair, for in 1888, when Salt decided to write his *Life,* he collected, through letters and interviews, every scrap of evidence he could find on the supposed romance. These letters and the notes of his interviews have been preserved, enabling us to examine and judge the basis for the Matilda Weller legend.

Salt began his investigation at the only place he could begin it, interviewing Charles Bradlaugh, through whom he learned, for the first time, Matilda's name and age: "She was a pretty, but not strikingly beautiful child of about 13." Bradlaugh repeated his earlier assertion that the romance was a "poetical invention on Thomson's part"; ridiculed the idea of an engagement, which Salt, after reading Thomson's poem, "The Fadeless Bower," assumed to have existed; and added the new information that Thomson's sorrow was an "idealisation," that he had "formed ideal attachments to several women, especially one in Jersey." [17] The most startling thing about this interview, however, was not what Bradlaugh had to say, but that Salt, when writing his biography, did not utilize a single word of it. We may be sure that he was delighted to learn the girl's name, and he immediately began a search for her relatives. He was, perhaps, somewhat shocked to learn her actual age, although he soon discovered that her youthfulness was a fact, disconcerting as it may have been, which he could not deny. Yet he refused to give the slightest credence to anything else Bradlaugh had to say about the man with whom he had been intimate for more than twenty-five years; the simple, if somewhat harsh, truth of the matter seems to be that Salt wanted the Matilda Weller legend to be true. Dobell, who had invited him to write the biography, had already painted a portrait of Thomson as a man who loved but once and, losing love, struggled bravely on through his "joyless and hopeless" existence. This was the man Salt had heard about and this was the man he intended to write about—not one who had invented a poetic romance about a thirteen-year-old child while having relations with mature women. For this reason, halfway through his research, Salt wrote to Dobell in great jubilation:

> My best stroke of business has been going over to Winchester and seeing William Weller, the brother of Matilda. He is a very nice man, and his not writing had only been due to lazyness apparently, as he was very willing to give information. Bradlaugh is *quite* wrong about the Ballincollig affair, the story as stated in your Memoir being substantially true.[18]

From Salt's notes of the interview with Weller, it is difficult to understand his jubilation. Weller's first reply must, in fact, have been most discouraging, for although he had said he would be glad to tell anything he knew about "James Thomson, who was an assistant schoolmaster at Ballincollig in the year 1852," he admitted that he had never read anything by Thomson, asked for the name of his publisher, and suggested Salt should try to see Charles Bradlaugh since he "was rather intimately associated with him at that time."[19]

It would be most interesting to know if Weller, when Salt finally interviewed him two months later, had read Thomson's works, particularly *A Voice from the Nile and Other Poems* which contained Dobell's memoir. Certainly it is not unreasonable to assume so, and to assume, perhaps, that he was pleasantly surprised to learn that his sister had played so important a role in the life of a man about whom a book was to be written. In any event, during the interview he established the date of Matilda's death (July 19, 1853); confirmed Bradlaugh's statement as to her age (about "fourteen or fifteen" when she died); and showed Salt a daguerreotype of the girl taken around 1850 which Salt described in his notes (and in his biography) as a picture of "a quite young girl, about thirteen in appearance, very pretty, with long fair curls," but in a later letter as "the portrait of a mere child," about "eleven or twelve" in appearance.[20] Weller also stated that he had been a student of Thomson's at Ballincollig in 1851–52 (his army documents reveal he was ten years old at the time), and that he recalled seeing Thomson again in Dublin several years later.[21] As to the supposed engagement between his teacher and his sister, he had to admit that he personally had never heard anything about it, but claimed that "before his mother died she spoke of it to her daughter-in-law, his wife," and that "it was a distinct engagement"—which was, apparently, the reason for Salt's jubilation in the letter to Dobell. Certain facts, however, were now clear: Thomson was sixteen when he arrived in Ireland, and Matilda, either twelve or thirteen; when he left Ireland and the couple had supposedly formed their "distinct engagement," he had just turned eighteen, while she was, at the most, fourteen. Her twelve-year-old brother had known nothing of the engagement between his sister and his teacher, and Thomson's closest friend in Ballincollig had insisted that there was no romance, much less an engagement. Yet Salt chose to believe, and published that belief in his biography, that Thomson's love and subsequent grief were so intense that, although he had published poems that presumably related the most intimate details of the affair, he had been unable to speak about it, even thirty years later, even to his closest friends; that Bradlaugh had maliciously lied in his statements; and that the fourteen-year-old Matilda, presumably just before her death, had told her mother she was engaged to marry the schoolmaster apprentice who had been returned to London six months earlier, the mother, who had not seen fit to mention the engagement to her son, relating it to a daughter-in-law who had apparently never even known Matilda.[22] Of such stuff are legends made.

In any event, Salt was unable to discover additional documentation on the affair. Although he questioned everyone he could find who had even vaguely known Thomson,[23] the best he could do when writing up the romance was admit that "there is a great lack of detailed information," and then print precisely what Dobell had printed five years earlier: the sonnet to the Barneses, Harriet Beecher Stowe's description of Little Eva, and Thomson's description of the blond girl in "Vane's Story." His conclusion, a slight variation on Dobell's earlier assertion, was that "it was the death of this young girl that, above all other single circumstances, fostered and developed the malady to which Thomson was predisposed, and that in this sense, at least, it was a cause of his subsequent despondency." His only significant addition to what had been previously written was a statement that "The Fadeless Bower" was "a poetical description of the scene where the young lovers first plighted their troth"—a statement that he excised from later editions of the biography.

External evidence in support of the romance appears, then, to be highly inadequate. I suggest that we can say with conviction but two things: Matilda Weller was a pretty girl who died in Ireland on July 19, 1853, at about the age of fourteen; Thomson, while stationed in Ballincollig, had been acquainted with her. Anything else is conjecture based on a reading of his poetry. There is, of course, no reason to doubt that, even had he known her only slightly, he would have been fond of her, for there is adequate evidence throughout his life to prove his love for children; moreover, we can certainly assume that her death caused him grief, for who, even mildly acquainted with a pretty child, would not be sincerely grieved if that child died at the age of fourteen or fifteen? But there is simply no basis for the claim that he was deeply in love with and engaged to marry her, and, unless that was so, it is difficult to see how her death could have been "the root of his misery."

It remains, however, to comment briefly on the poetry

on which the Matilda Weller legend was based, as there is excellent reason to believe that the dead girls who appear in some of Thomson's poems had their origin, at least in part, in the girl who died so young in Ireland. To fully understand these dead girls it must first be recognized that Death, as an allegorical figure, and dead people—men, women, infants, and, to be sure, young girls—are commonplace in his work. Death and separation are, in fact, the dominant themes in his gloomy poetry, which is not at all surprising when we consider that his only sister died when he was five, and that, when he was eight, his mother also died, leaving him to be placed in a school for orphans where he was separated from both his infant brother and his father, who was by then, as the result of a stroke, himself more dead than alive. In one sense, then, Thomson used the dead girl, not as an expression of personal grief for any particular real girl, but as the most dramatic example he knew of death and separation, and in this he was certainly not unique; dead girls are far from uncommon in Victorian literature—Little Nell, Evelyn Hope, Pompilia, Lucy Desborough, Maggie Tulliver, and Dora Spenlow being just a few of the more obvious examples. When, therefore, Thomson has a funeral procession for a dead girl ("The Doom of a City") or has a young man kneeling before the corpse of a "woman very young and very fair" ("The City of Dreadful Night") or has "Death" separate two young lovers while they dance ("A Festival of Life"), we cannot assume that these incidents refer to Matilda Weller or to any of Thomson's "loves"; Thomson clearly indicates that the dead girl in such situations is specifically related, not to dead love, but to dead faith and dead hope. In Section II of "The City," for instance, when the man revisits the places where his faith, hope, and love had died, it is faith, not love, which had been lost in the cemetery; and this association, far from being peculiar to Thomson, is again typical of nineteenth-century literature, for the cemetery was, of course, a nightmare to the Victorian who was afraid of losing, or had already lost, the traditional religious faith.

There are, however, in Thomson's works a group of some half-dozen poems written between 1858 and 1864 in which we find a dead girl who is specifically described, and who serves a different purpose from that suggested above. These poems ("The Fadeless Bower," "Mater Tenebrarum," "The Deliverer," "Vane's Story," and the sixth sonnet to Joseph and Alice Barnes), along with the prose phantasy, "A Lady of Sorrow," form the cluster on which the Matilda Weller legend has been based, and there is every reason to believe that Matilda was, at least in part, the inspiration for the dead girl who appears in them. If, however, we look closely at this girl—young, blond, white-robed, and thoroughly angelic—it is obvious that she is not a real girl at all, but simply the traditional description of what Thomson actually called her—an angel. In "A Lady of Sorrow" he was explicit on this point; not only did his introduction explain his method, somewhat apologetically noting that "some men see truth and express truth best" through imagery and symbol, but within the body of the phantasy he stated that his angel was

> simply the image in beatitude of her who died so young. The pure girl was become the Angel; the sheathed wings had unfolded in the favourable clime, the vesture was radiantly white with the whiteness of her soul, the long hair was dazzling golden glory round the ever-young head, the blue eyes had absorbed celestial light in the cloudless empyrean.

As an angel, she symbolized all those things that angels traditionally symbolize, but specifically she represented the concept of platonic love which Thomson had discovered, and been fascinated by, in his reading of Shelley. In "Epipsychidion," for instance, Shelley had written:

Spouse! Sister! Angel! Pilot of the Fate
Whose course has been so starless! O too late
Beloved! O too soon adored, by me!
For in the fields of Immortality
My spirit should at first have worshipped thine,
A divine presence in a place divine.

It was passages such as this which apparently first inspired Thomson to use the angel figure. In the 1857 "Bertram to the Most Noble and Beautiful Lady Geraldine," the first poem in which the blond girl dressed in white makes an appearance, she is so "holy-pure" that her lover, with more than just a touch of Shelley in him, is forced to cry out:

The Vision sways me; I must speak or die:
Life of my life! I see, I know, I feel;
The inspiration cannot err or lie;
Passion doth its own truth with pure fire seal;—
God from the depths of all Eternity
Created us One Soul, in woe or weal,
In life and death, in union or apart.

This particular girl was not dead, nor, I suspect, was she inspired by Matilda Weller, but insofar as she symbolized platonic love, she was the prototype of the figure that, in the year after this poem was written, sprouted wings and became the Dead Girl–Angel. In the 1858 "The Fadeless Bower" she was halfway to Heaven; in the 1859 "The Deliverer" and "Mater Tenebrarum"[24] she was a permanent resident; and by 1862, in "A Lady of Sorrow," she was making periodic visits to her soul mate on earth, who explained how

> as we wandered, like two children, sister and brother, straying in delight solemnised by awe through the palace and the measureless domains of Our Father, our beings were ever in most intimate communion. Our lips scarcely moved, our hands

never gestured save in startled rapture, our eyes rarely expressed aught save reverence and gratitude and love of Him and to Him through whose realms we were thus enfranchised to wander as in our own heritage; . . . then first was I taught beyond all forgetting that there is a perfect interfusion of soul with soul, when the pure fire of love has utterly consumed matter and space and time.[25]

Sometimes, however, the Dead Girl–Angel served a more specific function; as a symbol of purity and goodness, she was also considered to be Thomson's "Guide" or "Deliverer," as in the poem titled "The Deliverer" where she was sent by God as the "Dear Angel of divine deliverance" and appeared wearing a crown of crystal, crested with a white dove, on which was written the word "Love." This function is also implied in most of the other Dead Girl–Angel poems, the speaker often calling out to her for help or advice, but it is explicitly stated in that oft-quoted but apparently seldom read sonnet to the Barneses, when Thomson calls her his "Guide," his "own Good Angel"; as the symbol of purity and goodness, she had led him to the "love-lit Faërie Land" which joins earth to paradise, and without this ideal of purity, he felt he had "wandered lost in blackest stormy night." This function was, in fact, all that the sonnet claimed for Matilda Weller, for in it, nine years after her death, she was simply playing the role she had for years been playing as the guardian-angel symbol of Thomson's Shelleyan poetry.

The 1878 "I Had a Love" is apparently another matter. This unpublished poem, having been written twenty-five years after Matilda's death, seems to fall outside the main cluster of Dead Girl–Angel poems. The title is, indeed, a tempting one, and the marginal comment in the manuscript that the poem is "more truth than poetry" has often been exhibited by Matilda Weller enthusiasts as primary evidence in support of Thomson's undying love. The truth is, however, that the title was conceived many years before the poem was written, possibly in the early sixties,[26] and, far from being a profound personal admission, was either inspired by or adapted from Elizabeth Barrett Browning's "Aurora Leigh," for Thomson's title line,

I had a love—it was so long ago,

is clearly related, consciously or not, to Aurora's outburst in Book I:

I had a father!—yes, but long ago.

"Aurora Leigh," published just a few years before the Dead Girl–Angel poems were written and, along with all Mrs. Browning's works, greatly admired by Thomson,[27] clearly influenced the main cluster of those poems—in combination, of course, with Shelley influences already noted. Thus "Bertram to Geraldine," although owing much to Shelley, was intended as a sequel to Mrs. Browning's "Lady Geraldine's Courtship"; "The Fadeless Bower," which is a "vision" poem (the one Salt called a poetical description of the scene where Thomson and Matilda "plighted their troth"), may have been partly inspired by Mrs. Browning's "A Vision of Poets" and "The Lost Bower"; and in Thomson's sonnet to Mr. and Mrs. Barnes, what he called Matilda—"my own Good Angel"—is almost exactly what, in Book IX of "Aurora Leigh," Marian Erle had called Romney—"My great good angel."

In any event, the relevant point—one that most commentaries ignore—is that "I Had a Love" is not, in any conceivable sense of the word, a love poem, but one of the bitterest of all Thomson's bitter poems on the theme that there is no God and that life is pointless. In this first-person narrative the important thing is not that the speaker had a love who died, or even, as in the "Good Angel" sonnet, that had she lived she might have saved him from "blackest stormy night," but that life is so cruel and meaningless that even if he could recall his dead love to life—that is, even if he could resurrect his Shelleyan ideal of platonic purity—he would not do it:

What profit from all life that lives on earth,
What good, what use, what aim?
What compensation for the throes of birth
And death in all its frame?
What conscious life hath ever paid its cost?
From Nothingness to Nothingness—all lost!

This is the point of "I Had a Love," and this, not the dead love, is the "more truth than poetry" of the poem;[28] the only "truth" we can really document is that long before 1878 Thomson was convinced, as he had written in "The City of Dreadful Night," that

The world rolls round forever like a mill;
It grinds out death and life and good and ill;
It has no purpose, heart or mind or will.

Perhaps, years after her death, Thomson did like to imagine that had Matilda lived (or, as he stated in a letter to his sister-in-law,[29] had his three-year-old sister lived), she might have saved him

from the Desert sands
Bestrewn with bleaching bones,
And led me through the friendly fertile lands,
And changed my weary moans
To hymns of triumph and enraptured love,
And made our earth as rich as Heaven above.

But there is simply no evidence to suggest that Thomson, even when writing these lines from "I Had a Love," imagined he had ever been in love with the girl, or that she had been in love with him, for the "poetic romance" he built around her memory was definitely platonic. That she never was considered to be more than a symbol of purity and goodness is indicated in the two works that climaxed the Dead Girl–Angel cluster; in both "A Lady of Sorrow" and "Vane's Story," when the Dead Girl–Angel had to appear in a situation involving not platonic, but physical love, Thomson changed the symbol by having his angel alter her appearance. In "A Lady of Sorrow" the angel appeared only in Section I, and later the same figure, having to lead Thomson through a "mad and lawless" orgy, became "The Siren"; in "Vane's Story," when the angel came to visit Vane and they were to kiss, frolic, and go off dancing, she came, not in her angel costume, but as a dark-eyed brunette wearing black lace. Vane's first startled comment was:

> Why have you left your golden hair,
> These gorgeous dusky braids to wear?
> Why have you left your azure eyes
> To gaze through deep dark mysteries?
> Why have you left your robe of white,
> And come in cloudy lace bedight?

The answer is obvious, as the Dead Girl–Angel would simply not do in "Vane's Story"; by the time Thomson had completed this poem, he was satirizing his rejected theories of platonic love, and the final moral, as expressed in the poem's epilogue, was

> Glory warms us in the grave!
> Stupid words, that sound so brave!
> Better warmth would give to us
> Molly Seagrim amorous,
> Slobbering kisses lips and tongue,
> And yet reeking from the dung.

This is Heine, not Shelley, and the two would, to be sure, make strange bedfellows—as strange, no doubt, as Molly Seagrim and Matilda Weller. The angel figure therefore had to shed her wings and don black lace, for her main feature had been her absolute purity, the Shelleyan purity which one might feel for one's soul mate, or one's sister, or even for a beautiful young child still playing with dolls.

It was, moreover, precisely this note of purity which Thomson stressed in the one poem we have which does seem to have been addressed to Matilda, an unpublished poem dated October, 1852,[30] just three months before he left Ballincollig:

> This is a strange and mystic tenderness
> With which I feel whene'er I think of
> thee:

What power is this with which thou swayest me?
I worship now thou loving gentleness—

I, with my hopeless, hard, cold, bitter heart!
I am with thee as gentle as a child;
Feelings and thoughts and actions all are mild,
And pure, and full of love.

This is the relationship he later expressed in the Dead Girl–Angel poems, particularly in the sonnet to the Barneses, which is the core of the Matilda Weller legend, and there is no reason so suspect, from either external or internal evidence, that the platonic role she played in his poetry differed from the platonic role she played in his life. There is, however, excellent reason to believe that within a few years of her death, at least by the time Thomson had reached the age of twenty-one, he had formed a most unplatonic interest in a girl named Helen Gray, and that, in later years, he did indeed, as Bradlaugh claimed, form "attachments" to several women.

As I am not writing a biography of Thomson, but merely attempting to clear ground for a study of his intellectual development, this is not the place for a discussion of his mature love affairs. It does, however, seem advisable to comment briefly on his relations with Helen Gray, who has long been confused with the troublesome Matilda Weller legend. When, as an eight-year-old child, Thomson was placed in a school for orphans, he was befriended by old friends of his parents, the William Grays of London. For almost ten years, until he was sent to Ballincollig for his army training, he was indirectly under their care, living with them during all his school vacations and thus growing up with their two daughters, whom he apparently thought of as his sisters.[31] Agnes, the younger of the two girls, later recalled that Helen (who was five years Thomson's junior) had been his "special favourite," that "her will seemed always law to him," that whatever she "said or did won appreciation from him," [32] an attitude that is confirmed in a unpublished poem dated 1855,[33] when Thomson was stationed in Plymouth on his first assignment as a schoolmaster:

Far-far away, my "Sister" dear,
The forms I saw around you move
Are fading in my memory,
But clearly shine the eyes I love.

The poem goes on to recall the "happy days that once had been," each stanza reverting to a description of the eyes he loved so well:

I see them now look painful doubt,
Wide-oped yet shrinking from the light;
She dreads, I say, that far away,
I do or shall forget her quite.

But, Dear, I never can forget
Thy truth, thy love, thy nobleness:
Oh, let them shine out clear again
In quiet musing anxiousless—

And then I see them mournful-sad,
And dim as if surcharged with tears;
I say, she grieves that I am gone,
And may be gone for many years.

Although the conclusion is that they are "not truly parted" since his spirit often yearns for her, the poem is obviously not a declaration of love—but it seems certain that Thomson's interest in Helen was becoming something more than brotherly, for a year later, when she was seventeen and he, as a twenty-two-year-old schoolmaster, was about to be transferred to Dublin, her parents would not allow him to correspond with her. Whatever his relations with her may then have been, and whatever her parents' reasons for wanting to separate them, soon after his arrival in Dublin he wrote, in quick succession, three poems on the theme of separated lovers: "Tasso to Leonora," in which Tasso has been parted from his "heaven-created wife" through station; "Marriage," in which the speaker calls out to his "noble wife" to come to him, for "time is long since we were parted"; and the previously discussed "Bertram to Geraldine," in which Geraldine (quite unlike Mrs. Browning's heroine) is a girl Bertram had known well in hours long faded when her breath had filled his frame and her dark eyes had shone with passion and bliss. At a dance, while "weaving gay vesture for an old despair," he had met her again, "her whom he had not sought since Youth," and had suddenly realized that God had made them "One Soul," although he feared, as Tasso had feared, that because she was of a higher station they might never meet again.[34]

I am not suggesting that these poems are entirely autobiographical, for the Shelley and Browning influences which I have already discussed are their most important feature. But when, after returning from four years in Ireland and revisiting Helen Gray, Thomson wrote a poem titled "Meeting Again," the autobiographical note cannot be ignored. Although the poem was written in the same period as the Shelleyan Dead Girl–Angel poems, the girl involved was neither dead nor angelic. The poem begins by describing the parting, which had occurred "long bitter years" ago:

> Your eyes were burning with wild love and
>   woe;
>   They seared my inmost heart;
> We knew, we knew too well that I must go,
>   Yet could not bear to part.

This parting, which the poem goes on to describe, has, in fact, sexual overtones:

> One yearning overwhelmed all strength and
>   hope,—
>   That then and there we might
> Sink down, embracing, under heaven's cope,
>   Engulfed in death's deep night.

Now, after long years, they are again allowed to meet
And mingle henceforth all our sighs and tears
While these two hearts shall beat.

He has come from the "fearful world" where he had been "cast among the multitude"; she has come from the "sterner solitary life," waging strife with "woe and sin" (Helen Gray had been working as a "ragged school" teacher). He wonders if she can really love him, whom she knew so "weak and foul of yore":

Dear heart! *I* feel that evil long-ago
But makes me love you more.

Yet still that longing almost swayeth me,—
That we should sink down deep,
And side by side, from life's sore burthen free,
Sleep death's eternal sleep.

Whether Helen shared Thomson's desire to "sink down, embracing, under heaven's cope" is unknown; probably not, for during this "meeting again," Thomson learned she was engaged to marry someone else, and thus, during the visit, was "painfully depressed and silent." A few weeks later he was transferred to Jersey where he began writing "Ronald and Helen," a long narrative poem about separated lovers; but he never again visited or wrote letters either to Helen or to Agnes, or even to Mr. and Mrs. Gray who, for more than a decade, had been his foster parents. Some thirty years later, John Grant (to whom Thomson had never mentioned Matilda's name) was able to report that Thomson had told him he was "not much, if at all, in love with Helen Gray"; nevertheless, one of the last letters Thomson ever wrote attempted to discover information about Helen,[35] and a purse she had made for him, which he had "treasured many years after," went with him to the grave. In addition to this purse, a lock of hair was also placed in Thomson's coffin, and biographers, ignoring the fact that the purse was Helen Gray's, have always assumed that the lock of hair had belonged to Matilda Weller, Salt calling it Thomson's "one memento of his lost love" and a recent biographer emphatically stating that it was "a yellow curl, a souvenir of Matilda cherished for twenty-nine years." [36] The hair may, conceivably, have been Matilda's (the color is not described in the only record we have), but as the purse was definitely the treasured possession which Helen Gray had made for him years earlier, it seems likely that the hair was hers too. It is, however, interesting to speculate on the other possibility, since Matilda's hair in Helen Gray's purse would symbolize what I believe happened in a good many of the Dead Girl–Angel poems: whatever part Matilda played in the platonic love passages, Helen played in the passages treating physical love. "Vane's Story," in which the Dead Girl–Angel changes her garb and appears in black lace so she may frolic and dance, was, in fact, originally titled "Gray's Story." [37]

Probably Thomson's admission to John Grant was the truth—in reality he was "not much, if at all," in love with Helen Gray. But there is considerably more evidence to support a love for her than for Matilda, and, in spite of the loss of Thomson's early correspondence and the championing of Matilda by his biographers, there are still traces of at least four "other women" in his life,[38] which makes it clear that neither his unhappiness nor his pessimism resulted from a "lost love," an "only love," or any sort of love at all. Oddly enough, it seems that the truth about his love life was best stated by Bertram Dobell, the man who, more than anyone else connected with Thomson, had repeatedly attributed his friend's misery to a lifelong devotion for the dead Matilda. Long after Thomson's death, Dobell admitted that Thomson "was always attracted by, and attractive *to,* the female sex." [39] Although it is probable that most of his romances were, as Bradlaugh had claimed, "ideal attachments," that they did exist, in some form or another, seems sufficient proof that whatever role Matilda Weller may have played in his poetry, or his life, she was not the cause of his unhappiness.

Neither was a gloomy disposition or depression over poetic failure, and the true cause remains to be explored; the "desert sands bestrewn with bleaching bones" from which Thomson liked to imagine a dead sister "or someone else" might have saved him, is a reference to the fact that he suffered from chronic alcoholism—a condition of which everyone who has ever written a word on him has been more or less aware. The extent and the true nature of his alcoholism have not, however, been stressed by his biographers or, indeed, completely understood by many of them, largely because his friends (and his early biographers were indeed his closest friends) did their utmost to hide or ignore the unattractive details of his condition. Flaws, for instance, in the first published memoir, set the tone for a good many of the later comments by treating the subject as ambiguously as he possibly could: "Believing it a duty to be frank in such matters, I just went on my own discretion, veiling his vice sufficiently to avoid gratifying the enemy, though all who can read between the lines may know the truth." [40] Not many, however, did know the truth, or anything approaching it, and Salt himself, even after compiling a considerable number of firsthand reports on Thomson's life, did not have a complete picture of Thomson's condition until almost ten years after his biography had been published. By that time he too seems to have felt that nothing would be accomplished by printing details, or perhaps he was reluctant to disturb the more romantic explanations already presented as the cause of Thomson's misery; as a result, the nature of Thomson's alcoholism has always been distorted. The impression is that he "drank"; the truth is that his drinking was completely uncontrollable and came upon him, as one friend put it, like "fits of mania."

It began, apparently, while he was in the army, perhaps even as early as 1856. Bradlaugh claimed that Thomson's discharge in 1862 was due to his drinking,[41] and remarked that during their friendship he had "rescued him at least twenty times from delirium tremens and misery," but we do not need statements from his friends to document these "fits of mania"; just a glance through the diaries reveals the periods when Thomson had been hopelessly drunk, the neat entries breaking off abruptly and two or three weeks of blank pages following before, in an incredibly shaky hand, they begin again. At first, sometimes a year or more would pass without a breakdown, but in the final years the attacks were recurring with increasing frequency—three months of normal behavior, then ten weeks, then six weeks, then two weeks. In his last six months, months that were otherwise the happiest and most successful of his life, Thomson suffered four distinct attacks, beginning in January, 1882, when he was, as one friend put it, off on a "sad sad spree" and "shockingly bad." [42] By the end of the month he had recovered briefly from what he called his "damned infernal fit," and had sworn an oath never to touch alcohol again; but only four days later he was found on the street and relieved "of about ½ pint of firewater from various pockets, he protesting that 'how it was done' was beyond him." In February and early March, while visiting Harriet and John Barrs in Leicester, he had recovered enough to write his last poems, but near the end of the month he suffered a humiliating relapse in Harriet's presence, and it was not until April 22 that, with two black eyes, a broken nose, and a cut forehead, he found himself able to write a letter of apology:

> I can only say that I was mad. In one fit of frenzy I have not only lost more than I yet know, and half murdered myself (were it not for my debts I sincerely wish it had been wholly), but justly alienated my best and firmest friends, old and new, both in London and Leicester. As, unfortu-

> nately for myself at least, I am left alive, it only remains for me to endeavour my utmost by hard and persistent struggling to repay my mere money debts, for my debts of kindness can never be repaid. If I fail, as very probably I shall fail, the failure will but irresistibly prove what I have long thoroughly believed, that for myself and others I am much better dead than alive.[43]

Within two weeks, however, Thomson was again "on the loose," and on May 10, while hopelessly drunk, he set fire to the rubbish in his room, "calmly surveying the scene from his armchair, refusing any word of explanation." Two days later, under the name of John Turner, he was sentenced to fourteen days in jail; but immediately upon his release on May 26, he began drinking again. The following night he fell asleep at a friend's, awoke at one o'clock to arouse the whole house with the cry of "Brandy!" and then "lay in bed and chimed out as merrily as possible this one request and so on till four, when he got up, saying 'he would do it,' dressing minus boots and hat, and left the house, and has since been lost sight of." By May 31 his friends had written to Liverpool to make arrangements for placing him in a retreat, but four days later, as the result of a broken blood vessel, he was dead.

Ever since Salt suggested that it was the death of Matilda which "fostered and developed the malady to which Thomson was predisposed," critics have assumed that Thomson's drinking was caused by his unhappiness, whether that unhappiness be ascribed to lost love, literary failure, or "constitutional melancholia." I suggest that the opposite is true, that Thomson's unhappiness was not the cause but the result of his alcoholism, a condition that is today properly classified as an illness.[44] Thomson did not "drink"; he was, in fact, when not suffering from an attack, a remarkably temperate man. But he suffered from a condition that made him one of those alcoholics described in medical terms as "desperately sick individuals who have reached such an impasse through their uncontrollable drinking that they can see no possible way out of their dilemma, and, consequently, are either consciously or subconsciously toying with the thought of self-destruction." At present, medical science, having discovered that any normal person, any type of personality, can become an alcoholic, is thoroughly at a loss to explain the etiology of the disease, and we are free to choose between a physiologically oriented school which attributes it to a "biochemical defect of one kind or another which provokes an uncontrollable craving for alcohol," and a psychologically oriented school which considers it to be a "manifestation of neurosis based on deficient or arrested development of personality, rooted in childhood." Biographers who find themselves psychologically oriented are, therefore, free to develop theories that Thomson's alcoholism resulted from arrested development of personality, rooted in childhood, although I might suggest that, in spite of death and separation, there is no indication that Thomson, at least, was aware of such deficiencies of personality. He not only was a popular and precocious child, but considered his childhood days, particularly those spent with the Grays, to have been the happiest of his life. In any event, this is a far different thing from saying that he drank because of his unhappiness, and I trust I have shown that in his maturity there was little unhappiness that could be considered a contributing factor to an arrested personality. Far from being gloomy by nature, Thomson was a pleasant and agreeable companion to all who knew him; as a poet and critic, he had considerably more success than failure; and, with regard to love, he not only was always "attracted by and attractive *to* the female sex," but did not seem ever to have suffered severely from a lack of female companionship.

Apparently, then, all we can say with conviction is that Thomson was an alcoholic, cause unknown, and that although, as one of his closest friends has stated, "no mortal ever strove against an overpowering disease more grimly than Thomson did,"[45] his battle was a hopeless one. My suggestion that his alcoholism was the true cause of whatever unhappiness he suffered throughout his life does not mean that his alcoholism contributed to his pessimistic philosophy—an impossible conclusion because Thomson was suffering from chronic alcoholism before and during a decade when his philosophy was thoroughly optimistic. I do suspect, however, that his later philosophy failed to bring him either cheer or comfort, and that it caused him some lonely and unhappy moments, lonely not from a lack of close friends, but for a far more significant and far more frightening reason: Thomson awoke one morning to discover that he was alone in the universe without a god, flung through meaningless space on what he became convinced was a meaningless journey to death. It was certainly not an uncommon discovery in the mid-nineteenth century, but this was small consolation to the individual who had arrived at such conclusions and who found himself forced to disown his former views on God, on society, and on his own role in society. It is, then, with the development of Thomson's religious beliefs that I have chosen to begin my study.

2

Theist to Atheist

THOMSON celebrated his twenty-first birthday in the year 1855, coming of age midway through the decade which had begun with *In Memoriam* and was to end with *The Origin of the Species*. A study of his intellectual development must begin with this year, not because it is so splendidly appropriate a date, but because it was in 1855 that Thomson, picking up a copy of Arnold's latest volume of poetry and asking himself, as Arnold had asked a few years earlier when visiting the Grande Chartreuse—"What am I, that I am here?"—was inspired to formulate his earliest statement on religion, the long poem, "Suggested by Matthew Arnold's 'Stanzas from the Grande Chartreuse.' " We cannot, unfortunately, begin at an earlier stage of his life because, although he was undoubtedly concerned with religion, if not religious problems, before 1855, we simply do not know enough about his early years to be able profitably to discuss his childhood religious training. We know little more than that he was brought up in a Christian home and, like most children born in the first half of the nineteenth century, was taught to believe in the omnipotence, the omniscience, and, probably, the omnibenevolence of the Judaic-Christian Deity. As his mother was a devout follower of Edward Irving, Thomson may have been taught somewhat more than this basic tenet; in later years he recalled: "I remember well Irving's portrait under yellow gauze, and some books of his on the interpretation of prophecy, which I used to read for the imagery." [1] He also recalled how his father used to take him to chapels "where the members of the congregation ejaculated groaning responses to the minister's prayer, and to small meetings in a private room where the members detailed their spiritual experiences of the week," but as all this occurred before Thomson was eight years old, it is easy to overemphasize its importance, which was probably more on emotional and, to use the word loosely, psychological levels than on a purely intellectual one. It seems safest, then, merely to state that Thomson's religious background, even if somewhat esoteric, was "normal" as to fundamental Christian doctrine, and that his earliest beliefs are accurately reflected in the jingle he was taught when a child, and could still repeat decades later:

> I thank the goodness and the grace
> Which on my birth have smiled;
> And made me in these Christian days
> A happy English child.[2]

It would be of considerably greater interest to know precisely what religious training Thomson received between his eighth and sixteenth years, from 1842 to 1850, when he was a student at the Royal Caledonian Asylum, but again there is little information.[3] All we can say with certainty is that sometime during these years, or, more likely, in 1850–1854, when he was training to become an army schoolmaster, he began to have doubts about the faith of his childhood, and that by 1855 these doubts were clear enough to be formulated. By that time he was reluctantly beginning to suspect that the old faith, the faith represented by Arnold's Grande Chartreuse, was inadequate. Perhaps it was not completely dead; surely it was not, as Arnold had claimed, "dead time's exploded dream"; but all was not well in the state of Christendom and Thomson, for himself at least, was attempting to put it right.

This important, if somewhat painful, poem is understandably forgotten, and a brief summary is in order. In "Suggested by Matthew Arnold's 'Stanzas from the Grande Chartreuse,'" Thomson begins by admitting that the spirit of Christianity appears to be fading from the earth, that Arnold's "dirge for a mighty Creed outworn" befits his anguished time, for Christianity no longer appears divine except to the ignorant, to a few who recognize its past power and still cling to it with yearning faith, and to those who "win wealth and power and honours serving at Its shrine." But who, he asks, mourns the dead religion? Who mourns Christ? Even if Christ is no longer fit to lead "the modern march of thought," he was divine, and none of human soul can lead it on. Wandering shepherdless, we are rapidly losing "all Earth has of Heaven; bereft of faith; and living in Eternal Death." Blinded by material might, we lust after wealth; "God turns to Mammon at our cry," for our souls have become "wealth-crushed, dross-stifled." For those few who still have need of "more than earth or time can grant," there is no place to turn. The old God-given wells of life are dry, and one turns away in blank despair to scoff or weep as fits his mood. Black disbelief, substantial doubt, are in all faiths, and each creed, "senile, sick, half-dead," reviles the others. "Oh God in Heaven! We know Thou art Allwise, All-good—Teach us how to worship Thee!"

Yet, even if Christianity, that "great Form" which has "sublimely templed God," is really dead, Thomson pleads that we do not reject this shrine, for we must study it so we may recognize the "greater One" that will succeed it. He suggests that we be patient, meek, and pure, "unselfishly resigned to God's mysterious judgments," and adhere to Christ until a new "God-illumined One" appears to disperse the gloom.

> Yes, let us stay in loving grief,
> Which patient hope and trust yet cheer,
> Silent beside our silent Chief,

Till His Successor shall appear;
Till death's veil fall from off His face,
Or One annointed take His place.

Nay,—our adoring love should have
More faith than to believe that He,
Before Another comes to save,
Can leave us in blind misery
Without a Guide; God never can
So utterly depart from man.

The concluding plea is that we will "move onward," "still on our Holy War intent," trusting that life and saving power remain in that "dear Form" which perhaps, after all, but seems dead:

O God, revive the seeming Dead;
Or send Another in His stead!

So ends Thomson's poem, obviously conceived of as a prayer to the all-wise, all-good "God in Heaven," a prayer that, even in so brief a paraphrase, reveals two important aspects of his thought at this time: he was extremely confused as to his position on Christianity, and he was writing under the influence of Carlyle and the Romantic poets, particularly Wordsworth and Shelley. Basically, his complaint in this poem is simply that the world is too much with us, that we are laying waste our powers in Mammon-worship, that Christianity no longer suffices for the "modern march of thought," that is, for the "everlasting yea." There is no suggestion of science or the higher criticism, for Thomson was not, like the young Ruskin, hearing Geologist's hammers, nor, like the young Clough, suggesting that Christ had not risen. Religion itself was not dead; it was merely awaiting the new Prometheus.

Eastwards through busy streets I lingered
on;
Jostled by anxious crowds, who, heart and
brain,

Were so absorbed in dreams of Mammon-
gain,
That they could spare no time to look upon
The sunset's gold and crimson fires, which
shone
Blessing keen eyes and wrinkled brows in
vain.
Right in my path stood out that solemn
fane,
Whose soaring cupola of stern grey stone
Lifteth for awful beacon to the sky
The burning cross: silent and sole amid
That ceaseless uproar, as a pyramid
Isled in its desert. The great throngs pressed
by
Heedless and urgent: thus Religion towers
Above this sordid, restless life of ours.[4]

This sonnet was also written in 1855, and, although Thomson repeats the idea that men are "absorbed in dreams of Mammon-gain" and insists that religion towers above "this sordid, restless life of ours," he significantly makes no mention of the "dear Form" that had once sublimely templed God, except insofar as he again implies that Christianity was no longer an active force in the world around him. This was, in fact, the one thing about Christianity of which he did feel certain, and thus, in spite of his plea that we should stay in loving grief "silent beside our silent Chief," he soon began a long and, to be sure, futile search for a new religion, a seven-year search during which his views on man's relations with the universe shifted crazily between orthodox Christianity and a conglomeration of pantheistic notions which he had discovered in the Romantic poets.[5] As we might expect, such views were often contradictory, occasionally incoherent, and almost never satisfactory. These were indeed Thomson's years in the wilderness.

His new world picture was built upon two basic concepts which he was unable to relinquish from his Christian background, the first and most important being the idea that an all-wise, all-good God would never depart from man.

Cling, cling fast to this dear faith,
Rock of life in sea of death:
Our mazed web of doom is wrought
Under God's directing thought.

God's function, then, was never in doubt, but God's nature apparently was, for shortly after Thomson wrote these lines in his 1856 "Tasso to Leonora," his "God in Heaven" who was directing thought became Shelley's "The One," became, in fact, a "perfect Spheral Whole," a "spiritual life, which is Love and Truth," a "solemn Heaven of sapphire-burning noon," throbbing and burning through the universe. Yet, at the same time, this pantheistic "One" was still conceived of as being seated on an invisible throne with a complete entourage of angels, actually retaining the powers of the monotheistic Christian god in that he was aware of, and even judged, each change and pass which the many of his universe underwent.

The paradox seems to have resulted, in large measure, from the second of the Christian beliefs that Thomson was unable, or unwilling, to relinquish: the idea that the human soul is eternal and that, although it must necessarily change and pass, it retains individual identity after death. This belief was essential, not only to his world picture, but, as he wrote in "Tasso to Leonora," to his sanity:

For were life no flitting dream,
Were things truly what they seem,
Were not all this World-scene vast
But a shade in Time's stream glass'd;

Were the moods we now display
Less phantasmal than the clay,

In which our poor spirits clad
Act this Vision, wild and sad,
I must be mad, mad,—how mad!

Christian eschatology, however, with its fire-and-brimstone Hell and its seraphim-and-cherubim Heaven, seemed equally mad, and it was not long before Thomson evolved a new, and presumably more acceptable, eschatology which he claimed to be "the laws of Fate" as dictated by God.[6] The 1857 "Doom of a City" and essays and other poems of this period suggest the belief that God, when first creating man in the "Golden Age," had placed each immortal soul in a sphere (apparently social and economic) that was appropriate to its God-given nature. After death, if a man had led a worthy life, had "fought the noble fight," he might expect to obtain a brief rest in Heaven and then be reborn with a "loftier rank, with nobler power, with far more generous dower," so that he might "do and dare once more, heroic as before," continuing to fight the "Holy War" until, after many cycles of this "Life Eternal," he would eventually attain union with "The One." If, on the other hand, he proved, during his life on earth, to have been unjust or proud, to have squandered his treasure of human life on selfish pomps and pleasures, then he could expect to be reincarnated as an animal, with the consolation that if he did not sink deeper still, he might conceivably build again into a human soul. But if a man had become so poisoned with sin that his soul was no longer salvageable, then he would be punished by having his immortal soul placed in a nonlife state called the "Death Eternal," for to be deprived of union with "The One" seemed, to Thomson, to be Hell and enough for any sinner. A climactic passage from "Doom of a City" summarizes the process:

All spirits from their infancy's bland sleeping
Must struggle to a strong and noble prime
Through sins, dangers, anguish, terrors,—
ever reaping

Costly fruits in every season of swift Time:
From their fountain in its deepest dark foundation,
Glory-shrouded in the shadow of God's Throne,
Through all worlds to their highest-soaring station
By unrest all have grown.

Life *is* only by perpetual on-flowing;
Torpid rest is the true life-devouring death;
Through stern struggles all things ever are upgrowing;
Sighs and moaning prove a vital-throbbing breath.
One alone—Eternal, Infinite, All-holy,
Is in changeless rest; the Perfect grows nor grew:
Finite souls and all things live by progress solely,
All *are* but what they *do*.[7]

The last line was, of course, Carlyle's contribution, and it was, in fact, as a Carlylean poet-prophet that Thomson concluded this poem, for the narrator, who had overheard God delivering judgments on the inhabitants of a doomed city, returns to England with a fierce warning. Yes, England, thy power is great,

. . . but thy evil is great no less,
And thy wealth is poor to pay the debt of thy guiltiness;
And the world is judged with justice, and thou must pass through that fire
Which hath tested so sternly the glitter of Venice and Carthage and Tyre:
For no wealth can bribe away the doom of the Living God,

No haughtiest strength confront the sway of
His chastening rod.
Repent, reform, or perish! the Ages cry unto
thee:
Listen, oh listen, ere yet it be late, thou
swarthy Queen of the Sea!

The indictments against England were, for the most part, Carlyle's indictments: one is supposed to love one's neighbor as one's self, and there is ample wealth to clothe and feed all, but social laws dictate that one person should be corruptingly rich, another bitterly poor, another starving to death; trade is fretted by gambling greed, slimed by creeping fraud, poisoned by falsehood's breath; rulers and priests have scarcely one noble aim, are deaf to the holy voice of the conscience of the world, are blind to God's banner; the streets are filled each night with a holocaust of woes, sins, lusts, and blasphemies, and so on—an indictment, in brief, which Thomson undoubtedly considered to be very much in line with the "modern march of thought." Yet by the time he reached his attack upon the Church, that "mere Fossil of a Faith," he had become so carried away with his vision of what Christianity had once been—when the poor and mean were wealthy and dignified; when there was freedom, faith, chastity, peace, and love; when the noblest of men were wholly devoted to Him; when there was a real Hell with a Devil for His foe, and a God-ruled Heaven of triumph awaiting His followers—that the old Christian beliefs burst through his pantheistic ramblings, and he concluded this remarkable poem with the angry, almost biblical, prophesy that his countrymen were doomed

If ye do not all repent, and cleanse each one
her heart
From the foulness circling with its blood to
poison every part.

It is, of course, impossible to say how much of all this Thomson really believed, and how much simply reflected the growing pains of a young man struggling to make sense out of a seemingly senseless universe. His flirtation with reincarnation apparently continued through the fifties, for an 1859 essay on Burns again plays with such ideas, stating Thomson's belief that "Burns, before he arrived at this earthly inn, had been working vehemently for some half-a-dozen lives at statesmanship, philosophy, war, divinity, and what not, whereof we find dim reminiscences in the papers left behind him here." [8] The conglomeration of ideas blending Christianity with pantheism continued into the sixties; an article written in 1860 vigorously defended Shelley against the charge of atheism by arguing that the pantheism Shelley expressed in such poems as "Prometheus Unbound," that "apotheosis of the One Infinite Soul," differed little from "what is called pure Theism," though "of the Greeks rather than the Hebrews." [9] And even the 1862 "The Angel" section of "A Lady of Sorrow" has the Dead Girl–Angel resting in a "separate sphere divine," praising and giving thanks to God, communing with the holy mysteries of love, and making angelic visits to her soul mate on earth as she awaits the "Supreme Sacrament" of their union in Heaven. We may, in any event, be certain of one thing: whatever degree of importance Thomson placed on different aspects of these beliefs, he found his total world picture considerably less than satisfactory, for the conflict between pantheism and Christianity was indeed irreconcilable. As a result, the poetry of the late fifties and early sixties reflects his doubts with a poignancy seldom discernible in his later work, not even in the hopeless dejection of "The City of Dreadful Night."

An 1858 sonnet, originally titled "Heresy," later "A Recusant," seems to summarize the dilemma. As the speaker yearningly gazes upon the spire of a church, wishing he might be able to enter, to kneel and pray so that all disbelief and doubt might pass away, Conscience cruelly replies that "There is but one good rest, / Whose head is pillowed upon Truth's pure breast." Not only orthodox Christianity, but also Thomson's pantheistic Christianity, was apparently being denied by "Truth," and thus, just a few years after formulating the complicated eschatology of "The Doom of a City," his "Mater Tenebrarum" angrily demands the truth about the soul of his Dead Girl–Angel:

> Have they killed her indeed? is her soul as her body, which long
> Has mouldered away in the dust where the foul worms throng?
> O'er what abhorrent Lethes, to what remotest star,
> Is she rapt away from my pursuit through cycles and systems far?

The answer Thomson gave himself was emphatic: "She is dead, she is utterly dead": a denial not only of the "cycles and systems far," but also of the soul's immortality. Unless the soul was immortal, unless God rewarded good and punished evil, then there was

> No hope in this worn-out world, no hope beyond the tomb;
> No living and loving God, but blind and stony Doom.
> Anguish and grief and sin, terror, disease and despair.

As a result of such despair, and perhaps largely through a maddening curiosity to know, once for all, the "Truth," the poetry written between 1858 and 1860 reveals, for the first time, a fascination with death which becomes almost a death wish. In the 1858 "The Cypress and the Roses," for instance, the speaker has planted roses that have withered and faded from the "constant deadly shade" of a cypress tree:

> One black cypress shade will blight
> Myriads of roses of delight;
> One stern cypress will outlast
> Ages of roses withering fast,

Too well I see.
What is left me now to do?
What, but sink at the dark root too;
Let the baleful gloom and rue
Kill also me.

The following year, in the 1859 "A Real Vision of Sin" ("written in disgust at Tennyson's, which is very pretty and clever and silly and truthless"), Thomson almost seems to agree with the old hag who invites her mate to commit suicide with her:

Come, and this loathsome life out-smother,
No fear that we'll ever have another:
The rain may beat and the wind may wuther,

But we shall rot with the rotting soil,
Safe in sleep from the whole sad coil.

And by 1860, with allegory and narrative discarded, the death wish was given forthright expression in a poem actually addressed "To Our Ladies of Death":

Weary of erring in this desert Life,
Weary of hoping hopes for ever vain,
Weary of struggling in all-sterile strife,
Weary of thought which maketh nothing plain,
I close my eyes and calm my panting breath,
And pray to Thee, O ever-quiet Death!
To come and soothe away my bitter pain.

Even here, however, Thomson was still clinging to his "Doom of a City" beliefs wherein the eternal soul could rise through cycles to attain union with God; hopeless as this plea sounds, it was not addressed either to the Eternal Death figure (the Lady of Annihilation) or to the Eternal Life figure (the Lady of Beatitude), but to the Lady of Oblivion, the "Restful One," who cared for those "trodden down beneath the march of Fate." The death Thomson requested here was, in fact, merely a "perfect sleep,"

That when I thus have drunk my inmost fill
Of perfect peace, I may arise renewed;
In soul and body, intellect and will,
Equal to cope with Life whate'er its mood.

If, however, the Lady of Oblivion could not allow him this restful sleep, then he pleaded that she lead him back to Mother Earth where he could "die by abdication of my separate soul," relinquishing his rights to the long march of the Life Eternal, yet still avoiding the abhorrent prospect of Eternal Death.

So shall this single, self-impelling piece
Of mechanism from lone labor cease,
Resolving into union with the Whole.

Clearly, then, thought was, as Thomson felt, making nothing plain, and within a few years of this melodramatic plea for "perfect sleep" he was to reject completely these youthful impressions of a world about which he still knew remarkably little, and was to find himself, not praying mournfully for ever-quiet death, but shouting exuberantly, "Thank God for Life!" The first phase of the movement from theist to atheist was to be concluded, emphatically concluded, early in 1863 with an extremely important, although previously unnoticed, article in Bradlaugh's *National Reformer.*

Actually, the reversal of position probably began a few months earlier, in the fall of 1862, when, after being discharged from the army, Thomson came to live in London, determined to make a new life as poet and critic. He was, as it soon became apparent, dismally unprepared for such a role, at least within the intellectual milieu in which he then found himself. While living in Ireland and Jersey, weighing his Shelley in one hand and his Bible in the other, he had been relatively untouched by the new ideas surging through England, and, although it seems incredible that the man who had been corresponding with Charles Bradlaugh and had even been contributing articles to the

National Reformer [10] should have been ignorant of the latest scientific and scholarly achievements, a review by "B.V." which appeared in Bradlaugh's paper in January, 1863, indicates that this was precisely the case.[11]

The book under consideration was Frederic Harrison's *The Meaning of History,* two lectures, largely based on Comte, in which history was traced from prehistoric times, man being described in his early state as "nothing but the first of the animals." Thomson was shocked and outraged:

> What authority has Mr. Harrison or M. Comte for this charming picture? Do not the traditions of nearly all races lead us back to see our first fathers, not groping their way up from the pit, but descending from the empyrean? What antique records place the iron age before the golden? What savage tribes have been known to civilize themselves? . . . if God had planted the world on such a plan, he would have been worse than a Colonial Secretary peopling a new continent with scum; . . . the human boat, launched with such a hole in its bottom, must have floundered on the brink of the year one.

Thomson had admittedly never read Comte; he had obviously not read Darwin; but he undoubtedly read the following letter written to Bradlaugh by an incensed reader and published in the next *National Reformer:*

> Those who desire to know M. Comte's views of history and humanity should read Mr. F. Harrison's "Two Lectures on the Meaning of History," lately published, of which I am sorry to say a most flippant and unjust criticism lately appeared in the National Reformer, I cannot but think without the editor's knowledge. It was not written by a Secularist, but apparently by a Theist or Christian, as the writer adopted the fable of a "golden age."

Thomson did not defend his review, or the position he

had taken in it, but two years passed before he again attempted to write for the *National Reformer*. When he did, no one could ever have accused him of defending Christian fables, for during those two years he rejected all his old Christian beliefs. No one single factor seems to have been responsible; a great many influences were at work upon his thought during these two years and he was, no doubt, more than receptive to most of them. I suspect, however, that the most important of these influences was the *National Reformer* and its editor, for it was at Bradlaugh's home that Thomson lived during these years, it was in Bradlaugh's library that he read,[12] it was Bradlaugh's friends with whom he conversed, and it was Bradlaugh's London that became, for the most part, his London—not yet a city of dreadful night, but, in Thomson's eyes, a city already darkened by the volleys and thunders of the atheist freethinkers soon to become his closest friends. The cannons to the left were labeled "Science"; those to the right, "Higher Criticism"; and the banner proudly unfurled above the fray was that of the "dear old *N.R.*"

When Thomson arrived in London in November, 1862, the *National Reformer* was in its third year of publication, already an unusually long life for a freethought periodical. In spite of two major wrangles over editorship, Bradlaugh had managed to retain control, and, with circulation increasing weekly, was highly optimistic about the future of his paper.[13] I doubt, however, that Bradlaugh, even in his most optimistic moments, imagined that it would continue to appear weekly for the next thirty years, exerting an influence on the age which is impossible to calculate, but was probably far greater than most Victorians suspected or, at least, ever admitted, for Bradlaugh's intention was that the *National Reformer*

> should make war on all the religions of the world, because all the religions of the world are based, not on human knowledge, but on human ignorance.

> That it should advocate Atheism, because the word "God" has been used by bad men as an engine to oppress weak men, and because practical Atheism is the development of humanity. That it should specially attack the Bible, because the Bible is the book most hurtful in its influence on the young, and it is necessary that children should not be compelled to read it until their intellects are sufficiently educated to judge of its value. That it should give battle to Christianity, because Christianity has been for centuries a stumbling-block to European civilization, and is at the present day antagonistic to all real progress.[14]

Although early issues were occasionally sensational in method (headlines such as "Suicide of Another Clergyman" were not uncommon) and often ludicrous in content ("What Has the Bible Done for Women?" "Did Jesus Instruct His Followers Correctly?" "Was Moses Bacchus?"), for the most part an effort was made to present sober, intelligent discussions on current topics. Moreover, Bradlaugh, who wrote a good many of the early articles under his famous pseudonym "Iconoclast," was quick to realize that iconoclastic activity of a far more respectable and enduring nature was being developed on a good many other fronts, and the policy soon became to allow the authorities to speak for themselves. Thus, as early as 1860, notices, reviews, and summaries of *The Origin of the Species* began to appear; Huxley's retort to Bishop Wilberforce was reported to readers at once; and Darwin's introduction to the American edition of his classic was reprinted in its entirety. The Colenso controversy, *Essays and Reviews*, Renan's *Life of Jesus*—all were presented to readers, such a deluge of new material being available that by 1864 it seemed to the editor that "scarcely a week passes by without our being able to record additional admission on the part of Christians of the fallibility and errors of the Bible."

Such, then, was the intellectual environment surrounding Thomson when he arrived in London and took up quarters in what was for him still very much the camp of the enemy. It was, undoubtedly, not the sort of environment he had expected. Although he had been sending Bradlaugh articles for the past two years, he had never taken the *National Reformer* seriously, and his early contributions, although not outright satiric, seemed designed to antagonize both Bradlaugh and his readers. The only poem submitted was Christian in its orientation; a short article on Wordsworth was pantheistic; the previously mentioned letter on Shelley denied Shelley's atheism; and a longer essay on Shelley actually began with a quotation from the Bible, the poet's greatness being attributed to his having been "God-possessed." The only article directly relating to reform pointed out to the National Reformers that it was far easier to reform the world than to reform one's self, which was where Thomson insisted such activity must begin.[15]

Bradlaugh was no doubt distressed to receive such contributions from his old friend, but he published them all, not only through friendship, but because he had proudly boasted that his paper, unlike the Christian periodicals, would be a free platform where "Christian, Pagan, Theist, Pantheist, Atheist, all may say their say"; he shrewdly realized that such articles would not only attract a wider circle of readers, but would stimulate controversy, a healthy state for both the sifting and winnowing of truth and, to be sure, for circulation. In any event, the situation as Thomson saw it in November, 1862, was somewhat different, for it was one thing to amuse himself writing "heresies" for a heretical journal when he had been living hundreds of miles away from the city in which it was published, but quite another thing to do so when accepting the hospitality of the editor. To make things worse, Bradlaugh insisted on giving Thomson a feature article as a welcome-home present, a gift that Thomson had not the slightest idea what to do with. In his present position he could hardly ridicule the movement, and yet his beliefs, though increasingly torn by doubts, would not allow him to write the sort of anti-Christian diatribe that Bradlaugh wanted. The article that resulted, "The Established Church,"[16] was, therefore, hardly a rousing success; the main concession made to National Reformers was that, all things considered, there were probably just as many sincere secularists and atheists as there were sincere Christians. The article did refer to the Church as an "effete Strength," which at least sounded properly anti-Christian, but this was something Thomson had been contending for years, and, in general, the attack against non-Christian Christians was still very much along the Carlyle-Shelley lines already noted in his poetry. Perhaps as a slight apology for his inadequacy as an iconoclast, Thomson did allow Bradlaugh to publish "A Recusant," but in turn Bradlaugh accepted two poems, "E. B. B." and "To Our Ladies of Death," the latter piece somewhat out of line with the editorial policy, which wanted "really stirring, original poetry for the people." Thomson even attempted to review a book on Moses,[17] a short tract by J. Lotsky which contended that the Judaic concept of Jehovah had been derived from Egyptian religion; but that Thomson had any idea of the importance of the subject he was treating is doubtful, for the following week his review of the Frederic Harrison lectures appeared, and after that, silence.

> Beneath and around
> A long shuddering thrill,
> Then all again still.

The shock of the rejoinder to his Harrison review was, I suspect, immense; if Comte and Harrison were right about the early state of man, if God really had "peopled the earth with scum," where then was the divinity in the human soul? Where, in fact, was the human soul?

If life was nothing but a cruel war in which only the fittest would survive, without any reward for good or punishment for evil, then where, most important of all, was God? The lines just quoted, and those that follow, are taken from a short poem that Thomson wrote a year after the Harrison review, appropriately entitled "Desolate."

> He cried out through the night:
> "Where is the light?
> Shall nevermore
> Open Heaven's door?
> Oh, I am left
> Lonely, bereft!"

The night makes no reply. The voice rings out, but no "answering light" appears; no "syllabled sound" can be heard. Just that long shuddering thrill, then complete silence, nothingness. By the end of 1863, after a year of reeducation by the National Reformers and the current best sellers (Huxley's *Man's Place in Nature,* Lyell's *Antiquity of Man,* Spenser's *Principles of Biology* had all appeared in 1863), it seemed to Thomson, as he expressed it in one of the few poems written during this period, that "The Fire That Filled My Heart of Old" had completely burned out, that life was a "flat of sullen dearth," that it held for him

> No love, no hate, no hope, no fear,
> No anguish and no mirth.

In brief, his old world picture was shattered, and there was nothing to do but emphatically disown it. "Vane's Story," begun early in 1864 and completed in 1865, became the vehicle, a personal history of past and present beliefs and, at the same time, an anatomy of the universe.

The old cosmology had been based on the belief that "all *are* but what they *do,*" that men must "struggle to a strong and noble prime," must, in brief, work out God's will. Vane and Thomson wash their hands of the whole futile process:

But I am working out God's will
Alike when active and when still;
And work we good or work we ill.
We never work against His will . . .
All work, work, work! Why must we toil
For ever in the hot turmoil?

He had worked long enough, struggling to make sense out of a senseless universe. He was determined never again to be accused of perpetrating Christian fables about a "golden age" which, he was now convinced, every fool could see was mythical; determined never again to concern himself with the future of souls which, he now believed, simply did not exist.

. . . I beseech no more
That one and one may make up four,
When one and one are my assets
And four the total of my debts;
Nor do I now with fervour pray
To cast no shadow in broad day.

So much for Shelley's idealism, for prayer, for faith in God; it had become obvious to Thomson that

God exists, or not, indeed,
Quite irrespective of our creed;
We live, or live not, after death,
Alike whatever be our faith;
And not a single truth, in brief,
Is modified by our belief.

Thomson had, therefore, determined to approach life as a realist, to see things as they really were, as Darwin and Huxley were seeing them, as Heine, too, had seen them, for Heine, we recall, had provided the poem's epilogue:

Glory warms us in the grave!
Stupid words, that sound so brave!

The world was, no doubt, chaotic, but if that was "Truth," then that was the way Thomson was determined to see it. Thus, in "A Lady of Sorrow," the discarded phantasy on which he now resumed work, "The

Angel" who had been descending from Heaven to console her weary soul mate abruptly became "The Siren" —"more terrible than beautiful"; as she led Vane through the city,

> The churches dwindled before her into whitened sepulchres, the palaces were seen as dungeons populous with vermin; she showed the fire raging under the earth's thin vesture of green grass broidered with flowers, and the skeleton padded with raw flesh beneath the skin of the beautiful; her finger point seared the hidden folly of the wise and the secret terror of the brave; her glance transfixed the foul lust in the lover, and the core of sublimated selfishness in the holy ones; all the noble and mighty and reverend of the kingdoms she transformed into gibbering apes. She laughed back the world into chaos.

We might well expect that such an attitude would have led Thomson directly to agnosticism, and when the Lady of Sorrow returns in her third phase, as "The Shadow," her reply to Vane's questions about the nature and the purpose of the universe does indeed sound like the advice of a slightly theatrical Huxley: "Know this only, that you can never know; of this only be assured, that you shall never be assured; doubt not that you must doubt to the end—if ever end there be." But, in spite of such convictions, Thomson did not, at this time, become an agnostic, nor did he become an atheist. He became what he had been trying to become for the past decade—a pantheist who

> believed in the soul's immortality as a Materialist believes in the immortality of matter; he believed that the universal soul subsists for ever, just as a Materialist believes that universal matter subsists for ever, without increase or decrease, growth or decay; he no more believed in the immortality of any particular soul than the Materialist believes in the immortality of any particular body. The one

> substance is eternal, the various forms are ever varying.[18]

Pantheistic, to be sure, but a far cry from the romantic idealism of Shelley, and radically different from Thomson's former view of his relations with the universe; now the immortality of "any particular soul" was completely denied, and he believed that

> The universe can do without me, as *me*, though my being is part of its being. When I die, Nature seizes on my effects, administers my estate, duly distributing the property. I . . . still continue my interest in the general life by every particle of my being thus distributed, and by the enduring existence of all that I have ever rayed forth—from attraction of gravity, attraction and repulsion electrical, to thought and emotion of humanity. Nothing is lost, though the walls of the *Ego* have given way and let in the floods of the universe.[19]

Nothing in the universe was indispensable, nothing was sacred, except insofar as everything was sacred. There was no longer a merit system for ascending into higher spheres, no Judgment Day for handing out awards, no throne around which angelic souls might flutter, and, of course, no God to sit upon the nonexistent throne. God had not, in fact, created man; it was man who had created God; or so, at least, the Lady of Sorrow explained to the bewildered Vane. What you term God, she went on to add, is simply "universal life." "Why," she asked, as Thomson had undoubtedly been asking himself, "are you so unwilling to acknowledge your relationship with all the rest of the world and its creatures?" All things must decay and perish; every kind has its own aeon; when its time is fulfilled it becomes extinct. As today we study fossil relics of the past, so someday much higher races than ours will study our own relics, for Nature has no care for individuals, and races and times are simply individuals in a broader sense.

Obviously, Huxley and Darwin had been at work here too,[20] although neither of them was responsible for the new philosophy that Thomson evolved from his pantheism, a philosophy holding that, because the human animal was no more and no less than a segment of the universal life force, man had but one duty—he must "live." This obligation to live was what Thomson now saw as the great panacea, for he felt that for ages, while endeavoring to persuade themselves that their "minute glowworm soul-sparks" lamped infinity and eternity, men had not dared to "live" true life. To Thomson the discovery was nothing short of sensational, and, although the message was as old as *carpe diem*, he could not resist climbing on the soapbox to proclaim it to his fellowmen:

> If you really lived, knowing, and gladly accepting, and bravely working out your little part in the sublime economy of the universe; ever conscious of your insignificance as an isolated creature, but no less conscious of your lofty and even divine significance as one flame of the universal fire, one note in the infinite harmony; without arrogance, selfishness, delusion, disdain; without hope, or fear, or self-contradictory longing, yet burning with pure aspiration; then I would not preach to you thus.[21]

No longer a Christian soul created by a Christian God, fallen through original sin, redeemed by the blood of Christ, one day to sit at the right hand of God; no longer a separate soul placed in its separate sphere by a Shelleyan "One" who would judge its merit and raise it through increasingly higher spheres until it attained union with the Divine; now merely a flame in the universal fire, a note in the infinite harmony, Thomson felt that he was at last freed from past bondage, freed to live, to burn with pure aspiration. Thus, in the mid-sixties, the most prolific poetic period of his life, Thomson, as a pantheistic humanist, wrote poem after poem proclaiming this doctrine. The 1865 "Sunday up the River" reverberates joyously:

> Let my voice ring out and over the earth,
> Through all the grief and strife,
> With a golden joy in a silver mirth:
> Thank God for Life!

In "Sunday at Hampstead," also written in 1865, the lovers leave the "grief and strife" of the city to find the golden joy in the open country:

> Too grateful to God for His Sabbath
> To shut its hours in a church.

And as they travel merrily along in the train, the narrator points out the glorious moral:

> We will rush ever on without fear;
> Let the goal be far, the flight be fleet!
> For we carry the Heavens with us, Dear,
> While the Earth slips from our feet!

Heaven was no longer a goal to be worked toward, and perhaps attained, in an afterlife; it was carried, so to speak, in one's pocket, available to any man who merely had the courage to face the facts and live his life bravely. One must not worry about things of which nothing can be known with certainty. One must not even analyze or probe too deeply into those things that can conceivably be learned, for

> . . . those eyes alone see well that view
> Life's lovely surfaces of form and hue;
> And not Death's entrails, looking through and through.

This is the advice given in the 1866 "Philosophy," the moral of which is:

> If Midge will pine and curse its hours away
> Because Midge is not Everything For-aye,
> Poor Midge thus loses its one summer day;
> Loses its all—and winneth what, I pray?

And at the conclusion of the 1867 "Two Lovers," we find what is probably the most succinct statement of the entire philosophy:

Live out your whole free life while yet on
earth;
Seize the quick Present, prize your one
sure boon;
Though brief, each day a golden sun has
birth;
Though dim, the night is gemmed with
stars and moon.

Such, then, was Thomson's answer to the new philosophies which, in the 1860's, seemed to be putting all in doubt. It was not, however, enough, for if the new religious faith dictated that man's sole duty was to burn with aspiration as one flame of the universal fire, then Bradlaugh had been right all along, and it was indeed necessary to wage war on the religions of the world, to remove those great stumbling blocks—God, the Bible, and Christianity. Heine had seen this need; so had Blake, whose poetry, which Thomson first read in 1863, seemed to express so beautifully what Thomson now felt to be the simple reality of life, and whose message, as Thomson then understood it, coincided with his own desire to attack those priests in black gowns who had been binding with briers his joys and desires, and devastating his Garden of Life and Love.[22] In January, 1865, then, exactly two years after the Harrison review, Thomson's first anti-Christian satire appeared as the feature article in the New Year's issue of the *National Reformer,* a satire written, not, as has long been assumed, by a pessimistic atheist, but by an optimistic pantheist working in the interests of humanism.

The first victim seemed a fairly safe one, the already heavily attacked author of the Athanasian Creed. "What infidel," Thomson boldly asked his readers, "ever dealt with God more contemptuously and blasphemously than this creed has dealt with him?" Its author is like an anatomist who

> gets possession of the corpse of God (He died of starvation doing slop-work for Abstraction and

> Company; and the dead body was purveyed by the well-known resurrectionist Priestcraft), and cuts it open and expounds the generation and function of its three principal organs.
>
> This humble-minded devotee . . . expounds this Infinite with the most complete and complacent knowledge, turns it inside out and upside down, tells us all about it, cuts it up into three parts, and then glues it together again with a glue that has the tenacity of atrocious wrongheadedness instead of the coherence of logic, puts his mark upon it, and says, "This is the only genuine thing in the God line. If you are taken in by any other, why, go and be damned"; and having done all that, finishes by chanting, "Glory be to the Father, and to the Son, and to the Holy Ghost!"

Obviously, the entire concept of the Trinity had come under attack, although it was probably his treatment of "Go and be damned" which gave Thomson the most satisfaction; the idea of a hell lorded over by a pitchfork-holding Satan had annoyed him for years, and was, in fact, one of the earliest of his Christian beliefs to be discarded. "Vane's Story," written the preceding year, had contained a more complete statement of his disgust with the Christian idea of Hell, for he felt that

> If any human soul at all
> Must die the second death, must fall
> Into that gulph of quenchless flame
> Which keeps its victims still the same,
> Unpurified as unconsumed,
> To everlasting torments doomed;
> Then I give God my scorn and hate,
> And turning back from Heaven's gate
> (Suppose me got there!) bow, *Adieu!*
> *Almighty Devil, damn me too!*

Compared with the somewhat hysterical satire of "The Athanasian Creed," this passage seems a considerably stronger and more convincing expression of

Thomson's belief, suggesting that, in print at least ("Vane's Story" was in manuscript at this time), he still felt a little uncertain about his role as a National Reformer. A few months after the article on the Athanasian Creed appeared, however, Thomson came upon a passage in which John Stuart Mill had written: "I will call no being good who is not what I mean when I apply that epithet to my fellow creatures; and if such a being can sentence me to hell for not so calling him, to hell I will go." "Vane's Story" suddenly seemed sanctified, and Thomson at once wrote a letter to the *National Reformer* [23] in which he quoted the above passage from his unpublished poem, and pointed out the close relationship between his own idea and Mill's. He was elated as he wrote, and his mood was definitely playful, but I suspect he was completely serious when he noted that he had, before reading Mill, condemned his lines to "penal obscurity." If, however, the great philosopher could think, write, and, yes, even publish such ideas, why then so could James Thomson. Any qualms he might have had about iconoclastic endeavors now vanished, and a month later, in September, 1865, he began a personal crusade against Christianity which saw his work appearing in virtually every issue of the *National Reformer* for the next two years, years in which "B.V." attained, if not the poet-laureateship of free-thought periodicals, at least a reputation as the most talented essayist of the movement.[24]

It is not necessary to examine all these essays in detail. Although some were sober discussions and some were blasphemous satires, some extremely clever and some thoroughly tedious, they were all, for the most part, attempting to make the same point—that Christianity, in placing its entire emphasis upon a hypothetical afterlife, was preventing men from attaining glory on earth, from partaking of human heavens, the only heavens about which one could be certain. The first essay, then, was typical of most of those that followed;

through an analysis of "Mr. Kingsley's Convertites,"[25] it exposed Christianity as the antithesis of "living life." Its inspiration came, I suspect, from Heine, who had written that "when health is used up, money used up, and sound human sense used up, Christianity begins,"[26] for what Thomson rather ingeniously suggested was that Kingsley's characters were all "more or less naturally good but decidedly godless" at the beginning of the novels, but became religious at the end, "not when healthy, but when diseased." Alton Locke, Lancelot Smith, Raphael Ben Ezra, and Tom Thurnal were all thoroughly anatomized to show how religion serves as "a drug for the sick, not as wholesome food for the healthy," how Christianity is "a religion to die with, not to live with." The conclusion, in this delightful if somewhat distorted analysis of Kingsley's novels, is that if Kingsley's "Muscular Christianity" were to become the Church of the future and be composed of creatures like his "Convertites," then "Westminster Abbey must be turned into a Grande Chartreuse, and St. Paul's into an Hospital for Incurables, and the metropolitan Cathedral of England must be Bedlam."

Not all the essays that followed were so skillful as this one, nor were many of them developed on a literary theme, but they did, in most instances, attempt to be topical, particularly when they touched upon other aspects of religion, such as the Christian Hell, the Trinity, or evangelical enthusiasm,[27] which were, indirectly if not overtly, major stumbling blocks to living true life. To give but one example, when Gladstone delivered an address on "The Place of Ancient Greece in the Providential Order of the World,"[28] Thomson immediately jumped at the opportunity to expound his message. Gladstone's argument was that while the Jews were preserving reverence for God, the Greeks were preserving reverence for man, the two elements being united into perfection with the advent of Jesus. When we recall the position taken in the Harrison review, it is somewhat amusing to find Thomson beginning his attack by ridiculing the assumption that human history follows a providential order, much less that the consummation of such order was the advent of Jesus. His main points, however, were that if, as Gladstone claimed, the Greek element was most pure in the Homeric poems, and the Jewish element in the Mosaic laws, then why did the world have to wait a thousand years for Christ to unite them into perfection? Anyway, where was the monotheism in Christianity? "In the belief in three gods, Father and Son and Holy Ghost, with a Manichean devil thrown into the bargain?" Where was the humanism? "In the bitter contempt and hatred for the human body and this life which pervade the whole New Testament?" The essay concluded by asking Gladstone if it had occurred to him that at the time he was speaking more than eighteen centuries had passed since the consummating advent, and that "the company of the devil and his angels having become utterly bankrupt so long ago, the official liquidator seems to have been rather dilatory in winding up that evil association and distributing the property."

This conclusion pleased Thomson immensely and led to three essays which may briefly be examined as final examples of his iconoclastic endeavors during these years. The first two, "The Story of a Famous Old Firm" and "Christmas Eve in the Upper Circles," were both satires which, although neither was particularly clever nor, to be sure, in good taste, became classics of freethought literature.[29] In "The Story of a Famous Old Firm" the object of attack was, once again, the Trinity, a drawn-out analogy being formed between the triune God and a business firm manufacturing the Bread of Life. "Christmas Eve in the Upper Circles," the more successful of the two, was a portrait of God as a doughty old man envious of Zeus, for, although the Olympians had perished, they at least had known how to live and love. At the conclusion, that "solemn prig" Christ is trying on his lamb costume for the morrow's Christmas festival, and a thoroughly disgusted God sneaks off with his favorite chaplain (Rabelais) and with two friars (Swift and Sterne) to feast on a bit of ambrosia and nectar which he had hidden away after the sack of Olympus. Obviously, both satires were blasphemous, and, although Thomson had a Heine precedent for such blasphemy (he had, in fact, just been translating several similar satires from the *De l'Allemagne*), perhaps the most interesting thing about them is that they reveal the extent to which he was willing to go in his role as an iconoclast, as either could have led to prosecution under the blasphemy laws. Some twenty years later, his friend G. W. Foote was to spend a year in prison for publishing a cartoon considerably less blasphemous, and it was only through good fortune (and perhaps the rather limited circulation of the *National Reformer*) that Thomson escaped a similar fate. That he was fully aware of the possible consequences is revealed by his notation in a memorandum book just before the second satire appeared: "Wrote to Watts [the subeditor of the *National Reformer*] that B. agrees with me that *Xmas Eve in the Upper Circle* should appear as I sent it with my usual initials, I taking full responsibility for it." [30]

In any event, this particular attack on Christ seems to have troubled Thomson; fearing that some readers might have misinterpreted his satire, a few months later he published a third, and far more effective, essay [31] in which he made it clear that he had not been attacking Jesus (the most sublime of mystics and a heroic and saintly martyr), but the falsification that had turned him into a "self-schemed, sham-sacrifice of a God." Heine's influence was again at work, for the essay was little more than an elaboration of the epigraph, a passage from the *Reisebilder:* "These hereditary enemies of the Truth . . . have even had the art to degrade this first preacher of the Mountain, the purest hero of Liberty; for, unable to deny that he was earth's greatest man, they have made of him heaven's smallest god." Thomson's emphasis, however, was on the idea that Christianity, in making Jesus a god, was "trampling on Man" through assuming men could not possibly be so good as Jesus was, which actually twisted Heine's idea back to Thomson's pantheistic plea that Christianity was a stumbling block to man's efforts to "live" the only life he had. Although Christians were shocked at the outrage offered humanity by the theory of evolution, they themselves committed a far greater outrage: "Little matters whence we sprang; we are what we are. But much matters to what we may attain. If the Development Theory plants our feet in the slime, the Christian Theory bows our head to the dust."

For two years, then, Thomson continued his attacks, pounding away at the same basic idea. By the end of the two years, however, his essays began to appear spasmodically and then, in May, 1867, they stopped altogether. For a few more months some of his poems, mainly rejects from the "respectable" periodicals, were given to Bradlaugh for publication, as were three translations from Heine and the long since completed phantasy, "A Lady of Sorrow." But except for these few pieces, National Reformers had to get along without "B.V.'s" assistance; although his name continued to appear, his role as an iconoclast was over for the time being, and his contributions became limited to translations of the work of one man, a reformer of sorts, but of a very different kind. Thomson had discovered Leopardi.

It has often been assumed that the Italian pessimist exerted a major influence on Thomson's thought, turning him, if not from theist to atheist, at least from optimist to pessimist—and certainly the assumption is understandable. Thomson's studies of Leopardi began in 1867, in the same months in which he abruptly terminated his iconoclasm;[32] his first translation of a Leopardi dialogue was published in November, 1867, within a month of the completion of "Two Lovers," the last poem in which Thomson ever expressed the "live life" philosophy; for the next two years, 1868 and 1869, almost his entire effort went into translating the *Operette Morali* and the *Pensieri;* [33] and, more than a decade later, his first volume of collected poems was dedicated "to the memory of the younger brother of Dante—Giacomo Leopardi—a spirit as lofty, a genius as intense, with a yet more tragic doom." Yet, in spite of all this, I do not believe that Leopardi was the actual source of the atheism that replaced the pantheism, nor of the pessimism that followed the optimism of the mid-sixties; a man who has spent five years claiming his "divine significance as one flame of the universal fire" and singing "Thank God for Life!" simply does not pick up a book of dialogues written in a foreign language and suddenly decide to change his tune. I feel, in fact, that Leopardi did little more than confirm a latent pessimism which was present even during Thomson's most joyous declarations,[34] for two major obstacles to the philosophy had begun to loom on Thomson's horizon, and, as he approached the Leopardi years, it became increasingly apparent that both of them were insurmountable.

The first concerned the problem of liberty versus necessity. In an 1866 essay,[35] when the matter was being hotly debated by the National Reformers, Thomson had vehemently argued against the necessitarian's position, for if a man was to live life bravely and burn with pure aspiration, it was obviously essential that he have complete control over his fate, that he be morally and intellectually responsible for his actions. Although several necessitarians attacked "B.V.'s" essay (one letter stated that although the remarks "of so highly intelligent a critic . . . could hardly fail to be of interest," "B.V." did not, unfortunately, understand the problem), Thomson never replied, and the matter, on the surface at least, was allowed to drop. But that it still troubled him is obvious, for his beliefs were completely absurd if it was really true that man did not possess a free will, if Fate and Chance could combine to condemn any given flame in the infinite fire—no matter how much that flame might wish to burn brightly—to a lifetime of sputtering sparks.

Even more frightening was the second obstacle. After almost five years of preaching the glory of living, Thomson was beginning to suspect that, taking it all in all, testing the best of moments against the worst, life in itself was really not a very good show. As he was to express it a few years later, "of what happiness there is among men the greater part is on such low levels that a thoughtful man may well account it worse than his misery."[36]

One of the first Leopardi dialogues that Thomson chose to translate (*National Reformer,* Dec. 1, 1867) was that between a Natural Philosopher and a Metaphysician. The Natural Philosopher rushes up to his friend shouting, "Eureka," he has discovered the art of living long and has just written a book expounding that art.

Metaphysician: Take my advice. Get a small casket of lead, shut that book in it, bury it, and before you die remember to leave record of the spot, so that the book may be brought forth when the art shall be discovered of living happily.

Natural Phil.: And in this way?

Metaphysician: In this way your book will be worth nothing. I would value it more if it contained the art of living but a short time.

Natural Phil.: That has been already known some few years; and it was not difficult to discover.

Metaphysician: At any rate, I esteem it more than yours.

Natural Phil.: Why?

Metaphysician: Because if life is not happy, as until now it has not been, it is better for us to have it short than long.

The dialogue concludes with the following comment by the Metaphysician:

> If you would in prolonging life be really useful to men, discover an art by which their sensations and actions shall be multiplied in number and vigour. You will thus veritably increase human life; and filling those interminable spaces of time in which our existence rather endures than lives, you may justly boast that you prolong it. . . . But full of leisure and tedium, which is as much as to say vacant, it gives us cause to believe true that saying of Pyrrho, that there is no difference between life and death. The which if I believed, I swear to you death would terrify me not a little. But in fine, life should be vivid; that is, true life; else death surpasses it incomparably in worth.

A month after Thomson's translation of this dialogue had appeared, he began writing the strange narrative "In the Room," a poem in which the furniture of a lonely room relates the tale of its unhappy inhabitant who, we learn at the conclusion, has just committed suicide:

> It lay, the *he* become now *it*,
> Unconscious of the deep disgrace,
> Unanxious how its parts might flit
> Through what new forms in time and space.
>
> It lay and preached, as dumb things do,
> More powerfully than tongues can prate;
> Though life be torture through and through
> Man is but weak to plain of fate:
> The drear path crawls on drearier still
> To wounded feet and hopeless breast?

Well, he can lie down when he will,
And straight all ends in endless rest.

Leopardi and Thomson had both reached the same conclusion: when life is lived with wounded feet and hopeless breast, when it is no longer "vivid," then it is simply better to have it short than long.

On November 4, 1869, two years after the appearance of the first Leopardi translation, Thomson celebrated his birthday a few weeks early, if one may call it a celebration when the party consisted of Thomson sitting alone in his room and, for five solid hours, burning all his old letters, papers, manuscripts—everything, in fact, except a few recent notebooks and copies of the work already published. He felt that he had "climbed half-way up a long rope"; he was to be thirty-five in a few weeks, and, as he looked back on recent years, he decided he could do no better than consume the past in order better to face the future, "come in what guise it may." The past two years, Leopardi notwithstanding, had probably been the unhappiest of his life. As a man, he saw himself becoming increasingly alcoholic; as a poet, although his "Sunday up the River" had just appeared in *Fraser's Magazine,* his laboriously worked-over "Weddah" had been rejected by every periodical to which it had been submitted; as a crusading essayist, he undoubtedly felt (and rightly so) that his work was already doomed to obscurity in the back issues of the disreputable *National Reformer.* His "live life" philosophy now seemed a mockery. Life had no meaning; that was all right; he had come to terms with that cruel fact. But if it also had no happiness, no joy, then why live?

Would some little joy to-day
Visit us, heart!
Could it but a moment stay,
Then depart,
With the lustre of its wings
Lighting dreams of happy things,
O sad my heart!

This passage, written in the preceding year, 1868, is probably the most poignant outburst of Thomson's life, for these years were, beyond doubt, the darkest of his career. There was, however, another factor contributing to this sense of gloom, a factor that I believe was more important than personal unhappiness, necessitarian fears, and Leopardi's philosophical pessimism all combined. Having already come to terms with the imperfectibility of the universe, Thomson had finally become convinced of the imperfectibility of man. This conviction, I feel, is the key to the pessimism that was to earn him the title of the "English Leopardi." It is also the key to his interest in Leopardi, for Thomson considered that Leopardi's greatness lay in his recognition of the hopelessness of man's nature:

> Human nature is sanguine, and hoping for the best, argues for it; but, apart from the sanguineness itself, which is a real argument to the amount of its worth (and which, at bottom, is simply life's preference of the life it knows to the death it knows not), the facts of the world do not sanction the belief in a good tendency. Leopardi's greatness [lay] in steadfastly acknowledging these facts, so terrible and mysterious for us poor human kind; [in] his heroic self-restraint from all the frailties of vain hope which seduce even the best intellects.[37]

The story of Thomson's struggles to resolve the problem of man's relations with his fellowman is, however, matter for another chapter; for the present, it merely remains to establish the precise nature of his final position as an atheist.

When, in November, 1869, Thomson decided to burn his past and face the future anew, he felt he could best come to terms with his problems by writing a poem, as he had done five years earlier in "Vane's Story." We might well expect that Leopardi would have inspired such an effort, as Heine had done with "Vane's Story," but one of the strangest things about the Leopardi interlude was that it stopped almost as abruptly as it had begun. The long memoir of Leopardi began appearing in the *National Reformer* in October, 1869, but after eleven installments it was dropped midway, and Thomson never again made a serious effort to complete his project. Another Italian had taken over to guide his poetic endeavors, a poet who had also, on his thirty-fifth birthday, written a long personal allegory—Dante Alighieri. When Thomson began writing in January, 1870, it was, in fact, *The Inferno* that he had in mind, for he began by writing three short allegorical narratives in which the speaker was on a quest for the answer to life's mysteries, each of the three incidents treating one phase of Thomson's present predicament. Beyond this, the poem apparently had no real theme, no central organizing element, and it was only after the three narratives were completed that Thomson saw how they might be worked together into a long poem, one that he tentatively titled "The City of Night"—a gloomy poem, to be sure, as gloomy as his mood and his predicament, but not yet really "Dreadful." [38]

The first section (later to become Section II of the completed poem) was the one in which the speaker follows a stranger and sees him visit the three shrines where his faith, love, and hope had died. The cemetery was the scene of the first loss, for it was the realization of death's finality, without hope of immortality in Heaven, which finally destroyed Thomson's religious faith. Love had died at a villa, "stabbed by its own worshipped pair," perhaps an allusion to the Helen Gray affair, though it may also refer to one of the unknown romances of Thomson's middle years.[39] Hope had died in a "squalid house," the house, perhaps, in which he had lived after leaving the Bradlaughs, and in which "In the Room" had been written. Or perhaps it was the house in which he was presently living, for, if life held no joy and no happiness, then, since his world picture had been stripped bare of all else, there was indeed no hope. Blake had been the major inspiration behind Thomson's pursuit of joy, had given him the idea that a man could become like a little child again, pure and good and true. But now it was obvious that this dream was futile, that man could never regain childhood innocence, for man, he had decided, was hopelessly imperfectible. These ideas, then, were expressed in the second of the three sections written at this time, the section (later to become Section XVIII of "The City") that is not only based on Blake's drawing of Nebuchadnezzar,[40] but is a bitter comment on Blake's entire philosophy as Thomson had interpreted it. The old gray-bearded man crawling down his life-track in search of lost youth is vainly seeking precisely what Thomson had felt any man who but "lived true life" could find: "Eden innocence in Eden's clime." But the conclusion leaves no doubt that he now believed such attempts futile:

> For this is law, if law there be in Fate:
> What never has been, yet may have its when;
> The thing which has been, never is again.

The third section (later Section XX) is probably the most significant of all, for in it the speaker comes upon the two great statues, the angel-warrior facing the sphinx. As the monstrous lion-figure sits supreme—unmoving, cold, majestic, the symbol of Necessity—the angel-warrior challenges him with sword upraised (as Thomson himself had stood when a young man, "still on the Holy War intent," telling his fellowmen they must move onward). A sharp, clashing noise breaks the silence, and the angel's wings fall and lie shattered on the ground; but the figure of a warrior still stands, leaning on his sword (as Thomson had stood for the past decade, warring on the religions of the world which prevented men from living true life). Another clash, and the sword lies broken at the feet of what is now but "an unarmed man with raised hands impotent" (Thomson at that very moment, the victim of dead faith, dead love, dead hope). One last crash, the loudest of all, and then:

> The man had fallen forward, stone on stone,
> And lay there shattered, with his trunkless head
> Between the monster's large quiescent paws,
> Beneath its grand front changeless as life's laws.

Angel, warrior, impotent man—all were helpless before the monster of Fate. It was a frightening concept, a nightmare vision: not only had man lost God, lost Heaven, lost eternity; he had lost life itself.[41]

Other sections were written in 1870: a description of the city, now seen as the potential unifying element of the fragmentary allegories, a nightmare city of the mind, isolated on the east by a "shipless sea," on the south by waste marshes, black moorlands, and stony ridges, and on the north and west by a trackless wilderness of savage woods, enormous mountains, bleak uplands, and black ravines with torrent fountains. Within the city, the inhabitants were described as the "saddest and weariest men on earth," no one there completely sane, no one once entered, once realizing (as Thomson was realizing) the true horror of life, ever able to escape again. Everything grotesque, insane, horrible which Thomson had seen or read seemed to converge in these sections, the episode of the woman who carries her own bleeding heart, for instance, bearing traces of the bleak landscape of Hunt's "Scapegoat," of Blake's ghostly spiritual visions, of Doré's *Inferno* illustrations, even, perhaps, of Browning's "Childe Roland." [42] Thomson's own Dead Girl–Angel makes an appearance on her funeral bier in one section, and the climactic nightmare of the sequence sees a man attempt to escape by going to Hell ("Almighty Devil, damn me too!"), but being refused admission because he lacks the necessary hope which has to be abandoned at the gate. Thomson's hope too had been abandoned, and even the expression of that loss made no sense; with the most hopeless gesture of all, he cast aside the verses he had been struggling with for nine months—completely discarded his "City of Night." Almost three years were to pass before he would touch it again.

During these years Thomson went back to writing for the *National Reformer,* this time, however, primarily as an iconoclast on the social and political scene. Some anti-Christian essays did appear, but, for the most part, he had temporarily grown indifferent to religious iconoclasm; after the Leopardi interlude, his old attacks against the religion that prevented men from living true life no longer made sense. We find such comments as the following:

> For my own part, I have nothing worth mention to say against the book [the Bible]. . . . At the same time, I have no strong objection to another being put in its place. . . . In fact, for deep moral and spiritual lessons any one scripture is as good as any other: and I am persuaded that were we to found our National Church on Hamlet or Epipsychidion, on Tom Jones or A Tale of a Tub, on Euclid's Elements or Johnson's Dictionary, or on the whole half dozen bound together, we should with any one or with all flourish in religion even as we flourish now.[43]

Even political and social reform was futile, and the hopelessness Thomson felt in such writing is clearly revealed in the essay that climaxed his efforts, "Proposals for the Speedy Extinction of Evil and Misery." The cure proposed for these troublesome ills was a simple one—universal suicide. His spirits, however, if not his philosophy, became considerably more cheerful; "Weddah and Om-el-Bonain," reluctantly published in the *National Reformer* at the end of 1871, drew great praise from the Rossettis and Swinburne; he spent a happy nine months in America, living in the Colorado mountains while employed as secretary for the Champion Gold and Silver Mines Company; and when he returned home, it was as a mature pessimist and a confident atheist. All doubt had been erased from his mind, and he sat down at once to write his final statement on life, his great pessimist's manifesto. Realizing that the tortured fragments of his discarded "Inferno" could be used to document the message he had to offer, he began again on "The City of Dreadful Night," now truly dreadful, for, having "searched the heights and depths, the scope of all our universe," he brought "Good tidings of great joy for you, for all"—"There is no God":

> I find no hint throughout the Universe
> Of good or ill, of blessing or of curse;
> I find alone Necessity Supreme.

There was no hope, and but one consolation:

> Lo, you are free to end it when you will,
> Without the fear of waking after death,

a consolation that led the inhabitants of his city eagerly to exclaim:

> We yearn for speedy death in full fruition,
> Dateless oblivion and divine repose.

The poem, completed by the end of 1873, was published in the *National Reformer* (in spite of the objections of several subscribers) between March and May, 1874. Thomson still had eight years before he was to gain his own dateless oblivion and divine repose, but in terms of this aspect of his thought, the movement from theist to atheist, there is little to add. For three more years he continued to write for the secularist papers, and, in spite of his convictions as to the hopelessness of the task, his attacks on Christianity actually increased in fervor. An 1874 essay (*National Reformer*, Oct. 25), for instance, bitterly commented on "Jesus Christ, Our Great Exemplar":

> To sum up: This poor sexless Jew, with a noble feminine heart, and a magnificent though uncultivated and crazy brain, did no work to earn his bread; evaded all social and political responsibil-

ities, took no wife and condemned his own family; lived a vagabond, fed and housed by charity; uttered many beautiful and even sublime moral truths and more impracticable precepts; preached continually himself, and faith in himself alone as the one thing necessary; and died with the lamentable cry of womanish desperation, perhaps the most significant confession in history of a life of supreme self-illusion laid bare to itself at the point of death, My God, my God, why hast thou forsaken me?

> I have much love and reverence for him as a man; but am quite certain that if everyone really set about following his example, the world (which is surely mad enough already) would soon be one vast Bedlam broken loose.

Even more vicious was the satire Thomson based on his American experiences, "Religion in the Rocky Mountains" (*National Reformer,* March 30, April 13, 1873), an essay that proved too strong for even National Reformer stomachs. Bradlaugh was forced to withhold the final installment after the second had evoked the following letter from an irate gentleman in Northern Ireland: "The very mention of your name is enough to make the hair stand. . . . I showed your last number to a neighbor, who was so horrified that he said your paper, yourself, and all your supporters ought to be burned." For the first time in his life Thomson proudly proclaimed himself an atheist (" 'The fool hath said in his heart there is no God.' Fool, because saying it in his heart, he has not the courageous wisdom to publish it with tongue and pen"),[44] and insisted that "men of intellect, public spirit, and intense moral convictions cannot have a sphere of usefulness more suitable to them just now than that of open warfare, and warfare *à outrance,* against the degrading absurdities and anti-progressive dogmatism of the supernatural religion called Christianity."[45] He began a long series of articles under the title "Among the Christians," in which he picked through periodicals like the *Christian World* to find particularly delectable "absurdities." He attacked Moody and Sankey on the one hand, Arnold's "Church of England" essays on the other. He became involved in the fierce wrangles within the Secularist Party, and, siding with the younger men, Foote in particular, made bitter accusations against Bradlaugh and Annie Besant, especially when they brought out that most ludicrous of all secularist documents, the "Secular Song and Hymn Book." [46] And he became, eventually, sick of the whole dreary business:

> In short, the tearing the Bible to pieces, verse by verse, and over and over again, for the amusement of audiences and readers, mostly familiar with the process, and already converted from Christianity, is a mode of warfare which could only be paralleled by the captains of an army stopping to pull down brick by brick, for the amusement of their men, a wall in which they had made a practicable breach, and rebuilding the wall for the sake of pulling it down again, instead of storming straightway through to capture the citadel.[47]

Thomson suggested that secularists occupy themselves with the "natural and human arts and sciences," for, as far as he was concerned, the war on Christianity had already been won: "The time is coming, and is probably not far off, when it will seem as absurd to intelligent men to argue seriously about the truth of the myths and dogmas of Christianity, as it would now to argue seriously about the truth of the myths of Greece and the dogmas of Egypt." Finally, by the end of 1877, Thomson had completely dissociated himself from secularist writing, most of his late essays being concerned with vastly different subjects and appearing, under the signature "Sigvat" or "J.T.," in a periodical that was selling what now seemed a far more sensible commodity than reform, and a more satisfying one too—tobacco.[48]

"B.V.," whose militant atheism had made men's hair stand straight, was no more.

We might, however, in concluding this aspect of Thomson's intellectual development, note a passage from "A Voice from the Nile," a poem he completed just a few months before his death. In it, the Nile, surveying the human race, seems to summarize Thomson's final attitude toward religion:

> Poor men, most admirable, most pitiable,
> With all their changes all their great Creeds change:
> For Man, this alien in my family,
> Is alien most in this, to cherish dreams
> And brood on visions of eternity,
> And build religions in his brooding brain
> And in the dark depths awe-full of his soul.
> My other children live their little lives,
> Are born and reach their prime and slowly fail,
> And all their little lives are self-fulfilled;
> They die and are no more, content with age
> And weary with infirmity. But Man
> Has fear and hope and phantasy and awe,
> And wistful yearnings and unsated loves,
> That strain beyond the limits of his life,
> And therefore Gods and Demons, Heaven and Hell:
> This Man, the admirable, the pitiable.

There is, undeniably, a note of weariness in this passage, but there is also, I feel, a suggestion of contentment. Once the universe had become, not a hostile force, but simply an indifferent one; once Thomson was convinced that man had no relations at all with God, that this little life was all he must endure—then there was no longer a struggle, no longer doubt and despair. "We think on these truths," he had written in "The City," "and they comfort us."

There was, however, another struggle going on in his

mind during these years, one of equal importance and perplexity. Whatever might be man's relations with the universe, Thomson was, day by day, hour by hour, faced with the far more concrete problem of the truth about man's relations with man. We have not, in fact, come to terms with the "English Leopardi," have not really understood his final position as an atheist, until we have examined the development of his ideas on Man—"most admirable, most pitiable."

3

Optimist to Pessimist

In 1883, the year after Thomson's death, his friends in Leicester decided to erect a "B.V. Memorial" in their new Secular Hall. Donations were solicited from secularist and nonsecularist alike, the list of contributors including Meredith, Morris, Swinburne, Garnett, and William Rossetti, in addition, of course, to most of the Secularist Party notables. Bradlaugh's name was conspicuously absent from the list; although he had donated 1 pound "In Memory of Bysshe Vanolis and Ballincollig," he did not wish to be associated with the project because he objected, strange as it must have seemed to the freethinkers who had long admired Thomson's work in secularist journals, to placing a "B.V. Memorial" within, of all places, a Secular Hall: "If you are honouring a fine poet and prose writer you do well. If you are honouring a freethinker for his devotion to the cause you are utterly wrong."[1] Bradlaugh was utterly right, for in spite of the fact that most of Thomson's work appeared in free-thought periodicals—*National Reformer, The Secularist, The Liberal, Progress*[2]—he vigorously condemned reform movements, refused to join the National Secular Society, was suspicious of anyone who called himself liberal, and, for at least the last ten years of his life, considered progress, in any lasting or worthwhile sense, an impossibility. He repeatedly denied interest in politics or social problems, referred to the articles he wrote on current issues as "nonsense," and, apparently feeling that the pseudonym "B.V." afforded inadequate protection, published such articles under the signature "X." [3] And yet, throughout his life he was, at heart, a reformer of the first order, the difference between his "cause" and Bradlaugh's being that Thomson was not a reformer of society, but of men. He believed, as Christian and atheist, as optimist and pessimist, that if problems of humanity were ever to be solved, they must be solved, not through social or political reform, but through reform of human nature. He was, in brief, a moralist, and although he was to relinquish his early Shelleyan belief in the perfectibility of man, he never relinquished his belief that each man had a responsibility at least to attempt the "reform" of human nature through reforming himself.

Thomson's position as a moralist did not, of course, remain unchanged throughout the three decades of his literary activity. When his views on God were altered, his views on human relationships and responsibilities were necessarily adjusted to correspond with the all-important theological beliefs. To understand his development from optimist to pessimist, a change closely paralleling the movement from pantheist to atheist, it is therefore necessary to return to the 1850's and to examine his ideas on man's relations with his fellowman within the context of his then prevailing Christian (or Christian-pantheist) view of the universe. During this early period, however, believing, as he did up to his rejection of Christianity in 1862, that the "world-scene vast" was "but a shade in Time's stream" and that the soul's "substantial life" existed only after death, he really had very little to say about man in society. In spite of an occasional grumble about the inequality and the inadequacy of certain unspecified "laws of justice," there was little that Thomson wanted to see changed in the social, political, or economic makeup of England, an attitude that is not surprising in light of his belief that the prevailing system was part of a divine plan as ordained by an all-wise, all-good God. Thus, there was cause for neither optimism nor pessimism as regards the future of the human race, for if, in mid-nineteenth-century England, society was not working as intended, the fault could not be with God's plan, which must necessarily be fulfilled, but with man's failure to recognize and to cooperate with that plan.

At first Thomson believed monarchical government to be an essential part of the divine plan, and his earliest extant essay treating problems of man in society, the 1859 narrative "The King's Friends,"[4] supports government by a benevolent monarch. Probably influenced by Carlyle, Thomson gives his good king absolute power although, significantly, the monarch is elected by popular vote, the citizens being free to debate the merits of prospective candidates and even to suggest alternative systems of government. An enthusiastic young republican suggests such a change:

> Cannot we exist unmastered? There is kingliness in all of us, though undeveloped. To be swayed nobly is good, but it is better to sway ourselves nobly; to reverence others worthy is good, but it is better to reverence ourselves worthy. . . . There is now one king; let there arise a serene republic of kings.

To Thomson in these years such a prospect was idiotic, and the young man is at once rebuked by another citizen:

> What wise folly do you speak? You are yet young, but I am old and have learnt too well how stern and how dreadful is this long, long conflict of our life. In some few hours we are sufficient for ourselves—throughout the years we need the curb and protection of fixed laws, and the tribunal of a supreme power. Your serene republic of kings would be a delirious fever of mobs.

To avoid mob rule, to retain order in an orderly universe, Thomson felt that men needed, and consequently had been given, the "tribunal of a supreme power," it being the duty of each individual to be willingly subject to such a tribunal. Moreover, because God had placed each soul on earth in a sphere "appropriate to his own nature," it was perfectly natural that society should be a mixture of weak and strong, poor and rich, evil and good, ignorant and wise, for not all souls were of equal status. Still, no soul need complain about his earthly lot, as it was not only "appropriate" to his nature, but was a necessary part of the "perpetual onflowing" of life, the progression upward through "cycles and systems far" to the eventual attainment of the Life Eternal.

England's ills, then, resulted, not from any flaw in God's plan, but from the individual's failure to fulfill that plan; monarchs and sages and poets and preachers and merchants and even workingmen were seeking, not a Life Eternal in Heaven, but self-gain, self-glory, and self-power on earth. Pride, covetousness, lust, anger, gluttony, envy, sloth—these were the evils plaguing England, not unfair taxes, rotten boroughs, long working hours, or overpopulation. Englishmen, both ruler and ruled, had become "poisoned with sin," and Thomson's remedy, as naïve as his diagnosis, was simply that sinners should "repent" and cleanse their hearts from the "foulness circling with its blood to poison every part." Even in the 1857 "The Doom of a City," the work that most explicitly develops this message, Thomson does not suggest that the system itself is at fault. Rulers are criticized, not because they hold power over their fellowmen, but because they "rule for the good of themselves alone"; the rich are condemned, not because they possess riches, but because they are selfish; the poor are chastised, not because they have failed to organize in the cause of freedom, but because they have felt "but their bread-distress," because they have failed to recognize their proper place in the divine plan and have refused to look to Heaven for their true rewards.

Not surprisingly, then, Thomson's writings of this

early period make virtually no reference to current events.[5] During the years when he was either unaware of or indifferent to the new discoveries in science and scholarship, he was also indifferent to social and political changes going on around him. For the most part, what he said was wrong with the world was what he had read was wrong with it—in Shelley, perhaps, or in his other favorites, Carlyle or Dante or Shakespeare. It must not be imagined that when Thomson lost his parents he had, like a Dickensian orphan, received an education in the streets struggling against a hostile society; even before his mother died he was comfortably established in the Caledonian Asylum, and the security of that school, followed immediately by the security of army life, was no doubt largely responsible for his intellectual insularity, the emphasis on "rank" and the high degree of order in both places perhaps even contributing to his ready acceptance of a hierarchical divine plan. In any event, whatever he may have seen of life in London as a boy, or in Ireland as a young schoolmaster, so long as he believed that "Our mazed web of doom is wrought / Under God's directing thought," he felt there was no need to concern himself about his fellowman beyond inquiring into the state of his soul. It was not until the end of the 1850's, when his doubts as to the reality of God had become pronounced, that Thomson began to suspect that his message—"repent ye"—was considerably less than adequate.

In "The Dead Year," written in November, 1860, Thomson looked back upon the past year and imagined it joining its predecessors in the icy regions where dead years reside, apparently, like Coleridge's albatross, somewhere near the South Pole. When "1860" was asked by the other years about the state of affairs on earth, whether there had been any improvement of late, whether man was "less steeped and brutalized in lust and blood," the reply was in line with views already noted: a "wild waste of restless thought" was sapping the old foundations around churches, palaces, castles, and polities; the war of classes was growing more intense; rulers were "cowardly and blind," teachers "barren as the wind," traders "full of lies and fraud," and so on—all of which attested to the true cause of the problem, "the People's inward rottenness." A new note was struck, however, when "1860" expressed hope that things might soon get better, for the past years were more than skeptical; they actually ridiculed such a prospect:

> The pure, the wise, the beautiful, the brave,
> The darlings of Earth's golden youth, are—
> where?
> Deep-trampled, rotted in the formless grave;
> Though still, wan ghosts, they haunt the
> upper air.
> Are wiser, purer, braver, breathing there?
> Plato's broad brow frowns homilies for-
> lorn;
> Nay, Helen's lips smile all your hopes to
> scorn.

No one on earth could ever hope to be wiser, purer, braver than men had been when fresh from the hand of the Creator, and if man had not attained perfection after the "Golden Age," was there really any hope for salvation at this late, sin-tormented date? Thomson was beginning to doubt it, and in his essay on Shelley, also written in 1860, he anticipated the position he was to take many years later when he stated that Shelley had been mistaken about the perfectibility of human nature and the attainment of "a heaven on earth realized by the noble endeavours of man himself." His poem to Shelley, written the following year, does, in fact, reaffirm the old position, that the poet's work had not been in vain:

> Thou hast *not* failed; where holy love and
> truth
> Contend with Evil failure cannot be.

But even here, while again expressing his dismay with a world that has "no loyal service, no revering awe," Thomson, for the first time, stated that the monarchy, which had been considered false only insofar as individual monarchs had been sinful, was a "bloody pall to stifle Freedom," and that the laws, which before had needed only slight revision, were "iron nets to hold the poor and mean." Clearly, the doubts that were to culminate in his denial of God were encompassing his views on man and society, and so in the following year, 1862, his belief in a divine plan and his message of "repent ye" were rejected along with his faith in the monotheistic God. They were to be replaced with a different "message," one that was part and parcel of the new pantheism, one that was to require a vastly different attitude toward man in society.

Although science and secularism, largely operating through Bradlaugh and the *National Reformer*, had combined to convince Thomson that Christianity was a myth and that the universe operated without an omnipotent deity at the controls, Bradlaugh and his friends did not exert a similar influence on his views of man in society. Thomson was, no doubt, susceptible to virtually any social or political creed that would replace his old beliefs, but the National Reformers were, for the most part, far too busy destroying God to take much interest in reforming man. In theory, Bradlaugh's policy was threefold—"in religious matters, Atheistical; in politics, Republican; on social questions, Malthusian"—but in reality he believed, at least until the end of the sixties when he began his long struggle to obtain a seat in Parliament, that theological iconoclasm was of primary importance; his convictions were that "men can never be free, socially or politically, while they are slaves to a creed" and that "a superstitious people can never establish a firm and enduring Republic." [6] This is not to say that Bradlaugh was uninterested in social or political problems during the early years of the *National*

Reformer, for, indeed, there was little happening at any time or any place which did not interest him. But that any of his enthusiasm for republicanism or Malthusianism rubbed off on Thomson, at least at this time, seems unlikely; although "B.V." willingly joined in on the fun of hurling bricks at the God who was no longer there, in political and social matters he was determined to remain outside the realm of immediate practice. He did, in fact, become a republican of sorts, at least insofar as he expressed opposition to the monarchy,[7] and he probably felt that birth control was commendable, but concrete admissions on either of these points are extremely rare, the most pronounced statements being a mild defense of the notorious *Elements of Social Science*, and a comment after the Hyde Park riots that "Whigs and Tories, rich and noble, will never help the populace; the populace must help itself." [8] Only two poems, the 1863 "A Polish Insurgent," which resulted from his brief employment as secretary to the Polish Committee, and the 1864 "Garibaldi Revisiting England," may be classified as republican, and neither piece is particularly effective, for Thomson, as he proudly proclaimed in the 1864 "Vane's Story," never mixed in "our vile nether politics." [9] And although "Vane's Story" also insisted that

> Now my gross, earthly, human heart
> With man and not with God takes part;
> With men, however vile, and not
> With seraphim I cast my lot:
> With those poor ruffian thieves, too strong
> To starve amidst our social wrong,
> And yet too weak to wait and earn
> Dry bread by honest labour stern;
> With those poor harlots steeping sin
> And shame and woe in vitriol-gin,

he did not, as this passage suggests, take any noticeable interest in the social wrong; only once, in the 1865 narrative poem "Low Life," did he attempt, poetically at least, to sing the song of the shirt.[10] Whatever good intentions Thomson may have had when writing "Vane's Story," what he actually did in taking part with man and not with God was to convey a new message of hope to his fellow sufferers. After years of preaching repentance, of preparing himself for death and warning others to do likewise, he had a new gospel to "ring out and over the earth / Through all the grief and strife," good tidings that, in line with his newfound pantheism, consisted of that single glorious word—"Live!"

In treating Thomson's views on man's relations with the universe, in tracing his career from theist to atheist, I have already discussed some of the reasons behind the development of this "live life" philosophy, and have attempted to explain its relationship with his anti-Christian iconoclasm of the mid-sixties. In the present context, however, the philosophy requires somewhat closer examination, for it was one thing to tell a starving beggar to repent, but quite another to tell him that all his troubles would cease were he but to "live." Indeed, the drunken clod wandering the flaring streets with one of the "thousands of harlots abroad"[11] might well claim to be doing precisely that, and, although those poor girls steeping sin in vitriol-gin were now being considered in a more favorable light, this kind of life was obviously not what Thomson had in mind by "living." It is not easy, in fact, to say precisely what he did have in mind, for much of his writing at this time seems little more than an expression of exuberance over freedom from the old despair. I suggest, however, that the key to his message can be found in his understanding of nature, and of man's place in a "natural" society.

During these years (roughly 1863 to 1867) when, as a pantheist, he believed that life was a sort of universal fire in which all living things were but flames, an "infinite harmony" of which all creatures were but single notes, "Nature" not only meant everything that was "natural"—the naked beauty that was truth, the naked truth that was beauty—but at the same time personified universal life in its totality, replacing the biblical God as an object of veneration. As the "great Mother" she was not, as God had been, "Allwise," but she was definitely "Allgood," for Thomson believed, when first expounding his new doctrine, that life, in its "natural" state, was harmonious and peaceful, that man had once frolicked joyously with both lamb and lion, and that, by "living true life," such Eden innocence could again be attained.[12] It was for this reason that Blake made so strong an impression on him during these years, natural innocence and purity being an essential part of Thomson's belief that men could live harmoniously in a state of nature.

At least half a dozen poems written in the mid-sixties could be cited as Blake-inspired, but the strongest case in point is the 1866–67 "The Naked Goddess" in which a goddess, living in an Eden-like forest surrounded by wild but friendly animals, is one day discovered by the natives of a nearby town. The people gather to gaze upon this spectacular creature, and eventually a priest and a philosopher approach her, each attempting to persuade her to put on his robe and follow his teachings. She dons the priest's gown, but immediately bursts through it and flings it off, saying:

This cerement sad was meant
For some creature stunted, thin,
Breastless, blighted, bones and skin.

The sage's robe is also discarded, for she stumbles in its long folds:

This big bag was meant to hold
Some poor sluggard fat and old
Limping, shuffling wearily,
With a form not fit to see!

With both robes cast aside, the goddess stands proudly before the townspeople, once again utterly naked:

Naked as the midnight moon,
Naked as the sun of noon,

Burning too intensely bright,
Clothed in its own dazzling light.

In great anger, she forsakes the forest, and that very night both the priest and the sage die, "accursed in sombre rage," as evil falls upon the entire town and countryside. Only two children, who had instinctively understood her message, manage to survive the ordeal —children who grow up "beautiful and bright," and then, as lovers, sail off together to form a new Atlantis where they live happily ever after, "living life."

In one sense, then, Thomson was advocating a "return to Nature," although not as the eighteenth-century or even the early nineteenth-century Romantics had intended. Daffodils, nightingales, autumn leaves, and the west wind had little or nothing to do with Thomson's message of "living"; his interest was solely in what he considered the "natural" state of man, man when thoroughly "alive," active, vibrant—"burning," as he liked to put it, "in naked truth and beauty." It was the Elizabethans, then, not the Romantics, who best exemplified what Thomson meant by "living life." Although the Elizabethans, like the Victorians, had manufactured "strait-waistcoats" for Nature, they were "far too naturally and instinctively wise to dement themselves by constant efforts to compel Nature to wear them when manufactured," and thus "the great Mother laughed at their pretty dolls-dresses, and took these her robust and passionate children to the embrace of her naked love." Men like Spenser and Sidney "naturally and instinctively" seemed to have burst through the social and political and religious barriers of their age, and attained an intimacy with nature which, Thomson felt, his own age had never begun to realize. They were "robust and passionate"; they were "alive"; they "burned with pure aspiration." Wordsworth (the once greatly admired Wordsworth) had never lived so intensely, and, although Victorians were praising him as "the wisest and purest of poets, and incomparably the most intimate with nature," Thomson now saw him as little more than a "highly respectable English Sunday School Teacher, toiling up Parnassus with a heavy bundle of sermons and hymn-books and moral old clothes on his back, resolved to convert and civilise those poor shameless heathen Muses." There was nothing vital in that picture, nothing heroic and sublime; the real heroes were those who understood

> that in the whole range of the universe, from highest heaven to deepest hell, there is no thing or circumstance, creature or being, dreadful to man; that out of himself there is nothing which a man need fear; that no nature can be born into a realm unconquerable by that nature; and, moreover, that the most dazzling lightning of ecstacy leaps from the blackest storm of danger.

This was what Thomson meant by "living life bravely"; and, in the heat of his enthusiasm, he optimistically believed, or at least tried very hard to believe, that such an attitude toward life could solve Victorian ills.[13]

When, as self-appointed physician to the human race, the disease Thomson had diagnosed as poisoning the human soul was "sin," his prescription had been "repent ye." But now that the remedy read "live ye," a new disease was at once apparent—pernicious, malignant, and so thoroughly complex that it required a new name. Thomson decided to call it "Bumbleism," his own term to describe a mental attitude not much unlike Arnold's Philistinism, for Bumbles, like the Philistines, were "slaves to routine, enemies to the light, stupid and oppressive, but at the same time very strong."[14] The "essence of the potency of Bumbleism" was, in a word, "Dulness"—dulness that represented and encouraged the opposite of everything Thomson meant by "living." There were some concrete dangers, such as censorship; since Bumble "hated a new idea, or even the semblance of a new idea, such as a novel opinion," any newspaper or book that ventured beyond the bounds of Bumbledom's restrictions in religion or morals could be effectually suppressed by Bumble's refusal to buy it. But in the broadest sense, Bumble being "at home with the middle classes" and the middle classes ruling England, Thomson feared it was virtually impossible for Englishmen (including, of course, Bumbles) to "live life," for Bumble was the antithesis of life. To him, Thomson insisted, "the naked beauty is obscene and the naked truth is blasphemous."

The problem, then, was not how to destroy Bumble, but how to cure him, and the method Thomson recommended was shock treatment, waking him from his lethargy by bluntly revealing truth and beauty as objects of veneration. The role, not surprisingly, fell to the poet, the "per contra" to his essay on "Bumble, Bumbledom, Bumbleism" being titled "The Poet, High Art, Genius." As used in the sense, "High Art," although obviously sacred, was not a very specific commodity; it meant merely the "loftiest expression of the Beautiful, in which more or less latent are involved the Good and the True." The "Poet," who was to expound the message, was therefore "the Priest of Beauty in general, whatever material he consecrates to its service." Browning, as a Poet who also happened to write poetry, had expressed the message in what Thomson called "one pregnant verse": "Sing, Riding's a Joy!—for me, I ride," but actually a Poet did not need to write a single line,[15] for the true Poets were the opposites of the true Bumbles, men who "intensely live, rejoicing supremely in the harmony and beauty of the world." They were the real keepers of the flame, the true children of light, for they realized "in flesh and spirit" the "loftiest dreams in marble and verse and sound and color of the men we commonly call poets." When, however, the age produced a true Poet who was also capable of writing things that shocked Bumble into an awareness of the naked truth, then indeed there was cause for singing in the streets; when in 1866 the Swinburne controversy developed, Thomson at once published a vigorous defense of *Poems and Ballads,* praising Swinburne as a true Poet, not because of the quality of his poetry—indeed, Thomson admitted in his defense of the book that he had not even read it!—but simply because Swinburne had "outraged propriety and shocked Bumbledom."

Thomson, of course, also attempted to shock Bumble by attacking the sacred cows of Victorianism, although his efforts were mainly confined to Christian satires such as "Christmas Eve in the Upper Circles" and "Story of a Famous Old Firm." In the 1867 essay "Indolence,"[16] (significantly subtitled "A Moral Essay"), he did, however, attack a purely secular idol, a doctrine that had long been a favorite of his own—the doctrine of work.

> In England, the passion for work, which pervades and to a certain degree ennobles the lust for wealth, has become an irrational idolatry; labour is prized for itself, not as the means to an end. Thus it is now quite a commonplace to extol the blessing veiled under the curse, "In the sweat of thy face shalt thou eat bread." Good people know better than God, and inform him and us that he was quite mistaken, that like Balaam he came to curse but really blessed, that Paradise Lost was in fact a Paradise Gained.

Even when writing this essay (in 1867), Thomson still considered Carlyle to be "intelligent and vigorous young England's" prophet, and felt that "taking him all in all, few generations have had a nobler." But Thomson could no longer accept a doctrine that condemned men for their reluctance to work; although a decade earlier he had been convinced that " all *are* but what they *do,*" he now suspected that Carlyle's

> continual cry of Work! Work! Work! is simply the Imperative mood of a doctrine which, couched in the quiet Indicative, reads, "Mankind is a damned

> rascal." . . . If we humbly inquire, Why work, work, work, in this furious fashion? we shall find that the ultimate because is to the following effect: To save yourselves from yourselves; to overwhelm and exhaust the natural (sinful and foolish) man in each of you; to occupy all your hours and make them pass as swiftly as possible, thus distracting yourselves from vain talk and thought and self-consciousness, until you are got into the quiet grave, and securely covered over, impotent for further mischief.

Obviously this would never do, for it was essential to Thomson's philosophy that "natural" man be, like Nature, instinctively wise and worthy, not sinful and foolish, and he also believed that men should be "living" every moment of life to the utmost of their ability, not overwhelming themselves with work so that the hours might pass swiftly. He was not, of course, advocating all play and no work, but he did feel that less work and more play would provide an antidote to Bumble's blind devotion to work for work's sake, for what Thomson most strongly objected to in the doctrine of work was "busy" work, work that wasted one's energies and dulled the awareness of life's beauty. The hero of Longfellow's *Excelsior* was an "Ineffable Ass" and an "Infernal Idiot." "What possible good," Thomson asked, "could he do himself or anybody else by planting that banner with the very strange device on the top of that mountain?" This was "busy" work of the most absurd kind, encouraging the grouping together of such infernal idiots and leading to a "plague of busy-bodyism" which passed itself off as a reform movement.

There is, I believe, a close relationship between Thomson's distrust of work in these years and his increased disgust for reform groups; he believed, and probably with some justice, that the great majority of the leagues and societies in Victorian England were little more than an outlet for energy that had no place else to go, the not particularly well-meaning Bumbles who ran them encouraging the dangerous belief that "hurry and bluster" were the sole symptoms of progress, that every step was a step in advance. Even if no great harm were to result from any one given movement, Thomson was convinced that no worthwhile good could come from it, as the whole machinery of a propaganda-spreading, speech-making, petition-presenting organization was not only annoying and obnoxious, but thoroughly futile. It was, he felt, as absurd to petition for curing mankind's ills, which could be corrected only through the individual's reforming himself, as it was to petition Mother Nature for a change in the course of the planets. In his 1866 phantasy, "A Walk Abroad,"[17] when he wanders through the universe and meets an "other-side-of-the-moon-man" who is complaining that the side of the moon earth can see holds an unfair monopoly, Thomson's advice is: "Employ yourself in getting up a monster petition, and don't let any one sign it more than twenty times, and if you can keep the fictitious names in the minority do so. Couldn't you make a demonstration from our side of the moon?" Although he agrees wholeheartedly with his moon friend that great injustice and inequality are prevalent throughout the universe, on earth, at least, such inequalities are soon to be corrected:

> Cheer up, let us both cheer up, O other-side-of-the-moon-man, this state of things cannot last much longer. For we have now societies numerous and powerful for the extinction of all wrongs, real and imaginary: Missionary Societies, Bible Societies, Religious Tract Societies; Societies for the Prorogation [*sic*] of the Gospel, the Confusion of Useful Knowledge, the Perversion of the Jews; a Temperance League, a Reform League, a National Secular Society, an International Society: and the least of these stupendous and glorious associations intends to accomplish things much more difficult

> than this slight alteration in your mode of revolution.

The sense of futility, the discordant note of bitterness which is noticeable even in this lighthearted satire, is indicative of a new stage in Thomson's thought, one that becomes increasingly apparent in the essays of the sixties, even as he was most vigorously expounding his "live life" philosophy. For Thomson was beginning to realize that whatever brave, true things he might write about the idiocy of Bumbleism, he could not walk the streets of London, could not witness the truth and the beauty in the real world around him, without coming face to face with the blind beggar or the starving child to whom "awake and sing" was meaningless advice. In "A Walk Abroad" he records his encounters on the streets of London:

> A poor woman offered me a box of matches; as I didn't want any, she begged a penny, which I gave. A girl well dressed asked for sixpence or a drop of gin, as she was perished with cold, etc. I gave her six-pence, but told her that in my humble opinion such hours and habits were scarcely conducive to health and morality. A whining man asked for twopence to get a bed, and a penny to get a roll; I gave him threepence. A ragged boy, thin-faced and large-eyed, asked for twopence to get some coffee and toke; I gave the twopence.

How, Thomson began asking himself, could such conditions exist, if the "great mother" Nature were really all-good, if men really were intended to live harmoniously and peacefully together? The horrifying answer was that men simply did not care, did not "sympathize" with their fellowmen, a realization that struck at the heart of Thomson's belief in an innate harmony in Nature.

> We see a blind beggar, and pity him, and give him alms. Does our pity deserve to be called sympathy? Can we, without the grossest exaggeration, pre-

> tend that we *feel with* him the miseries of his blindness? Assuredly not. . . . If our feeling of the blind beggar's misery approached in intensity his own, it is plain that, instead of giving him pence and passing on, we should do our utmost to ensure his subsistence for life and lavish on him daily the tenderest cares.[18]

The realization that "intense and comprehensive sympathy" was, except in a handful of heroic saints, *un*natural in man, seemed indeed, as Thomson admitted, "a strangely unpleasant bit of wisdom to carry about with one." But it was, I suspect, the "bit of wisdom" which, more than any other, led him from the "live life" optimism of the sixties to the "City of Dreadful Night" pessimism of the seventies. If there was no true sympathy among men, what sort of harmony, what manner of communion, was really possible with Nature? In 1865, when first proclaiming his doctrine, Thomson had insisted on a "natural" harmony between man and Nature:

> Let us praise the impartiality of our Mother Nature, the most venerable, the ever young, the fountain of true democracy, the generous annunciator of true liberty and equality and fraternity; who bestoweth on all her children alike all things most necessary to true health and wealth, the sunshine, the air, the water, the fruits of the earth; and opens to rich and poor alike the golden doors of enfranchisement and initiation into the mysteries of heroism, purity, wisdom, beauty, and infinite love.[19]

Yet little more than a year later, Thomson's views underwent radical alteration:

> Nature is savage enough, and is likely to continue so; I don't think that she has made her arrangements specially for our placid and inane comfort, nor do I find that the saints and the goody philosophers are her darlings. We must have teeth, and

> strong and sharp ones, to crack the hard nuts she throws to us. To think that there are grown men always talking treacle and pap! men who have seen and heard a thunderstorm and are not ignorant of the existence of shark and crocodile and tiger! [20]

And by 1868, when writing "Proposals for the Speedy Extinction of Evil and Misery," Thomson was bitterly condemning the once amiable Nature:

> The animals she brings forth (not to speak of the plants and the minerals) are in many cases ugly, unamiable, ferocious, and tormented with monstrous appetites, which can only be satisfied by devouring their fellow-creatures; nearly all of them are quite selfish and immoral; and the few of them that are philanthropic (such as surly old lions, tigers, wolves, sharks, vultures and other sweet carrion fowl; all genuine lovers of man) are almost as disagreeably so as our human philanthropists themselves.

The savagery in nature, in both animals and humans, was the realization Thomson had been pushing into the background while outwardly clinging to his belief that "living life" could produce natural harmony on earth. The theory of evolution had, for the most part, come to him as a blessing, for it had released him from bondage and restored meaning and order and harmony to Nature—but the survival of the fittest was a factor he had refused to recognize. Blake's *Songs of Innocence* had inspired him to proclaim an idealistic message of love and hope, but he had ignored the *Songs of Experience;* he had concentrated on the little lamb while shutting out the fearful symmetry of the tiger. When he finally did recognize both aspects, his optimism as to mankind's future collapsed along with the pantheism; he had discovered the tiger not only in nature, but in the heart of man. Savagery was considerably more serious than "sin," a malady that could not be cured through repentance; it was, in fact, incurable, for the savagery of nature was inseparable from life itself.

By 1867, then, Thomson was ready for Leopardi. The "live life" philosophy he had been expounding for the past three years was ironically concluded by placing lines from Leopardi's pessimistic "Alla Primavera" as an epigraph to his own supremely optimistic "The Naked Goddess" [21]—more epitaph actually, than epigraph, and completely appropriate, for Leopardi too had realized that "human society has inherent and essential elements of imperfection, and that its various conditions are bad more or less, but none can be good." Thomson was convinced that the Italian had seen precisely what he had seen—"the nature of man in all its strength and weakness and marvellous inconsistencies, . . . the evil destiny of man in its naked and terrible truth"—and, like Leopardi, feeling utterly impotent before this realization of an unharmonious universe, a hostile Nature, an imperfectible human race, he decided that he too would "laugh at the ills common to us" rather than begin "sighing and weeping and wailing." [22] Thus, in 1868, he began his great satiric essay on the human race, "Proposals for the Speedy Extinction of Evil and Misery." [23] If life was but a joke, he had determined to laugh at it.

Although this essay repeats much of what I have already noted about the "live life" philosophy, including the insistence on reform beginning with the individual, the irony is that it also ridicules such notions. Although Thomson was still convinced that this was the only logical solution to reform, he now believed that man was no more capable of reforming himself than he was capable of reforming nature, for both were savage at heart and were destined to remain so. The proposal is presented, as Swift, who influenced many of Thomson's satires, had presented his own "Modest Proposal," through the pen of a practical reformer who had given a good deal of thought to the problem and decided that to bring about the speedy extinction of evil and misery would involve "simply a universal change to perfection of nature and human nature; of which I think that we as men should enterprise the latter first." Previous reformers had failed in their attempts through endeavoring to make a large number of men and women believe and act as they themselves did, but this scheme modestly limited each man to reforming only himself. The proposition called for just three virtuous and intelligent readers to step forward and perfect themselves, a task requiring only that they put off the seven cardinal and all minor sins, follies, and defects, and put on the seven cardinal and all minor virtues, wisdoms, and graces. The then perfect three would form a provisional committee to set up Universal Perfection Company, Unlimited, which, once established, would be joined by all other societies of reformers and world reformers, as well as most earnest and intelligent peoples of all religions and all sects, for "every one who has faith that his own doctrine is true and his own plan of life good, must have faith that the better and wiser men become, the more will they believe his doctrine and adopt his plan of life." Thus strengthened at the start by such numerous and powerful accessions, in a few years perfect men would be in the majority, and it would then be a simple task to decide whether to tolerate the imperfect minority, allow them to die out gradually, or promptly exterminate them. With every human perfect, evil would be extinguished, and the remaining task would be merely to eliminate suffering by correcting Nature's imperfections. But could Nature be compelled to perfect herself? Oh yes, says the honest reformer, for at present the human race, as the scientists have proved, is the head of Nature. Since Nature's one ruling passion and principle is her love of life, and the one thing she abhors and shrinks from is absolute death, men could force Nature to perfect herself simply by threatening to cut off her head if she refused. Thus the practical corollary: "*That the human race, so long as no other is ready to supersede it, can compel nature to do what it pleases, by resolving on instant universal suicide in case of her refusal.*" And should Nature refuse, could "any thoughtful and conscientious man, candidly considering our state and that of the world, doubt that such universal suicide would be the one best and most beatific action we could perform for ourselves and our (potential) posterity and our world in general?" In conclusion, fascinated readers were reminded that "it is only our *universal* suicide which would prove a panacea for all the ills our flesh is heir to; individual suicides can do little or no good, save to the individuals themselves." It was, however, confidently asserted that once man became perfect, Nature would surely not refuse him anything, and that in just a few short years, at least by the twentieth century, "evil will be extinct by the perfection of man, and misery by the perfection of nature, and everybody will be thoroughly good and happy everywhere for evermore."

"Proposals for the Speedy Extinction of Evil and Misery" is probably Thomson's best prose satire although, its "message" being, to say the least, unpleasant, it has never received the attention that it deserves. Thomson himself seems to have been reluctant to give open expression to his conviction of the inevitability of evil and misery; after beginning to write the essay, he set it aside for three years, as he had done with "The City of Dreadful Night." Unlike the delay in completing "The City," however, the gap in composition in the "Proposals" may have been largely caused by the "terrible years" at the end of the sixties which had drained Thomson of both inspiration and, perhaps, the courage needed to continue writing in such a vein. As he had done at the end of the fifties, when pleading to the Lady of Oblivion for an interlude of "peaceful rest," he had again decided to sit back and reappraise the situation, telling his fellow workers on the *National Reformer:* "I will rest here that I may the better meditate and realize and acclaim your daring and devotion." And in another passage from this same essay ("A National

Reformer in the Dog Days"), he related an anecdote that succinctly summarizes his position at the end of the decade:

> A certain officer in the great American War (who most likely had no business in the rear himself) discovered a poor devil prostrate far behind while the battle was raging in front, and called out, Hallo there! are you dead? And the warrior faintly moaned, No. Are you wounded? No. What the hell is the matter with you, then? I am utterly demoralised. Deeply do I sympathise with the poor devil of a warrior, for indeed I am myself in precisely the like case.

In tracing Thomson's views on religion, I have already discussed how he had remained "utterly demoralised" throughout the years in which he was translating Leopardi, the Italian's attitude toward *noia* corresponding with and perhaps contributing to Thomson's ennui. In 1871, however, he finally completed and published his "Proposals for the Speedy Extinction," and when, after the interlude in America and Spain, he found himself back in London completing and publishing "The City," it was as a new man, vigorously, if not enthusiastically, about to begin what would prove to be the final phase of his life. Now, for the first time, he found himself able objectively to appraise and comment upon man in society, for he no longer felt that he had to rationalize the insurmountable obstacles obstructing man's path to Utopia. As a confident atheist, a confirmed pessimist, Thomson was convinced that Utopia could never be, and thus his views on man in society in these final years provide a striking contrast to the position he had taken as a young man.

As might be expected, Thomson, throughout the final decade of his life, continued to react against his youthful admiration for monarchical government. Although he did not consider England's "gingerbread monarchy" to be a serious threat to society, and expressed the conviction that "the whole thing will be pitched to Limbo if ever the people get mature enough to put away childish things,"[24] he nevertheless wrote several heated satires attacking the Queen and the royal family. Such attacks were, of course, quite fashionable in the sixties and seventies, and much of what Thomson had to say was commonplace. In 1870, however, even while "utterly demoralised," he had managed to throw off his lethargy long enough to write one of the cleverest of all the attacks on Victoria, an essay, a minor free-thought classic, entitled "A Commission of Inquiry as to Complaints against Royalty," in which an enterprising committee, after thoroughly investigating all the causes and results of Victoria's long period of mourning, conclude that the "gracious Sovereign could not do better than she is now doing, in doing nothing." As to her assuming the title of empress, it is suggested that since the title of queen has a "certain strength and stability in the habitudes if not the affection of the people," and the title empress has none, our "beloved monarch," in taking on the new title, is working consistently toward the great end of her reign—the speedy abolition of monarchy and the establishment of a republic. In like manner, the 1872 poem, "Our Congratulations on the Recovery of His Royal Highness," rejoices over the Prince's recovery from illness:

> If we wished him well we might wish him
> gone;
> As it is, we rejoice in his breath;
> For his life is likely to damage the throne
> Such a good deal more than his death.

Criticism of England's monarchy was, however, merely one facet of the broader, far more vicious, attack on despotism, in whatever country it might exist, and in whatever form. The despot Napoleon, for instance, had been "the monster of genius and falsehood and selfishness,"[25] and it was mainly because Thomson felt that France, at the start of the Franco-Prussian War, was being "true only to herself as represented by Chauvinism and Napoleonism" that he sided with Germany.[26] His best-known attack on despotic rule is "L'Ancien Régime," a poem in which he suggested that love, justice, truth, and loyalty are unwanted by kings, that servility, war, harlotry, and lies are the "gifts" kings desire, but that the best gift for "our lord the king" is death. This poem was written somewhat earlier, in 1867, but there are numerous "Jottings" in the secularist periodicals in the seventies in which Thomson reiterates this theme, and the last poem he ever wrote, just a few weeks before his death, was "Despotism Tempered by Dynamite." [27] In this poem a Russian prince, realizing that the "anarchic west" has made an impact upon his people, looks with terror to his coronation:

> My palaces are prisons to myself;
> I taste no food that may not poison me;
> I plant no footstep sure it will not stir
> Instant destruction of explosive fire;
> I look with terror to each day and night—
>   With tenfold terror to my crowning day.

Yet, in spite of his opposition to despotic rule, in spite of his attacks on royalty, Thomson did not become a champion of republicanism; even though he admitted to being a republican "in principle," he was "by no means in a hurry for a Democratic Republic in Great Britain, preferring to wait until we are taught and trained into something like fitness for it." [28] Even in advocating "freedom" he seems to have been advocating it "in principle," and probably meant no more than what he felt Whitman meant in singing the "Song of the Open Road," for Thomson too saw the open road as one that

> every man must tread who would not remain dungeoned in stark old conventions, the road leading none knows whither, save that it leads to freedom and self-reliance; nor has he who urges his comrade . . . to travel it, the least notion whether

> they shall be victorious or utterly quelled and defeated.[29]

Perhaps the key to his meaning may be found in his linking freedom with "self-reliance," which suggests his old belief that reform must begin with the individual, each man containing his own salvation within himself. In any event, Thomson saw nothing in the political movements of his age to encourage the hope that such freedom was attainable for society as a whole. He viewed the two-party system with distrust, and felt that the old party traditions "taught and still teach that our government is a game of cricket, whose innings are for the Tory and Whig aristocracy by turns, while the perpetual outings are for the insignificant residue of the nation." [30] After Gladstone had shattered the Liberal Party by his dissolution in 1874, Thomson had no use for him, and suggested that he should either have retired altogether or else gone to the House of Lords, where "he might outroll his pent thunders with the slightest possible disturbance of anyone or anything in the working world." [31] Disraeli and the Tory administration fared even worse, and by 1879 Thomson was calling the Prime Minister the "Dictator of Our Degradation":

> Never before, since old enough to take interest in our national policy, have I, for one, as a Briton, felt so vilely and wantonly insulted and humiliated as during these last three years; in which for our manifold sins and stupidities we have been delivered over to the scourging domination of an alien Charlatan, cutting his ignominious capers and posturing with yet more preposterous solemnity to the amazement of the world, on the solid platform of the dense wooden heads of an abjectly servile Parliamentary majority.[32]

Thomson had a good many specific complaints against the Tory administration,[33] but it was primarily Tory imperialism, and particularly jingoism, which infuriated him and made him feel that England had aligned herself with all that was "blind, deaf, senile, effete" against all that was "young, active, vigorous, and promising." In spite of, or perhaps because of, his long service in the army, Thomson had always hated aggression of any sort, had considered the Crimean War to have been "a mere selfish haggle for the adjustment of the balance of power, badly begun and meanly finished," and even as early as 1865 had condemned "the humbug of certain popular writers (the two Kingsleys, Tennyson, *Tom Brown, Guy Livingstone,* together with a solemn swarm of female novelists) anent the Crimean War." "Was English manhood really in so rotten a state," he wondered, "that these people are justified in soaring into ecstasies of admiration because an English Army with its officers did not act like a drove of cowards (though in many instances exceedingly like a set of fools) during a rather severe and longish siege?" [34] Sixteen years later, when Disraeli was in power, Thomson reread his comments on the Crimean War and, republishing them in *Essays and Phantasies,* added a footnote:

> The general acclamation and worship of that vilest Blatant Beast, Jingoism, the most dastardly as it is the most vauntful and rapacious and bloodthirsty of big Bullies, have revealed an immeasurably deeper degradation of our English manhood than could have been foreboded sixteen years ago. The Court, the Senate, Pall-Malldom, the majority of the nobles and clergy and middle classes, have vied with the slums, the music halls, the hirelings of the Press, and the cosmopolitan gamblers of the Exchange, in despicable glorification of this hideous Idol, whose front is of brass and the rest of it clay tempered with blood. We have crouched at the feet of the sons of Levi for discipline in English honour and patriotism; our Queen has hailed our fitting Tyrtaeus in a bard of vulgar comic

> songs. Soldiers successful—or even unsuccessful!—in brutally iniquitous battue-wars against tribes of ill-armed savages, have been bepraised and honoured and dowered as if they were the heroes of another Waterloo. All signs point to a thoroughly disastrous and disgraceful collapse of our whole military system should we find ourselves involved in a European war.

In brief, then, Thomson, appraising the state of the nation in the 1870's, found the national policy to be "vilely and wantonly" humiliating, considered imperialism, as perpetrated by the jingoes, to be an abomination, and even questioned the desirability of the inevitable democratic republic, fearing that to give control of government to an uneducated populace would result, not in freedom, but in the "delirious fever of mobs" which he had long dreaded.[35]

To a certain extent, Thomson did, however, align himself with the uneducated populace, even though it is unlikely that he ever felt any of the "sympathy for ordinary life and vulgar occupations" or the "feeling of brotherhood for all rough workers" which he professed to admire in Whitman.[36] Far more likely, he simply considered the lower classes less objectionable than the others, for the middle class was made up of men "sufficiently well off to be conscious of social inequalities, and not sufficiently well educated to understand their real character," whereas Tory and Whig aristocrats were men

> sufficiently well off to be unconscious of social inequalities all and always in their own favour, or else sufficiently well educated to understand their real character as a Divine Providential arrangement in accordance with the text whose right reading is, "The earth is the Lords' and the fulness thereof." [37]

Occasionally, then, we find Thomson complaining about

the plight of the working classes, as when he reproached Northcote for saying, in his defense of the present taxation, that the working class had no reason to complain:

> . . . if he who uttered this, and the portly, many-acred country gentlemen behind him who approved, could realise how callous, how heartless the "not much reason to complain" sounds in the ears of the moiling over-burdened millions, who stagger through hopeless life to the not unwelcome grave, where is neither hunger, nor thirst, nor taxation, nor toil, whose fruits are mainly for others —why, I think, that even these honourable and wealthy legislators would feel some abatement of their sublime satisfaction with themselves and things in general.[38]

For the most part, however, Thomson, always the confirmed opponent of reform movements, refused to write in support of even the obviously worthy efforts being made to alleviate the conditions of the working classes, the one notable exception to his antireformism being his interest in education. Education was, in fact, the one dim hope that he felt remained for the human race, and it was vital that such education be purely secular. One of his most vigorous outbursts came during the 1876 elections for the London School Board, when he feared that the state church was trying to gain control of the board, and that the "great work of educating the poor children whom the church had hitherto neglected" would not be continued:

> If these priests and their partizans could have their will our children would not be allowed to learn that three times one are three, without learning at the same time that one is three and three are one; nor learn that man has existed for myriads and myriads of years, without also learning that he was first created less than six thousand years back; nor learn that the laws of nature are uniform and inviolable, without also learning that they have been

> frequently violated for the most petty, or silly, or ferocious purpose. Whatever they were taught of science would be contradicted or confused by something taught in the Bible; they should read and believe that the sun and the moon stood still, in order that one semi-barbarous race might have light to continue the slaughter of another, that the sun went back ten degrees in sign that a sick king should recover; that an ass spoke; a woman was turned into a pillar of salt; iron floated up to the surface of water; a man was swallowed by a whale, and lived three days in its belly; a virgin conceived by a spirit, and remained virginal after carnal child-birth; that a living body of flesh and blood walked on the water, and floated up and away from the earth; that many dead bodies arose from their graves. And on the strength of these and such-like absurd and incredible stories, they would be taught to put unquestioning faith in certain dogmas as to supernatural beings, immortal souls, everlasting punishments and rewards, concerning none of which, or whether they really exist, no man ever has known anything, while most of the dogmas are repugnant to reason or conscience, or both—*i.e.* to the undefiled reason and conscience enlightened by purely secular knowledge.[39]

"Secular Science," Thomson felt, had finally forced the admission that "the people will be and must be educated," and he was determined to do his best to see that "springs of useful knowledge" would not be adulterated with "old Hebrew legends," for such hope as the poor and underprivileged had, rested in education. After admitting this, he had, however, little else to say on the social problems of his age, and even as late as 1881, when he addressed his secularist friends at the opening of their new hall in Leicester, the only advice he had to offer as to social melioration was contained in the following couplet:

> Our creed is simple, All men are one man!
> Our sole commandment, Do what good you
> can.

Though hardly profound or even very helpful, this suggestion was, I suspect, Thomson's sincere belief, even when he was convinced that nothing good was likely to result from "doing good." This "sole commandment" partly explains, however, why he continued to write as a moralist, even when the only real hope he had to offer men was, as expressed in "The City of Dreadful Night," that they were free to "end it when they will," a concept that in itself deserves attention, for his attitude toward the value of human life was clearly related—in all his various phases—to his reluctance to become involved in "social work." When he had been a Christian, life itself, he had felt, was insignificant, and one's social position a matter of no importance, for the true life was to come in Heaven; when a pantheist, life itself was all important, so important, it seems, that he believed men should simply burst through social, political, and religious barriers and "live life" in spite of their present conditions and immediate surroundings; but as an atheist and pessimist, life became not only meaningless, but also, since it could never really be "good," worthless. That is to say, it was neither worth having nor, it seems, worth preserving, and thus it made little sense to Thomson to struggle to improve, much less perfect, the imperfectible. It is, in fact, because of his belief that life was worthless that he approved of capital punishment ("We are . . . absurdly reluctant to extinguish a nuisance when the nuisance is a man or woman. . . . We preserve hardened criminals alive, though their lives are noxious to themselves and others"), euthanasia ("children born idiotic, scrofulous, deformed, etc., are kept alive to be a nuisance to themselves and others, when an early dose of chloroform would avoid all"), and, of course, suicide:

> If a man feels that his life is useless or worse than useless to himself and others, or that it does more harm than good; and especially if he has reason to expect that it will grow more miserable, more dependent, more ignoble, more vicious, with advancing years, the best use he can make of his life is to end it.

Moreover, since he felt that "in most cases the responsibility of engendering human life is far heavier than that of extinguishing it," he implied, at least, that birth control could solve most of the problems of the poor and needy if such classes would simply abstain altogether from breeding; he felt there was "insane recklessness in engendering human life . . . when its probabilities are almost certainties of evil, to itself and others."[40] In brief, as pessimist and atheist, Thomson seems to have believed that the one simple solution to all man's problems—social, political, economic—rested with the individual, who was capable of solving them all, at least for himself, with the barest of bodkins.

Thomson never tried to force these beliefs on anyone; even in "The City of Dreadful Night," where wise men said

> We yearn for speedy death in full fruition,
> Dateless oblivion and divine repose,

he made it perfectly clear that he was not writing for the "hopeful young" or for those men who could still "foresee a heaven on earth." Nor, in spite of his pessimism, did Thomson ever become a misanthrope; even in his final prose phantasy, the 1877 "In Our Forest of the Past,"[41] his heart was "sick and sorrowful to death" with the vision of all the past lives that had been frustrated by Nature or crushed through man's inhumanities to man. This phantasy may, in fact, be taken as a summary of Thomson's final views on man, for in it he had a dream in which he is guided through a great forest containing all the men who had ever lived, conveniently grouped according to their sufferings in life. Only a handful are found whose lives had not been waste and frustrate, a pitiful few in comparison with the "countless moaning multitudes" whose lives had never been fulfilled. "Must it always be so?" he asks, and his guide replies:

> Did Nature destroy all those infants? did Nature breed all those defects and deformities? did Nature bring forth all those idiocies and lunacies? or, was not rather their chief destroyer and producer the ignorance of Man outraging Nature? And the poor, the prisoners, the soldiery, the ascetics, the priests, the nobles, the kings; were these the work of Nature, or of the perversity of Man? And I asked: Were not the very ignorance and perversity of Man also from Nature? And he replied: Yes; yet perchance, putting himself childlike to school, he may gradually learn from Nature herself to enlighten the one and control the other.

This passage suggests both Thomson's belief in education and his discarded pantheistic dream of a harmonious nature, but his reply to the suggestion is indeed ominous; instead of commenting, he abruptly concludes the phantasy by waking from his vision: "Then the dolorous moanings again filled my ears, even in the moonlit valley of peace; and I awoke in the moonlight and heard the moaning of the gale swelling to a storm." The voice of Nature was replying for him, a voice inextricably mingled with the dolorous moanings of the wasted lives in the forest of the past. A few months after this essay was published, Thomson broke completely with the secularists and, with but a few exceptions,[42] never again wrote on the social or political problems of his age. There was simply nothing more to say.

I cannot, however, leave this phase of Thomson's intellectual development without making a few observations on his pessimism, about which there has been a good deal of misunderstanding. G. W. Foote, whose comments, taken all in all, are more valuable than those of Thomson's other friends, was only half right when insisting that the pessimism was "not a mood but a philosophy"; although it was most definitely not a mood, it was not a philosophy either, not, at least, in the sense that, as in Leopardi, it provided the basis for a "system" expounding life's meaning and purpose. Thomson's pessimism was, in fact, little more than a conviction as to the impossibility of progress, and it was based entirely on his experiences with and his understanding of weakness in the individual man. Virtually everything he ever had to say about man in society pivoted, not on society, but on the individual, who alone could take the necessary corrective action, whether that action was repentance, "living true life," or suicide. The machinations of government, of economics, of social theory, of philosophical systems—none of these interested Thomson in the slightest; throughout his career he believed that the human race could operate no more effectively than the individual was operating within himself. The general impression that the loss of God was responsible for his pessimism is completely erroneous, for that loss was a blessing, a release from doubt and despair which had been tormenting him for almost a decade. Indeed, when Thomson "lost God," far from becoming a pessimist, he celebrated the event by writing some of the most optimistic poetry ever written in the nineteenth century, poetry expressing a supreme faith in man's capacity for sublime thoughts and actions.[43] It was when he lost this faith, his faith in man, that he became a pessimist, the great shock coming, not with the realization that man had evolved from an animal, but that man, as an animal, was fully as savage as all other animals in nature. Once Thomson believed that the individual man, as a naked savage, a creature of "vanity and nothingness," was incapable of improving himself, was unable to alter his natural animal savagery, then, and only then, did he become "hopeless of any improvement in mankind." If the individual could not improve, then society could not improve, and thus, even were mankind to be dragged out of one pitfall, it would "immediately stumble into another as deep and dangerous." [44]

We do not have to dig very deep to discover weaknesses in Thomson's beliefs on God and man, for he was neither a profound nor an original thinker. He did, however, read widely, and when he felt he had discovered truth, he made no attempt to avoid or circumvent it, however unpleasant the implications may have been. His great weakness was a tendency to grasp at, rather than to grasp, a major concept, refining and simplifying it until shadings were removed and it became all black or all white. Yet perhaps this very tendency to absorb and simplify great ideas explains, to a large extent, why Thomson continues, both as man and as poet, to exert a fascination that far exceeds any value to be found in either his message or his poetry; living as he did in the middle third of the nineteenth century, he was, in a way, a catchall for the major intellectual trends of three vastly different generations. As a boy his inheritance was, for the most part, eighteenth-century evangelism, and the views of man and God which he learned from his parents and at the Caledonian Asylum can be traced back to Wesley and Whitefield just as surely as they can be traced to Edward Irving. In his young manhood, early nineteenth-century Romanticism washed over him, erasing the biblical God and leaving an empty universe wherein men could but join hands and huddle together, pretending the heap itself was God, believing that they all were gods. Like Heine, Thomson could make no use of that god of the pantheists, for he seemed interwoven and blended with the world, imprisoned therein, gaping out without will or power. But unlike Heine, Thomson could not return to the old God, for the secularists and the scientists of the latter half of the century convinced him that "all the divinities have fled, and on high there dwells but an old woman with hands of iron and disconsolate heart—Necessity."[45] She was the "Melencolia" who ruled over "The City of Dreadful Night," that one nearly great poem which links Thomson to the twentieth century, not only because its message bears a close relationship to more recent messages of despair, but because without it we would probably never have discovered a mind that had incorporated some of the best, and, inevitably, some of the worst that had been known and thought in the nineteenth century.

Thomson lived for eight years after writing "The City," a life without hope and without fear, for, as he had written in his masterpiece, "no hope can have no fear." By 1877 he had relinquished his role as an expositor of man's relationship to God and as a sideline commentator on man in society, but he never relinquished his role as poet and critic. Asking himself why, as a confirmed pessimist, he continued to work for the improvement of the human race, the reply he gave was, "First and foremost, because 'it is my nature to' "—which is, apparently, nonsense, until it is viewed in the light of his views on the function of criticism and the place of the poet in society.

4

Romantic to Realist

IT IS NOT KNOWN when Thomson began to write poetry. Friends who knew him at the Caledonian Asylum, between his eighth and sixteenth years, remembered him as being a somewhat precocious mathematician, but make no mention of him as a budding poet. It is possible that during those years he privately indulged in an occasional Byronic outburst, for even as a child he admired the Romantic poets,[1] and his earliest extant poems, written the year after he left school, do not seem to be first efforts. In any event, the few pieces that remain from the early years, 1852 through 1856, give no reason to suspect that he then considered himself to be anything more than an admirer of poetry who, in idle hours, enjoyed writing verses.[2] In 1857, however, Thomson's attitude toward his poetry apparently underwent a radical change; in that one year alone he wrote well over three thousand lines, several of the longer poems indicating that, at least in his own opinion, he had stopped "writing verses" and had become "A Poet":

> Poets are the hierophants of an unapprehended inspiration; the mirrors of the gigantic shadows which futurity casts upon the present; the words which express what they understand not; the trumpets which sing to battle, and feel not what they inspire; the influence which is moved not, but

> moves. Poets are the unacknowledged legislators of the world.

This is, of course, Bysshe Shelley, not Bysshe Vanolis, but the famous passage is singularly relevant to a study of Thomson's early attitude toward poetry; as he frequently admitted, Shelley was "from my youth up, a perennial source of delight and inspiration." Shelley was, in fact, "the poet of poets and the purest of men," and when, in those years in which orthodox Christianity still dominated his world picture, Thomson wrote that Shelley had been exalted "to sit with Isaiah and Dante, as one of that small choir of chief singers who are called transcendent," I suspect that he meant it literally.[3]

It is, therefore, not surprising that the earliest poem relevant to this aspect of his thought is the 1857 allegory, "A Festival of Life," a long poem in which Shelley's "dome of many-coloured glass" is realistically constructed as the stage for life's festival. It is Thomson's earliest "vision" poem, the first of many in which the poet, as narrator, can "see" things which ordinary men cannot. In one scene, for instance, when two figures personifying death appear in the midst of the dancing throng, they are invisible to the multitude but not to the poet:

> . . . power to me was given
> To see, to pierce the gloomy robes austere,
> Which . . .
> Concealed these Two in undistinguished shade.

This is the concept that separates "A Festival of Life" from Thomson's earlier poetry, for when he began to sense that he had been given a power denied to other men, it followed that, like his famous namesake,[4] perhaps even like the great Shelley, he too may have been "chosen" to be the hierophant of an unapprehended inspiration. Moreover, in those years in which Thomson believed that such divine power could be granted only by the "Allwise, Allgood" God (Shelley himself had written that "poetry is, indeed, something divine"), the prospect of being a "true poet" was not only a vision of delight, but a call to duty. In the holy war being waged between Good and Evil, "all *are* but what they *do*." If poets were really God's messengers, it was inconceivable that one could "do" more than be a poet.

In "The Doom of a City," written shortly after "A Festival of Life," Thomson gave free rein to this idea that the poet is God's messenger. In "The Doom of a City," the poet, after suffering intensely, deserting his home, sailing through storm-tossed seas, and finally reaching the visionary city where all men had been turned to stone, is absolutely certain that God has been directing his course of action and that some important use is about to be made of his poetic gifts:

> Some revelation from the awful Throne
> Awaits me surely: if my life, torn free
> From dire Egyptian bondage, has been led
> In safety through the all-devouring sea;
> If, lost in foodless deserts, it was fed
> Though murmuring ever; hath it truly trod
> Such paths for nothing? Shall it not be brought
> To stand awe-stricken 'neath some Mount of God
> Wrapt in thick clouds of thunder fire and gloom,
> And hear the Law of Heaven by which its doom
> To good or evil must be henceforth wrought?

It shall, and it did, for as the poem develops, the poet not only hears God's judgments and attains a glimpse of Heaven's gates, but is given the grave responsibility of carrying God's message back to England. Returning home in his Shelleyan bark, the "Burden of the Message" lies heavy on his soul, but, as Shelley had made it clear that the poet's inspiration is unapprehended, Thomson's sacred messenger need not, indeed could not, do anything but lean back in his little boat, until suddenly

> That Spirit which will never be withstood
> Came down and shook and seized and lifted me,—
> As men uplift a passive instrument
> Through which to breathe whatever fits their mood,
> Stately triumphal march or war-note dread,
> Anthem, gay dance, or requiem for the dead;
> And through my lips with irrepressible might
> Poured forth its own stern language on the night.

Included in the "stern language" Thomson addressed to his countrymen was a specific reprimand to "poets who sing their own lusts instead of hymns of the Lord," an idea that is central to a third significant 1857 poem, one revealingly titled "A Happy Poet." Here, while elaborating still further on the importance of inspiration in poetic composition, Thomson also describes the poet's position in society. It was, indeed, an exalted position, for the poet was considered to be an honored guest at life's feast:

> O happy-dowered Soul! Whom God doth call
> To life's imperial Banquet as a guest.

Although the tumult of life "whirls forever to and fro," the poet "can see it all in vision" and, as a result, lives a "self-fulfilling" life apart from the cares of the world. He gazes upon the actors "with reverent love, with unaccusing thought," waiting patiently, disinterestedly, until suddenly

> . . . the heavenly light doth dawn and grow
> And thrill my silence into mystic psalms.

With the heavenly light dawning and growing, the poet is compelled to sing, to sing of everything he "feels" and "knows"—of nature, of his "human kin," of the "secret sympathies that bind all beings to their wondrous dwelling-place," of the "perfect Unity" of life. And as he sings the mystic psalms, robing them "in full verse-folds dark with awe," it is even asserted that he can "glimpse the law ineffable, eternal, veiled behind," learning

> New secrets more impassioned, crowning
> them
> With golden words, a fulgent diadem.[5]

In brief, by the end of 1857 the twenty-three-year-old Thomson considered the poet to be a man who had, not a craft, but a calling, and although he could not be certain that he himself was among the chosen, he evidently decided to sing the hymns of the Lord and hope for the best. For five years, then, obsessed with the idea that, like Shelley, he too might be a divine hierophant, Thomson carefully patterned his subject matter after what he considered to be Shelley's "great subjects," writing upon the beauty and harmony of the visible universe ("A Happy Poet," "The Lord of the Castle of Indolence"), the existence of God ("Suggested by Matthew Arnold's 'Stanzas from the Grande Chartreuse'"), the moral law of the universe ("The Doom of a City"), the immortality of the soul ("The Deliverer," "The Fadeless Bower"), the independent being of what is called the material world ("Tasso to Leonora," "A Festival of Life"), and, finally, the perfectibility of man ("The Dead Year," "Shelley"). Never for a moment did Thomson relinquish his idea that the poet was God's messenger, and even as late as 1861, in the poem titled "Shelley," he pictured Shelley as having been a seraph in Heaven who had volunteered to come to earth as a divine messenger in order to "preach the Gospel of our Lord above." In fact, in this poem he even included a footnote directing readers to *The Defense of Poetry* from which he quoted, almost as if to say "I told you so," the concluding lines about poets being the unacknowledged legislators of the world.

Undoubtedly the most important aspect of these early views, however, was the role that inspiration played in the creation of true poetry. The final test of a great poet was whether his treatment of great subjects was such as to entitle him to the epithet "inspired," for without "spontaneous musical utterance" the divine touch was lacking. Again and again Thomson insisted that God, not James Thomson, was the true author of his verse:

> My friend, I have no power to rule my
> voice:
> A spirit lifts me where I lie alone,
> And thrills me into song by its own laws.[6]

Elaborating upon Plato's idea that "poets utter their beautiful melodies of verse in a state of inspiration, and, as it were, *possessed* by a spirit not their own," Thomson, in the essay on Shelley, insisted that true poetry, whatever its mood, was "not self-possessed but God-possessed; whether the God came down serene and stately as Jove, when, a swan, he wooed Leda; or with overwhelming might insupportably burning, as when he consumed Semele." This was the vital point in the entire philosophy, and this, of course, was the Achilles' heel that, in 1862, caused its downfall; since God was, in effect, the heart of the inspired singer, Thomson, when finally convinced that God did not exist, lost not only God, but also the "singer's heart."

In the five years before 1862 Thomson completed at least thirty-five poems, well over seven thousand lines of poetry; in 1862 and 1863 he completed six poems, less than 350 lines.[7]

> Ah! life's blood creepeth cold and tame,
> Life's thought plays no new part:
> I never cared for the singer's fame,
> But, oh! for the singer's heart.

Obviously, his entire philosophy of poetry had been shattered, and before he could write again, it was necessary that his views on the nature and the function of the poet undergo complete revision.[8] The above lines from "The Fire That Filled My Heart of Old" were written in February, 1864, the year in which he began to evolve, not only new attitudes toward God and man, but toward poetry. It was the beginning of his journey from Romantic to realist.

The first thing to be discarded from the old beliefs was, of course, the idea that the poet was inspired by a divine spirit. As Thomson had declared in "Vane's Story," he was now determined to take part with man, not God, and since it was now man, not God, who was going to have to do the work, inspiration was replaced by intellect, Thomson noting, for the first time, that

> it is astonishing what a large part of even a good modern book has been written without any exercise of the faculty of thought. Without going back to Shakespeare and Bacon, we may select works from a literary epoch upon which we affect to look down, works such as Pope's *Essay on Man* or Swift's *Tale of a Tub,* wherein nearly every sentence has required a distinct intellectual effort, and which thus, whatever their faults, shame by their powerful virility our effeminate modern books.[9]

"A distinct intellectual effort"—that was the crux of Thomson's new philosophy of poetic composition, and if Blake and Heine, not Pope and Dryden, became the new heroes, this did not alter his conviction that the poet, far from spontaneously overflowing in a moment of inspiration, must carefully select, construct, refine, and, in brief, "create" a poem rather than, as previously believed, give birth to it. The process is explained in detail in the 1865 essay, "The Poet, High Art, Genius," written shortly after "Sunday at Hampstead," a poem in which four young couples are picnicking in the country:

> Let a poet be of the party in some merry picnic. Do you think he enjoys it as thoroughly as it is enjoyed by the simple youths and thoughtless girls, or even by the stout matrons and old fogies, around him? The probability is, that he proves about the dullest person in the party. He is reflecting and

> observing while the others are enjoying; he is so used to reflect and observe that he cannot throw off these staid habits and plunge into the glittering stream of the revelry. Yet some days or weeks afterwards, musing upon the elements of delight which existed in the company and the excursion, he distils them into a poem exquisitely delightful, a poem overbrimming with the pure joyousness which he ought to have felt but did not feel, and which the commonplace people about him really did feel; though they could give it only fugitive expression in chatter and laughter and dancing and romping, while he can give it quasi-enduring expression in lovely verse.

Poetry had become a craft. No longer did the poet lean back in his Shelleyan bark until the glorious moment of inspiration descended upon him; he was constantly reflecting and observing, going through life, as it were, with notebook and pencil in hand, ready to swoop down on his material, gather it up, take it home, sort it out, and then distil it into an exquisitely delightful poem. He did not sing about all he "feels and knows"—he did not, in fact, "feel" anything; commonplace people did that, for the poet, with his "staid habits," was beyond feeling. He was still, in one sense, a guest at life's feast, but no longer an honored dignitary; the poet had actually become a martyr, sacrificing his own pleasure to help others enjoy life.

As might be expected, this view of the poet as martyr was to prove even more disastrous for Thomson than the earlier view of the poet as divine hierophant. Although it was one thing for the poet, as God's servant, dutifully to remain apart from life's tumult, it was quite another for him, as man's servant, willingly to remain outside "the glittering stream of the revelry." This is precisely what Thomson had been doing in that prolific spring of 1865, collecting his material with scientific detachment during weekend pilgrimages to Richmond and Kew Gardens, or up to Hampstead, then taking it home and distilling it into more than a dozen "live life" poems.[10] That the method was rejected after only four months is not surprising, for writing poetry in this way obviously could not be reconciled with Thomson's other views, with the new philosophy wherein every man was to burn with pure aspiration, "living" every single moment of his life. By the summer of 1865, then, this brief poetic outburst ended abruptly as Thomson unhappily concluded, not only that the poet as martyr was unable to "live life," but that only a man incapable of "living life" would ever choose to become a poet.

> The man we call a Poet . . . sings of that which he cannot enjoy, cannot achieve; if at any time he can enjoy it, can achieve it, be sure that he is not then pondering or singing it. Where and when rich life is present, it lives, and does not content itself with shadowing forth and celebrating life. When and where rich life is not present, the shadowing forth and celebration of life may partially console for its absence, or may even partially illude into the belief in its presence. Yet life remains and ever is as superior to art as a man to the picture of a man.

Had Thomson left it at that, he might very likely have continued to write poetry, at least whenever the rich life was not present, for the basic idea in this passage, as restated in his 1865 "Art," is simply the Victorian commonplace that

> Statues and pictures and verse may be grand,
> But they are not the Life for which they
> stand.

Thomson, however, did not leave it at that, but labored this idea until he had reached the logical absurdity that unless art is pursued simply as relaxation or as the least irksome mode of earning the daily bread, "artistry accuses weakness and lack of vitality in the artist." The argument ran something like this: Life is superior to art; living is superior to creating art; one creates art only when one cannot live; the serious artist, being incapable of living, is weak.

Thomson had come a long way from the poet as hierophant of an unapprehended inspiration to the poet as a man who is weak and lacking in vitality, but he had not yet reached the argument developed in "The Poet, High Art, Genius," where he also accused the artist of lacking intelligence, courage, energy, sympathy, fortitude, and wisdom.

> If a man, being poor, can earn more and earn it more easily and pleasantly by painting pictures than by ploughing and reaping, let him paint. But in this case he paints to live, he does not live to paint; his art is purely a trade, not a divine mission and holy vocation, as so many of us in these years regard it. If a man, being rich, finds happy filling up of idle hours in making verses, let him make verses: but let us clearly understand that his art is simply a hobby and a pastime. If the poor man and the rich man were endowed with keener intelligence and more puissant vitality, they would prefer a trade and a hobby bringing them into closer and warmer relations with the living world and their fellowmen, demanding more courage and energy and sympathy and fortitude and wisdom.

We well might wonder how Thomson could reconcile such a belief with his intense admiration for poets like Shakespeare and Shelley; the answer is astounding, for we are told that

> the very greatest geniuses, those whom we really reverence in their complete manhood, have worked at their art with a distinct consciousness that it was but a trade, an apology for better work from which they were shut out by hostile circumstances; or a pleasant relaxation, a hobby to carry them at a canter through dull hours.

Thus, Dante wrote poetry only because defeat and exile

had driven him from his native town, the "petty and transitory interests" of which were his real love; Milton's true devotion was to his age and country, and his first poems were but "refined amusements of youth," his last poems, "the consolations of a defeated partisan"; Shakespeare "wrote no more when he could afford to live without writing"; and even Shelley, who "yearned for the direct action of political life," had found himself "disabled and outcast into the mere life of poetry." [11] In fact, all these men had evidently realized, as Thomson himself now admitted, that the poet as

> slave of a sublime mission, the instrument of a divine inspiration, "the word which expresses what it understands not, the trumpet which sings to battle and feels not what it inspires" . . . is considerably less than a man; weak, diseased, mutilated, and more or less silly.

The epigraph to this essay completes the story, for once Shelley had been reduced to the disabled state where he was outcast into the "mere life of poetry," once the poet had become "weak, diseased, mutilated, and more or less silly," Thomson could only throw up his hands in disgust and agree with Hotspur that

> I had rather be a kitten and cry mew,
> Than one of these same metre ballad-mongers.

I doubt, however, that Thomson, even while writing this essay, really believed everything he suggested in it, for, at least in 1865, he neither burned his books nor gave up writing poetry. It was, nevertheless, increasingly difficult for him to continue writing, for this was a blind alley affording no exit for a man who persisted in calling himself "Bysshe Vanolis." Between the completion of this essay in mid-1865 and the end of 1866 he wrote only two short poems,[12] and, although he did complete four poems late in 1866, and four more in 1867, he never denied the main premise behind "The Poet, High Art, Genius"; it was this essay, not the 1860 essay on Shelley, which he chose to republish less than two years before his death. Several of its major ideas were, in fact, repeated elsewhere, notably the idea that poetic "inspiration" is nonsense. In his 1879 review of Garth Wilkinson's *Improvisations from the Spirit,* Thomson stated that Wilkinson's belief in his poems as having been divinely inspired was

> not only a delusion but a delusion very noxious to them and to himself. A delusion, because in essence it is that claimed in common by all the loftiest poets, and conceded by the loftiest philosophers; a noxious delusion, because it has prevented him from using his natural faculties to correct and perfect conception and expression, and because it has impelled him to yield his natural sanity to the absolute sway of uncontrolled fantasy, following this flitting marsh-meteor as if it were the lode-star of truth.[13]

In like manner, Thomson continued to hold the belief that the poet was, physically at least, "weak, diseased, mutilated"; and this is perhaps the main reason for his attraction to Whitman, for a supreme poet "supremely embodied" was worthy of joyous contemplation:

> The greater part of our noblest modern poetic genius have been shrined in disease or deformity; Shelley never had good health, Keats died of consumption at twenty-four, Byron and Scott were lame, Schiller with difficulty kept alive till forty-six, Heine lay helpless in paralysis seven years before his death, Lenau died young in a madhouse, Alfred de Musset was an old man at forty, Leopardi was irretrievably shattered at twenty; and I, for one, cannot remember these, with others only less illustrious, and yet contemplate without joy and admiration a supreme poet supremely embodied.[14]

This was written in 1874, but the idea reappears in an 1879 notebook entry: "How small and weak are all the *singing* birds!"—an observation repeated in his "Notes on the Genius of Robert Browning," the paper read before the Browning Society on an evening when Thomson was recovering from what a friend described as a "sad sad spree," and was himself too "small and weak" even to attend the meeting.[15]

In any event, that Thomson's theories on the nature and the function of the poet affected his poetic output in the late sixties and the seventies is undeniable. In a period of fourteen years, between March, 1868, and November, 1881, he wrote only four poems of any significance: the unpublished "Supplement to the Inferno," the discarded "I Had a Love," "Weddah and Om-el-Bonain," and "The City of Dreadful Night."[16] Moreover, although he did, during the last six months of his life, write some 1,600 lines of verse, this apparent prolificacy resulted from neither a shift in his attitude toward poetry nor from some sort of magical revival of poetic powers, for, discounting the four "little skits" he wrote for the *Weekly Dispatch*, all but four or five of the eleven poems he completed in this final phase were pieced together from old ideas and old fragments written more than a decade earlier.[17] Indeed, when Thomson again began to write poetry, it was mainly because, as he admitted, he was "in sad want of cash"; after taking "poetical stock" and discovering that he had practically exhausted his material in the 1880 volumes, he was forced to write again in order to fill the volume eventually published posthumously as *A Voice from the Nile and Other Poems.*[18] Ironically, then, although hailed in the eighties as a "new Poet," Thomson had almost completely stopped writing poetry at the end of the sixties, and although he is remembered today only because of his poetry, those pieces that are usually considered his best work—"The City of Dreadful Night," "Insomnia," "Weddah and Om-el-Bonain," and possibly "In the Room"—were not written in the fifties when, as hierophant of an unapprehended inspiration, he was writing hymns of the Lord, nor were they written in the early sixties, when he was "reflecting and observing" and taking part with man; they were written in the years when he had not only stopped being a "true poet," but had, to all intents and purposes, stopped writing poetry.

If, however, Thomson's active career as a poet may be said to have ended with the publication of "The City," his interest in literature was still very much alive, and it was in that year, 1874, that his career as a literary critic began. Just two months after subscribers to the *National Reformer* had received four installments of "The City," written "not for the hopeful young," but for the "desolate, Fate-smitten, whose faith and hope are dead, and who would die," they received the first installment of a seven-part essay on Walt Whitman, written, "not for the few who know Whitman, but for the many who knowing him not would be the better for knowing him." In line with his belief that secularism should occupy itself with the "natural and human arts and sciences," Thomson had determined to make his own disinterested endeavor to learn and to propagate the best known and thought, to introduce his readers to authors whom they would be "the better for knowing." During the next six years, then, he published eight such essays, not intended to be critical discussions, but simply "notes of introduction," long biographical studies of Whitman, Stendhal, Heine, Saint-Amant, Rabelais, Jonson, John Wilson, and James Hogg. Moreover, in the same period Thomson published no less than thirty-eight book reviews, most of which were also introductory essays, as the books he selected included the relatively unknown novels of Meredith and Flaubert, new translations of authors such as Uhland, Epictetus, and Schopenhauer, and critical studies of the English classics, including every volume of the "English Men of Letters" series published before 1880.[19]

Prior to the 1874 essay on Whitman, Thomson had, of course, written literary criticism, but his earliest critical studies, "Notes on Emerson" and "A Few Words about Burns," written in 1858 when he was pondering on divinely inspired hierophants, reveal little more than his obsession with "spontaneous musical utterance" and the "singer's heart."[20] In the pompously pedantic essay on Emerson, for instance, although assuring his readers that Emerson was "one of the noblest spirits of the age" with the "noblest philosophical intellect," Thomson had refrained from making "impertinent inquiry into the various individual opinions strown throughout the works of this philosopher," suggesting that "the instrument is noble, it is uttering grand music; let us not fuss about the name of the Tune." His theory, it seems, was that "the one good of reading is that it raise you to a grand sphere of thought, inspire you to a lofty mood," and thus, in the essay on Burns, readers were told, among a good many other silly things, that the great man's words were "but a cloud-medium through which burns an unconsuming sun." Although the essays are of some interest as regards Thomson's early belief that the poet is "inspired," as literary criticism they are, I fear, virtually worthless, a judgment that is, to a great extent, also true of the 1860 essay on Shelley. The essay eulogizes Shelley; praises the Brownings (who, far superior to Tennyson in all the other "noble qualities," lack his "singing voice"), Scott ("the poet of the past"), and Goethe ("the poet of the future"); and contains an interesting passage which notes that, in addition to studying Shelley for quintessential poetry,

> we must study Shakespeare for knowledge of idealised human nature, and Fielding for knowledge of human nature unidealised, and Carlyle's "French Revolution" as the unapproached model of history, and Currer Bell's "Villette" to learn the highest capabilities of the novel, and Ruskin for the true philosophy of art, and Emerson for quintessential philosophy.

None of these dicta, however, are documented or explained, and we are forced to assume that these heroes were simply considered men and women of "genius," more or less divinely inspired in their work.[21] The earliest essay that did attempt a thorough analysis of a poet's work, a review of *Men and Women,* was not written until 1862.[22] Here, probably for the first time, Thomson was forced to consider the role that intellect plays in the creation of poetry, and his analysis of Browning's work is, therefore, of considerable interest. Unable to deny that the "richest materials of poetry" were present in Browning's verse, yet aware that Browning was not writing the Shelleyan sort of divinely inspired poetry which true poets should be writing, Thomson concluded that Browning's failure to combine his materials into the "poetic form and brightness which is Beauty" was neither laziness nor the "lack of conscientious reverence for the Giver of his precious gifts," but a "restlessness of mind, resulting from the strength and activity of his talents as distinguished from, and often rebellious against, his genius." In other words, Browning was a gifted poet who suffered from an "intellectual fault," since his talents (by which Thomson apparently meant his "self-possessed" powers) ran away with his genius (the "God-possessed" part of the poet). But even though Thomson was still of the opinion that the intellect was incompatible, if not actually antagonistic, to the God-given powers, his admiration for Browning's down-to-earth realism was beginning to undermine his faith in Romantic inspiration. Even Browning's "loftiest idealizations" were recognized as being "embodied in that Shakespearean flesh and blood reality which is so cordial a contrast to the vague, dim, spectral productions of all but the supreme mystics," and once Thomson began to recognize "flesh and blood reality" as a cordial contrast to the work of all but the supreme mystics (the God-possessed poets who had "spontaneous musical utterance"), he was indeed well on the way to rejecting Romanticism. Whereas two years earlier Tennyson had been considered a better poet than Browning because he possessed the "singing voice," Thomson now felt, in concluding this review of *Men and Women,* that "Tennyson is a rare 'literary luxury' for us all, and especially our youths and maidens; but Robert Browning is indeed the poet of Men and Women." [23]

Less than a year after writing this essay, Thomson published his review of Harrison's *The Meaning of History,* which I have suggested was the turning point in his intellectual development, and shortly afterward, taking part with man, not God, he was writing his "live life" poems. However, before he could write poetry in which, as in Browning's, the intellect would be free to "reflect and observe" on men and women, it was necessary for him to come to terms with those "vague, dim, spectral productions" that, in the Romantic poets, he had long admired and imitated. It was Blake who seemed to provide a solution to his problem, for, on first reading Blake's poetry, Thomson was delighted to discover that here was both a realist, in whose early works "the spirit of the great Elizabethan age was incarnate once more," and a Romantic, in whose later works had been planted the seed of what was "half-consciously struggling towards organic perfection" and would eventually become the poetry of the future.[24] The essence of this poetry of the future was not, however, "inspiration," but "simplicity"—a "mystical simplicity" which, as Thomson saw it, could lead to the state of childhood innocence in which all men would "live life" naturally. Such an analysis of Blake, then, not only gave support to the "live life" poetry which Thomson had determined to write,[25] but served the more important function of redefining Romantic poetry, allowing him to revaluate the vague, dim, spectral productions of the inspired Romantics, rejecting them, or at least ignoring them, on the basis of their failure to possess this now-essential "simplicity." Wordsworth, although aspiring toward simplicity, never attained it; Coleridge, who had had much of it in his early work, supremely in "The Ancient Mariner," later lost it; Scott wrote altogether out of its sphere; Byron had none of it; Keats did not live long enough to attain it; and only Shelley, who carried on the work begun by Blake, "sinking its foundations into a deeper past, and uplifting its towers into a loftier future," really possessed it to the utmost.[26] Thomson, therefore, in one delightful stroke of nonsense, had disowned Romantic inspiration, spared Shelley, and discovered in Blake both an inspiration for his "live life" philosophy and a functional theory of poetic composition. I doubt that he appreciated the full significance of his comment when, at the beginning of this strange essay, he admitted that Blake's writings "were a revelation far richer than my hopes."

In any event, by mid-1865 Thomson had become hopelessly confused as to his critical position on the poet. In the essays on Bumbleism, even while designating the poet as the "High Priest of Beauty" whose task it was to combat Bumble, he was also ridiculing him, as "slave of a sublime mission," for being "weak, diseased, mutilated, and more or less silly." In attempting to fit the poet into his total world picture, Thomson had written his way into a jungle of contradictions and absurdities, and by the end of 1866 was not only telling himself,

> Most of your poetry is now dyspeptic,
> Most of your creeds and doctrines are he-
> patic,[27]

but was arguing against any sort of critical analysis:

> If you will analyse the bread you eat,
> The water and the wine most pure and sweet,
> Your stomach soon must loathe all drink and
> meat.[28]

Thus, after 1865, although he had a good deal to say about specific books and authors, Thomson never again attempted to survey a literary movement or to present a formal theory of literary criticism. Nevertheless, his comments in the later biographical essays and book reviews make it abundantly clear that the transition from Romantic to realist had been completed, for the guiding principle behind the selection of works that men would be "the better for knowing" was simply that they treat life realistically. Realism was the one thing needful. Whatever form it might take, whatever conclusions it might arrive at, a work of literature must attempt, as "The City of Dreadful Night" had attempted,

> To show the bitter old and wrinkled truth
> Stripped naked of all vesture that beguiles.

A survey of Thomson's critical studies from the 1874 essay on Whitman right up to the end of his life indicates, then, that in English literature it was the "robust and passionate" Elizabethans who, in general, best fulfilled this test of greatness, for they were "forever bursting through their own creeds and systems" and were, above all, "Men" who were "great integrally, in character and talents and genius, in body and mind and soul." As writers, they "pressed fearlessly all that they knew and loved into their works," and did not "first timidly inquire whether a thing was poetical" but "knew it and cared for it, and therefore used it." [29] They had, in short, that "Shakespearean flesh and blood reality" which no age since has possessed in greater measure. This essential realism was, however, lost in the seventeenth century, and the best Thomson could say even for Milton was that "Lycidas" was an "eloquent jumble of heady grief, which perhaps, however, had some heart in it," while *Paradise Lost* was simply that abomination in which "God and the Son of God, not to speak of an archangel or two, prose in the blankest of verse the most wretched and incongruous theological sophistries, like a dreary and bitter pair of cantankerous old Calvinistics." [30]

In considering the eighteenth-century writers, Thomson felt that satirists such as Pope, Fielding, Sterne, and Swift were again looking at life realistically, and Swift in particular was greatly admired because "for sheer strength and veracity of intellect" he was "unsurpassed, and scarcely equalled, in the whole range of English writers." [31] Burns, also a realist, was by far the century's greatest poet, and was expected to "live with the language"; on the other hand, Blake, who had formerly held so important a position in Thomson's critical theories, was seldom mentioned, for, in the final analysis, it was decided that Blake "never grasps or cares for the common world of reality." [32] It was for this reason that, with the exception of Shelley, the early nineteenth-century Romantic poets were also looked upon with slight favor, as, in fact, were most of the Victorians.[33] The Rossettis, Swinburne, and Meredith were praised, and the *Rubáiyát* was considered a "masterpiece of energy and beauty," [34] but only Browning and Tennyson received frequent mention in these later critical studies, with virtually all the comments on "our weak and exquisite Tennyson" being derogatory.[35] The poet laureate was considered to be "a pensioner on the thought of his age," and "nothing gives one a keener insight into the want of robustness in the educated English intellect of the age than the fact that nine-tenths of our best-known literary men look upon him as a profound philosopher." "The Lotos-Eaters" was his one great poem, and, in a comment with which many twentieth-century critics could agree, Thomson predicted that it would

> preserve his fame as an almost great poet when the hysterics and commonplace philosophy of his *Maud* and *In Memoriam* have passed out of memory, when all his *Idylls* are idle on the shelf, when nothing else of his save a few tender lyrics and fragments of description shall be cared for by the general public.

Browning, on the other hand, was the supreme genius, and *The Ring and the Book* was considered the greatest poetic achievement of the age, if not, in fact, of the entire century; it contained passages unsurpassed anywhere in Shakespeare or Shelley, in Dante or Leopardi—the highest praise Thomson could ever have given to any poem or poet.[36]

Nineteenth-century prose writers fared somewhat better than the poets, although, except for Coleridge, none of the Romantic essayists retained the high estimate they had held in earlier years.[37] Carlyle received less praise in the seventies than he had in the sixties, Ruskin was still greatly admired, and Huxley, as we might expect, was considered without equal as both writer and thinker. Mill, too, was an "acute and unprejudiced thinker," although never quite forgiven for having hidden the full extent of his religious heresy during his own lifetime; Newman, also a "great man," had, by abjuring his reason and "seeking peace in blind faith and abject submission to authority," deplorably "mutilated his mind." [38] Macaulay was another matter; his optimism was deplored, and his biographies and history were distrusted because they were not realistic but "put together in mosaic work, and on glass for the love of brilliancy." Thomson felt that although all the pieces had been diligently gathered, at the last moment they were put into the kaleidoscope of Macaulay's idiosyncrasy, and, after some rapid twirls and flourishes, no mortal could guess what strange shape they might take when finally settled for exhibition.[39] Arnold, too, was viewed with suspicion, particularly after "perpetrating" *Literature and Dogma,* and was reminded that his "proper fields are poetry and artistic literary criticism"; when this "Professor of Haughty Culture"

> descends into the arena of the brawling controversies of the day, he is apt to make us think of a mild and soft-speaking gentleman who should saunter about gracefully among the vehicles dur-

> ing the hubbub of a crush in Fleet-street or Cheapside, addressing words of sweet soothing and calm admonition to the exasperated and objurgating drivers, and only exasperating them the more.[40]

Generally, however, Thomson did not become vicious in his critical attacks until commenting on the novelists; he seems to have felt that the novel, when abused, was one of Bumble's most useful weapons for distorting reality, for hiding the naked truth and beauty.[41] Meredith was the supreme novelist of the century, and that it was Meredith's realism that attracted Thomson is clearly indicated in a passage written in 1879, when Meredith was still little known:

> He may be termed, accurately enough for a brief introduction, the Robert Browning of our novelists; and his day is bound to come, as Browning's at length has come. The flaccid and feeble folk, who want literature and art that can be inhaled as idly as the perfume of a flower, must naturally shrink from two such earnestly strenuous spirits. . . . But men who have lived and observed and pondered, who love intellect and genius and genuine passion, who have eyes and ears ever open to the mysterious miracles of nature and art, who flinch not from keenest insight into the world and life, who are wont to probe and analyse with patient subtlety the intricate social and personal problems of our complex quasi-civilization, who look not to mere plot as the be-all and end-all of a novel reflecting human character and life, who willingly dispense with the childish sugar-plums of so-called poetical justice which they never find dispensed in the grown-up work-o'-day world, who can respond with thought to thought, and passion to passion, and imagination to imagination; and, lastly, who can appreciate a style vital and plastic as the ever-evolving living world it depicts, equal to all emergencies, which can revel with clowns

> and fence with fine ladies and gentlemen, yet rise to all grandeurs of Nature and Destiny and the human soul in fieriest passion and action; such men . . . will find a royal treasure-house of delight and instruction and suggestion in the works of George Meredith.[42]

This passage not only reveals Thomson's opinion of Meredith, but rather succinctly defines what he was expecting from a successful novel. Obviously, a good many of the Victorian greats did not fit the pattern, and it is not surprising that, with the exception of some of George Borrow's work, George Eliot was considered the only novelist equal to Meredith.[43] On the other hand, Bulwer-Lytton, that "great bladder for dried peas to rattle in," that "dictionary with diarrhea," was insulted with unusual vehemence,[44] while the "shallow and underbred Cockney Dickens," along with Charles Reade, fared only slightly better; Dickens,

> who coincided at all points with the vulgar taste as exactly as the two triangles of the fourth proposition of the first book of *Euclid* with one another, carried to perfection the Low-Dutch or exhaustive style of description, which may be termed artistic painting reduced to artful padding; minutely cataloguing all the details, with some exaggeration or distortion, humorous or pathetic, of each to make them more memorable; so that every item can be checked and verified as in an auctioneer's inventory, which is satisfactory to a business-like people.[45]

Trollope was also bitterly attacked, his study of Thackeray in the "English Men of Letters" series being described as "pervaded by a misconception, so gross as to be ludicrous, of the relative magnitude and importance of its writer and his subject." Trollope was

> not like that great, idle, unsteadfast Thackeray; not he. Has he not informed the world that he can turn out morning after morning his regular amount

> of copy, with some insignificant variation allowed for a cigar or glass of wine more or less the previous night? just as a machine can be depended upon to turn out its regular amount of work day by day, with some very slight variance for fouling or lubrication. Little t. has thus over big T. all the eminent commercial advantages which steady-going machine possesses over a mutable man; with the additional advantage of being comfortably conscious of them! [46]

"Big T," however, was not rated very highly himself, for although *Pendennis*, at least, might have stood next to Balzac, the novel had been ruined through concessions to Bumbleism, and, although Thackeray had been "vulgarly charged with cynicism," he was

> less a cynic than a worldling of genius who had cynical moods. He had a great deal of genuine respect for the established, the customary, the common-place, and was altogether more ironical in tone than in fact when he classed himself among the Snobs he satirised so keenly, though he was certainly a very superior specimen of the class.[47]

A similar fate befell Kingsley. Although Thomson felt that Kingsley had been granted the rare gift of "seeing and picturing clearly, in words very simple and pregnant, all features and aspects of earth and sea and sky," once he had become Canon Kingsley, Thomson could only note, in a brief obituary notice, that "to us, unfortunately, he was dead and buried long ago"; his "fire was of thorns and green wood; it flared and spluttered and soon died out, leaving him charred to a black priest and chilled to the zero of Bumbledom." [48]

In the 1870's, then, Thomson believed there were few English authors who had satisfied the one thing needful, showing "the bitter old and wrinkled truth stripped naked"—the Elizabethans, Burns, Shelley, and Browning; Fielding, Sterne, Meredith, and George Eliot; Swift, Ruskin, Huxley, perhaps Carlyle and Mill—not, to be sure, a very long list. This opinion largely explains Thomson's increasing attraction to foreign literature, five of his eight biographical essays and almost half of the books selected for review in the secularist periodicals being concerned with foreign authors.[49] The men admired in the seventies were not, however, the same men admired in the fifties and early sixties. As the touchstone was now realism, it was Heine, not Novalis, Leopardi, not Dante, and Epictetus, not Plato, who became the new heroes; and even Emerson, once considered the "noblest intellect," was rejected in favor of Whitman and Melville, the only Americans who had really embraced "the common world of reality."[50] Moreover, for the first time, French writers began to receive praise and attention—not only satirists like Saint-Amant and that "supreme and Titanic Genius" Rabelais, but novelists too: Stendhal, Balzac, Hugo, and, above all, Flaubert, whose *Madame Bovary* was "unequalled for power and intensity in the fiction of his country," for it was more true than even Balzac and Hugo "to the essential realities of life."[51] None of these essays, however, throw additional light on Thomson's critical position, for whether writing on English or foreign authors, he was merely attempting to publicize those works he considered true "to the essential realities of life." He never claimed, in fact, to be doing anything else, for his final work as a critic was integrally related to his total world picture. From theism to atheism; from optimism to pessimism; from Romanticism to realism—the three were, to Thomson, inseparable. A realistic appraisal of life demanded a denial both of God's existence and of man's perfectibility—and this was, in large measure, the bitter truth stripped naked which he felt his readers would be the better for knowing.

Such was the intellectual development of James Thomson, a man who, as poet, critic, moralist, was both more and less than his contemporaries and his critics have assumed. One problem, however, remains unresolved, the problem that troubled Thomson for the last twenty years of his life, and has, to an even greater extent, disturbed a good many of his critics.[52] Why, believing life to be meaningless, considering human progress impossible, yearning for "speedy death in full fruition, dateless oblivion and divine repose," did he continue, not just to live, but to write essays that attempted to teach and persuade his fellowman? A good many answers are possible, but I believe the simplest solution, and probably the best, was provided by Thomson himself when, replying to the same question, he stated: "First and foremost, because 'it is my nature to.' "

> One works, one cannot but work, as his being ordains, exercising the faculties and attempting to gratify the desires thereof, whether he thinks that such exercise will produce what other people call good or ill, that such gratification implies what other people call happiness or misery. If one is a musket, he will shoot, and is right to shoot; if one is a dirk, he will stab, and is right to stab.[53]

I have suggested that this idea is apparent nonsense, for saying that "it is my nature to work as my being ordains" adds up to little more than saying that "I am what I am." In Thomson's case, however, there may be reason to suspect that his "nature" did play a major role in his decision to continue writing essays that would make men better long after he was convinced that the task was an impossible one. If we are willing to accept the idea that our "natures" are largely formed during the early years of our lives, we would have to recognize that Thomson's "nature" was formed between his sixteenth and twenty-eighth years, when he was serving as an army schoolmaster. Whatever degree of importance we wish to place on such influences, it seems undeniable that Thomson at least, in wearing the uniform of the regiment to which he was attached and in being subject to regular military discipline, considered himself to be what in effect he was—both teacher and soldier. I find it of interest, then, that in the above passage, when attempting to explain how one cannot help but work as his being ordains, Thomson should have selected the analogy of the musket that must shoot, the dirk that must stab—soldier's language from a man who, I suggest, throughout his life remained, not just a teacher, but a "soldier." Whatever intellectual phases he passed through, however radically he altered his views on God, man, and the poet, Thomson seems to have consistently viewed life as a "war" in which, whatever anyone else may have done, his "nature" ordained that he must fight on to the bitter end.

This attitude was, of course, strongest in his early years, for his army career exactly corresponded in time with the years in which his world picture was Christian oriented, when life was viewed as a holy war, a "bitter fate-deciding war constant between the Evil and the Good." Heaven, with its lofty band of angels "like stern warriors armed with shield and sword," was a reward only for "the soldier who has fought the noble fight," and in those years, whenever Thomson was overwhelmed with despair and feared he could not continue fighting, his pleas for help were always the cries of the wounded warrior, whether, as in 1857, he was calling to his Dead Girl–Angel to come down and "heal his wounds with heavenly balm" so that he might "fight undaunted, cheerful, this stern agony called Life," or, as in 1860, when, "weary of struggling in all-sterile strife," he was calling to his Lady of Oblivion to give him "peaceful rest" so that he might "arise renewed" and "equal to cope with Life."

Yet long after 1862, when the "Holy" war had ended, the battle still raged on; in the sixties, although no longer at war with evil, Thomson was "at War with Fate," and the symbol that haunted him was that of the two statues, the angel-warrior with sword upraised valiantly opposing the unrelenting sphinx.[54] Even when writing his most joyous "live life" poems he was unable to escape the imagery and language of the battlefield, and his well-known plea to

> Give a man a horse he can ride,
> Give a man a boat he can sail;
> And his rank and wealth, his strength and health,
> On sea nor shore shall fail,

is as much a part of the struggle as is this love passage, which also appears in "Sunday up the River":

> My love is the flaming Sword
> To fight through the world;
> Thy love is the Shield to ward,
> And the Armour of the Lord
> And the Banner of Heaven unfurled.

That such imagery should have occurred even in a love poem during the years when Thomson considered himself an active poet is not surprising, for, at least in the early sixties, poets were not only "the trumpets which sing to battle," but supreme warriors, even Elizabeth Barrett Browning having been given a soldier's tribute in the memorial stanzas Thomson wrote shortly after her death:

> Soldiers find their fittest grave
> In the field whereon they died;
> So her spirit pure and brave
> Leaves the clay it glorified
> To the land for which she fought
> With such grand impassioned thought.

It is surprising, however, that long after he had stopped being a poet, long after he had found himself, like Swift, cursing the day he was born, Thomson continued, as he felt Swift had continued, "fighting Titanically a Titanic battle." Whatever other reasons we may wish to consider, psychological or physiological, it appears that by the 1870's the idea of fighting ever onward was simply an irrepressible part of his "nature." For Thomson, of course, the battle was fought with pen, not sword, and thus, even when he no longer had a constructive philosophy to offer his fellow sufferers, even when the only consolation he could give was that they were free to end life when they would, he himself did not choose to end it but continued to fight undaunted, propagating literature that, as he suggested in reviewing Long's *Marcus Aurelius Antoninus,* might provide others with the strength and courage needed "for the stern unintermitted warfare of life." Perhaps this is why "The City of Dreadful Night" begins with a quotation from *Titus Andronicus,* for even in "The City" Thomson still saw himself in the role of soldier-teacher, addressing his "Sad Fraternity" as if he were standing before the troops, hoping that at least some

> Will understand the speech, and feel a stir
> Of fellowship in all-disastrous fight.

Like Titus Andronicus, Thomson was involved in a fight that would prove "all-disastrous," yet as a soldier he had no choice but to carry on the struggle to the futile end. At the conclusion of "The City," then, Thomson has its inhabitants turning to the "Melencolia" statue for "new strength of iron endurance," for "new strength of stern defiance,"[55] for the great Titaness was "unvanquished in defeat and desolation," was "undaunted in the hopeless conflagration," and, like Thomson himself,

> Baffled and beaten back she works on still,
> Weary and sick of soul she works the more,
> Sustained by her indomitable will.

In a drunken stupor in the last tortured months of his life, Thomson once threatened to join the inhabitants of his dreadful city by throwing himself into the "River of Suicides." He did not, however, attain his "dateless oblivion and divine repose" in the Thames, but in a hospital bed where the day before his death he was expressing confidence of recovery and determination to return home. And yet, had Thomson lived longer, I doubt that whatever he might have written would have appreciably altered or enlarged a study of his intellect, for his ideas in 1882 had changed little from his ideas of a decade earlier, and even his uncompleted projects—the Leopardi translations, a volume on Heine, a biographical essay on George Eliot—had all been planned or started many years before his death. No, once he had attained the position expressed in "The City of Dreadful Night," Thomson was trapped in a world of dead faith, dead love, dead hope, and although his final attempts to strike out blindly at an invisible foe may or may not be considered courageous, they were, for Thomson, completely futile. It would seem, therefore, that his deathbed utterance was little more than a succinct summary of the views he had expressed almost a decade earlier in "The City of Dreadful Night" —words of which we have no record, for his final comment on life was unprintable.

Notes

Chapter 1.

[1] Henry S. Salt, *The Life of James Thomson ("B.V.")* (rev. ed.; London, 1914), p. 142. Most of the comments by Thomson's friends have been taken from the notes Salt made when gathering material for his biography. These notes, and Salt's correspondence, are presently in the possession of the Rationalist Press Association, Ltd., London. I am indebted to Hector Hawton, managing director, for allowing me to utilize this material. For additional comments on Thomson's genial nature, see also Hypatia Bradlaugh Bonner, "Childish Recollections of James Thomson ("B.V.")," *Our Corner,* VIII (Aug., 1886), 65–74; G. W. Foote, "James Thomson: The Poet," *Progress,* III (June, 1884), 367–373; Bertram Dobell, memoir in *The Poetical Works of James Thomson (B.V.)* (2 vols.; London, 1895), I, lxxxvi; and Salt, pp. 14, 53.

[2] G. W. Foote, "James Thomson: The Man," *Progress,* III (April, 1884), 250–254; Bertram Dobell, memoir in *A Voice from the Nile and Other Poems* (London, 1884), p. xix.

[3] Salt, p. 5.

[4] Jeanette Marks, *Genius and Disaster* (London, 1928), pp. 77–128, has noted that "by actual count" Thomson wrote more poems "expressing joy than pessimism." This particular passage occurs in "Sunday up the River," a poem that Foote himself (in *Progress,* June, 1884) realized "must not be supposed to express the author's personal experiences. When I conveyed to him a lady's objection to the colors of the rower's costume . . . he replied with a slight sneer, 'do they think I ever went boating in that style? I write what I have seen.' "

[5] Introduction to "A Lady of Sorrow," *National Reformer* (July 14, 1867), reprinted in *Essays and Phantasies.*

[6] British Museum MS, Add. 38535.

[7] Bodleian Library MS, Don. d. 109/1, letter to William Michael Rossetti, Nov. 16, 1874.

[8] *Letters of George Meredith* (2 vols.; New York, 1912), I, 307. See also Henry S. Salt, *Seventy Years among Savages* (New York, 1921), p. 107. Swinburne's comment was made in an unpublished

letter to W. M. Rossetti and was reprinted without his permission on the inside cover of an 1881 Leek Bijou reprint, *What Must I Do To Be Saved?* See Appendix II in David Worcester, "James Thomson the Second: Studies in the Life and Poetry of 'B.V.'" (unpublished Ph.D. dissertation, Harvard University, 1933).

[9] *Poetry of the Victorian Period,* ed. G. B. Woods and J. H. Buckley (New York, 1955), p. 1018.

[10] Hoxie N. Fairchild, *Religious Trends in English Poetry,* IV (New York, 1957), 456–473.

[11] Worcester, p. 286.

[12] Gordon G. Flaws, "James Thomson: A Study," *Secular Review* (June 24, July 1, 1882). Although Flaws knew Thomson only during the last decade of his life, their friendship was apparently close, and it was Flaws to whom Thomson gave his manuscript copy of "The City." In the early years of Thomson criticism, therefore, Flaws's memoir was quoted frequently, particularly such passages as his description of Thomson's verse: ". . . an aeolian harp, through whose overstrained strings the zephyrs breathed melancholy music that now swells into all but a shriek of despair, and then dies in melodious whispers of resignation and wailing for eternal rest." It was Flaws who described how in Thomson's later years "tremendous fate" had "beaten great furrows into his broad brow, and cut tear-tracks downwards from his wistful eyes"; he also asserted that Thomson's later life was "a slow suicide, perceived and acquiesced in deliberately by himself."

[13] Bodleian Library MS, Don. d. 109/2, letter to Turnbull, June, 1882.

[14] This information came out in July, 1888, when Salt interviewed Grant for his biography (notes in the RPA Collection). At the time, the Barneses were both dead, and Salt could find no direct statement by either of them on the Matilda-Thomson romance. Their son, in reply to Salt's inquiry on the matter, was unable to find "any reference to the circumstances you speak of," although he sent Salt the original manuscript of the 1862 sonnets to his parents, suggesting that the passage that Dobell had already discovered in one of Thomson's notebooks and had published in his memoir in *A Voice from the Nile and Other Poems* might possibly be a reference. Grant's only other contribution to the legend was to tell Salt that he had heard from someone in Chelsea that when the news of Matilda's death reached Thomson, he did not taste food for three days. It was this comment, when Grant related it to Dobell in 1884, which caused Dobell (a pessimist poet himself) to remark that it could hardly be doubted that Thomson intended to starve himself to death.

[15] Charles Bradlaugh, "Reviews," *National Reformer* (Nov. 9, 1884). Bradlaugh and Thomson first met in Ballincollig when they were both about seventeen, Bradlaugh serving as an infantry soldier in the Seventh Dragoon Guards, of which Matilda's father, Henry Weller, was "Armourer as Serjeant." They remained the closest of friends for almost twenty-five years, Thomson writing long letters to Bradlaugh when they were separated and, when he was discharged from the army in 1862, living in Bradlaugh's home for four years. Thomson

spent every Christmas between 1862 and 1871 with the Bradlaughs, and it was not until 1875, when they had a violent disagreement, that the two friends parted company.

[16] G. W. Foote, "James Thomson," *National Reformer* (April 7, 1889).

[17] The interview occurred on June 5, 1888. Salt's notes (RPA Collection) seem important enough to quote in their entirety: "First met Thomson at Ballincollig in 1851—used to read Shelley, etc., with him: but no discussion of a controversial kind. Thomson used to walk at night with him, on picket duty. Matilda Weller was a pretty, but not strikingly beautiful child of about 13—The idea of a betrothal purely imaginary—a poetical invention on Thomson's part. His sorrow was an idealisation. Thomson formed ideal attachments to several women, esp. one in Jersey. Bradlaugh received many letters from Thomson from Jersey and other places, all very interesting. Gave them to a Miss Barnes who was in love with Thomson. The cause of his leaving the Army was connected with drink, T. having been under arrest more than once. His intemperance began early; & was inherited. Used to talk of DeQuincey with Bradlaugh (in London) & make experiments with opium; but no evidence that he took it habitually. During his friendship with Bradlaugh, their intimacy was complete. B. loved him as he has never loved any other man; & shared money & everything with him. Drink was the cause of the estrangement."

[18] Bodleian Library MS, Don. d. 109/2, letter dated Aug. 7, 1888. It must also be remembered that Salt had not known Thomson personally, and that his impressions were largely formed by friends who had taken Thomson's side when he had quarreled with Bradlaugh. The attitude toward Bradlaugh, then, was far from cordial; the following comment, written by Flaws in a letter to the American publisher, Thomas Mosher, when Flaws was trying to get Mosher to publish a book he wanted to write on Thomson (but never did), is typical: "While naming B.V. let me tell you that among other secrets and solemn charges he gave me in those horrible last weeks when no one but I saw him, was one little scrap of paper in Bradlaugh's hand, stating that he had discharged him for drunkenness. I was to avenge his memory on that; I did so till I left, but the crowning stroke will come in my book" (Bodleian Library MS, Don. d. 107, letter dated Feb. 8, 1893).

[19] Letter to Salt, June 9, 1888 (RPA Collection). The interview finally occurred on August 3, 1888.

[20] Bodleian Library MS, Don. d. 109/2, letter to Bertram Dobell, Sept. 12, 1888. Salt felt, in fact, that the daguerreotype gave so unfavorable an impression of Thomson's "only love" (although it was taken just a year before he met her) that it would not do for reproduction in his biography. He suggested that an artist might make "a satisfactory picture" by combining the daguerreotype and the "written description of the girl," surely the most ludicrous note in the entire Matilda Weller legend, as the written description Salt wanted to use consisted of Thomson's blond angel in "Vane's Story" and Harriet Beecher Stowe's Little Eva.

[21] Thomson had been stationed in Dublin between 1856 and 1860.

Weller was stationed there from December, 1858, to January, 1861. Weller was also an army schoolmaster, so it is not unlikely that they should have met again, although it is perhaps significant that the two men who presumably had so much in common never became friends.

[22] Weller's army documents reveal that he was not married until 1868, fifteen years after Matilda's death.

[23] In addition to interviewing John Grant (see n. 14, above), Salt talked to Thomas Carson, headmaster of the Royal Military Academy in Chelsea where Thomson had received his army training. Carson, however, admitted he had had no intimacy with Thomson, and had merely heard about the Matilda affair "from one source or another." A. A. Thomson (no relation), who had known Thomson intimately at Chelsea, stated that when he returned from Ballincollig "he seemed unchanged in character, nor was any change visible during his stay at Chelsea, till 1854," a year after Matilda's death. Harriet Barrs, who had known Thomson only in the last year of his life, said that once, while discussing the death of his young sister (she had died at the age of three, when Thomson was only five), he had apparently alluded to Matilda's death, which is reminiscent of a statement Thomson made (in a letter to his sister-in-law) that had his three-year-old sister "or someone else" lived, he might have been worth something (Salt, *Life of Thomson,* p. 4). Finally, Mrs. Annie Duncan, widow of another of Thomson's early friends, said her husband had once told her that Thomson brooded "over the death of a young and lovely girl whom he loved most devotedly, more as a saint than a mortal," which sounds as if Duncan had also been reading Thomson's poetry, for his widow added that she knew "some verses were composed in memory of her." Salt's notes on all these interviews, which occurred in 1888, are in the RPA Collection. For his own conclusions on the affair, see Salt, *loc. cit.*, pp. 11–14.

[24] "Mater Tenebrarum," although definitely involving the Dead Girl–Angel, is primarily related to Thomson's religious dilemma, and as such is dealt with in chapter 2. It has long been considered an autobiographical poem, for in it the speaker calls out in anguish from his bed for his love to come down from heaven and assure him that the soul never dies. A notation at the bottom of a manuscript copy which Thomson gave to his friend John Grant (Bodleian Library MS, Don. d. 108) reveals that it was, indeed, "written in an access of fierce emotion"—while Thomson was waiting for a friend to go to a dance.

[25] It will be noted that Novalis' *Hymns to the Night* also exerted an important influence on this prose phantasy; Novalis and Shelley, of course, had combined to form Thomson's famous pseudonym, "Bysshe Vanolis," which he first used in 1858, the year in which the Dead Girl–Angel poems were begun. There is also no doubt that Dante exerted an influence on the poems, for Bodleian Library MS, Don. d. 108, a notebook of Thomson's work in the late 1850's, contains many passages that Thomson had copied from Dante, most of them relating to Beatrice. A third literary source for the Dead Girl–Angel poems, one not previously noted in Thomson criticism, is

Matthew Arnold's 1852 "Faded Leaves." Thomson used two epigraphs for "The Angel" section of "A Lady of Sorrow." The first consists of the second quatrain of Arnold's "Longing," the final poem in the "Faded Leaves" sequence; the second epigraph, closely paralleling Arnold's lines, is taken from Thomson's own "Mater Tenebrarum," lines 5–10.

[26] British Museum MS, Add. 38533. This manuscript copy of "The City of Dreadful Night" was apparently written in 1870. On the back are sketched the titles of some poems Thomson had planned to write, including the first line of "I Had a Love." As this poem was planned at least this early, I suspect that it had been conceived with the other Dead Girl–Angel poems, probably in the early sixties. Thomson often composed in this manner, the 1880 "A Voice from the Nile," for instance, having been planned in the late sixties.

[27] One of Thomson's manuscript books contains a fragment written in 1858 which was apparently intended to be his own "Aurora Leigh," and when we recall that Aurora, like Thomson, had lost both her parents in childhood and had dedicated her life to poetry, the attraction is obvious. His youthful admiration for Mrs. Browning's works led, in fact, to virtual hero-worship; a diary notation dated October 29, 1861, reads: "A remarkable dream. Mrs. R. Browning appeared in the place where I was. She had in her hand a book written by herself—a book (in my dream) wonderfully fascinating. Her face was adorable—sweet, suave, benignant, wise. I passed her on the shore alone; she was reading" (Bodleian Library MS, Don. g. 5).

[28] Thomson never published "I Had a Love" (Bodleian Library MS, Don. e. 36), which is one reason for the confusion as to its importance as an autobiographical document. Until Anne Ridler, ed., *Poems and Some Letters of James Thomson* (London: Centaur Press, 1963), was published, only excerpts had been printed, and they had been selected by Matilda Weller enthusiasts (see Dobell's memoir in *Poetical Works* [1895], and Imogene Walker, *James Thomson (B.V.): A Critical Study* [Ithaca, 1950], pp. 154–157). In any event, Thomson requested that "I Had a Love" remain unpublished, not because it was an intimate personal revelation, but simply because he considered it a bad poem. His complete marginal comment is, "Too hard and harsh in both conception and execution for attempt at polishing —far more truth than poetry in it."

[29] See n. 23, above.

[30] Bodleian Library MS, Don. e. 37. The poem is simply titled, "To ———." In the final two stanzas, Thomson mentions the yearnings that the girl's presence inspires, and wonders if she ever "yearnest" for a common lot.

[31] The fragment of an 1858 poem which was to have been Thomson's own "Aurora Leigh" (see n. 27, above) is written in the first person. The narrator describes how both his parents died when he was young, his mother in childbirth (Thomson's mother died shortly after giving birth to his brother) and his father, a sailor (as was Thomson's), in grief. The narrator relates how he was raised by a friend of his parents in their home, growing up with their two

children. The younger is "darling little Agnes," a girl with golden hair and large blue eyes—Thomson's angel symbol in a child again. Helen's counterpart is not described at all, but is, in fact, a boy. The fragment breaks off as the narrator is beginning to relate the foster-mother's history.

[32] Practically all our information on Helen Gray came from her sister. When Dobell was writing his memoir (in *A Voice from the Nile and Other Poems*) in 1884, he located the sister and she wrote him everything she could remember about Thomson. In 1888 Salt also wrote to her and arranged an interview, the notes of which are strangely missing from the RPA Collection. The quotation in Dobell, Salt's summary, and several of the passages that Salt quotes from Thomson's letters to Agnes leave no doubt, however, as to the reality of the affair. In view of Salt's position on Matilda Weller, his admission that later discontinuance of visits to the Grays' was owing to "a revival of his early affection for Miss Helen Gray" is strong evidence as to the seriousness of the affair (see Salt, *Life of Thomson,* p. 29, and the Thomson letter Salt quotes in *ibid.*, p. 26).

[33] Bodleian Library MS, Don. e. 37. It is to be noted that this poem was written two years after Matilda Weller's death.

[34] Thomson left for Ireland in the summer of 1856. In November he wrote "Tasso to Leonora"; in January, 1857, "Marriage" and "Bertram to Geraldine." The poems "Marriage" and the earlier 1854 "Parting" have often been assumed to be Matilda poems. I suggest that they were actually inspired by Helen Gray, but were later slightly rewritten to fit into a four-part dramatic monologue (the fourth part was written in June, 1858), published in September, 1858, under the title "Four Stages in a Life." In the narrative as published, the wife appears to be already dead in the section titled "Marriage," although this section is rather strangely followed by the section titled "Parting." In any event, if these two sections are read separately, it is obvious that only slight changes would be necessary for them to be addressed to a living girl. Several of the Dead Girl–Angel poems were written, as already indicated, in 1858, and it is possible that, in organizing "Four Stages in a Life," Thomson realized he could adapt the two early poems to Helen Gray and use them in a Dead Girl–Angel sequence. On the other hand, I recognize the possibility that either or both of these poems were inspired by Matilda all along; as early as 1854, when "Parting" was written, Thomson may already have been using the dead girl in his creative writing. Bodleian Library MS, Don. d. 108, contains a single page of what seems to have been part of a novel, the extant passage describing a marriage ceremony between a young man and a girl who is, apparently, about to die.

[35] The admission to Grant came out in his interview with Salt, July 24, 1888 (RPA Collection). The letter was written to William Maccall, with whom Thomson had, as early as 1870, initiated a correspondence, only because Maccall had himself once been intimate with the Grays. Maccall, in fact, corroborated Thomson's romantic interest in Helen; in a letter to J. W. Barrs dated September 11, 1882, he wrote that Thomson was "very tenderly attached" to her

and in an article on Thomson, republished as *A Nirvana Trilogy* (London, 1886), Maccall again alluded to this attachment, noting how, in their correspondence, Thomson had "never tired of recalling" those "happiest days" of his life. Bodleian Library MS, Don. d. 109/2, contains a letter from Maccall to Thomson dated February 20, 1882, in which Maccall replies to a request by Thomson for the Grays' address. In the letter Maccall mentions that "Mr. Gray has a daughter who was prolific as a poetess. But she got married and was still more prolific as a mother." There is no way of knowing if this comment refers to Helen or Agnes, but Thomson's reply, for which we have his notations only, includes comments on "The Grays, Mrs. Gray," and "Self & daughter."

[36] Salt, *Life of Thomson,* p. 142; Walker, p. 172.

[37] Dobell's note in *The Poetical Works of James Thomson,* I, 368. Attempts by Matilda Weller enthusiasts to come to terms with the Helen Gray evidence are somewhat amusing. Worcester insists that all poems in which a dead girl appears are autobiographical, but feels that "Meeting Again" is a narrative, probably inspired by one of Browning's dramatic lyrics (although it is "barely possible" that it "records an unknown chapter in his life"). Walker concludes that Thomson was refused permission to write Helen Gray, not in 1856, but before his 1851 tour in Ballincollig. She suggests that Thomson could not possibly have been in love with Helen, as Helen was only eleven at that time, but that he could and did fall in love with Matilda during his eighteen-month tour in Ballincollig. Matilda and Helen Gray were the same age.

[38] Thomson's interest in Harriet Barrs during the last year of his life has been noted in all previous Thomson studies (see Thomson's poems "To H. A. B." and "At Belvoir"; also Salt, *Life of Thomson,* pp. 118–131; Walker, pp. 167–168; Worcester, pp. 265–283; W. Stewart Ross, "A Last Interview with a Man of Genius," in *Roses and Rue* [London, 1890]; Victor Neuburg, "James Thomson (B.V.)," *Freethinker* [Dec. 2, 1934], pp. 762–763). Three other women have not been previously mentioned in studies of Thomson. When interviewed by Salt, Bradlaugh mentioned two of them: a "Miss Barnes who was in love with him" and to whom Bradlaugh gave all Thomson's letters (since destroyed) and a woman in Jersey, to whom Thomson was especially attached. The former romance was confirmed by Miss Barnes's brother in a letter to Salt, although, being younger at the time, he knew "little of the circumstances." The latter may possibly be confirmed by a sonnet Thomson wrote April 15, 1862, while stationed in Jersey, a sonnet that later appeared as Section X of "Sunday up the River." Three copies of it appear in different manuscript books, and the earliest has the roman numeral "VII" in front of the title "To ———," suggesting it may be the only one of a series he chose to save when, in 1869, he burned all records of his past. A third romance is suggested in a letter Thomson's sister-in-law wrote to Salt in 1888: "I may say that should a copy of Mr. Thomson's answer to a letter from Miss Birkmyre have come into your hands, I am sure James would not wish it made public in any way. Her letters and his answers were in my possession

for a year or two, for the purpose of silencing any misrepresentation which might and did arise, but I gave them to him and evoked him to return them and visit at their house again thinking it might brighten his life a little having some of his own kin to go to occasionally. The mother never knew anything of the affair at all, and always made him welcome." Helen Birkmyre was a cousin of Thomson's who, when Salt wrote to her, replied that she had seen Thomson only once in London when they were both children, and again in London in 1867 for only a few minutes; she did, however, say that her mother met Thomson in London in either 1864 or 1869 (date illegible) and that they were "mutually charmed with each other."

[39] Bodleian Library MS, Don. d. 107, letter to Thomas Mosher, Feb. 19, 1893.

[40] Bodleian Library MS, Don. d. 109/2, letter to Bertram Dobell, July 2, 1882.

[41] Bodleian Library MS, Don. d. 109/2, letter to J. W. Barrs, Nov. 12, 1882 (or 1883). The reason Salt (*Life of Thomson,* p. 34) gave for Thomson's discharge is highly suspect. I have examined all extant records of Thomson's army career, but they reveal only that Thomson was court-martialed, and that two weeks prior to his trial he was in confinement. The War Office (in a letter of April 4, 1962) has told me that they are "unable to trace any record of a Court Martial involving James Thomson."

[42] This information is revealed in a series of unpublished letters addressed to John Barrs by Percy Holyoake and H. Hood Barrs, who report on Thomson's activities during the last six months of his life (Bodleian Library MS, Don. d. 109/2).

[43] Quoted in Salt, *Life of Thomson,* p. 137. Thomson's reference here to his "money debts" might suggest poverty as another possible cause of his "lifelong gloom." Thomson was, of course, never financially secure, but in spite of erratic employment and the expenses undoubtedly incurred because of his alcoholism, there is no indication that he was ever hungry or homeless. His salary as army schoolmaster and as city clerk was no doubt small, but Thomson seems to have been an unusually frugal man, and his letters indicate that he took his privations in good humor (see, for example, the 1872 letter to his sister-in-law, quoted in Salt, *loc. cit.,* pp. 49–50). Bradlaugh claimed that his friend had been well paid for his work on the *National Reformer,* and Thomson himself admitted that during the five years he worked for *Cope's Tobacco Plant,* the payment was "fair and regular" (Salt, *loc. cit.,* p. 96). He did, of course, have occasional debts; his diaries contain several references to borrowing money or to requesting advances from his publisher. But the debts all seem to have been repaid (even his funeral expenses were covered through royalties from his last volume), and occasional "money debts" would hardly support poverty as a cause of Thomson's pessimism.

[44] The following works were consulted for current information on alcoholism: Seldon B. Bacon, "Alcoholics Do Not Drink," *Annals of the American Academy of Political and Social Science,* vol. 315 (Jan., 1958); Donald W. Hewitt, *Alcoholism: A Treatment Guide for General Practitioners* (London, 1957); Mark Keller, "Alcoholism:

Nature and Extent of the Problem," *Annals of the American Academy of Political and Social Science*, vol. 315 (Jan., 1958); Oskar Kiethelm, *Etiology of Chronic Alcoholism* (Springfield, Ill., 1955); H. D. Kruse, *Alcoholism as a Medical Problem* (New York, 1956); and Ornulv Odegard, *The Etiology of Alcoholism* (Oslo, 1958).

[45] John Barrs, in a letter to Salt, July 5, 1886 (RPA Collection).

CHAPTER 2.

[1] Henry S. Salt, *The Life of James Thomson ("B.V.")* (rev. ed.; London, 1914), p. 4. In this 1882 letter to his sister-in-law, Thomson also mentioned that his mother was "mystically inclined" with Irving and had followed him from the Kirk when he was driven out. To my knowledge, Thomson's writings contain no other mention of Irving.

[2] "Some Muslim Laws and Beliefs," *Secularist* (Aug. 12, 19, 1876).

[3] Imogene Walker (*James Thomson (B.V.): A Critical Study* [Ithaca, 1950], pp. 7–8) went into this matter thoroughly, but all she seems to have discovered from early records of the school is that "due attention" was paid "to the morals and religion of the children."

[4] Bodleian Library MS, Don. e. 37. The sonnet, titled "The Approach to St. Paul's," is published for the first time in Anne Ridler, ed., *Poems and Some Letters of James Thomson* (London: Centaur Press, 1963), although Thomson quoted the concluding lines in his 1863 "Seen Thrice: A London Study," published in the *Secularist* (July 8, 15, 1876).

[5] The exact source of Thomson's pantheism in these years cannot be determined. Shelley and Wordsworth seem to have been primarily responsible, although Emerson probably contributed to, or at least confirmed, the main ideas. Essays on all three, emphasizing pantheism, were written and published between 1858 and 1860. It is also probable that Thomson had done some reading on Eastern religions. J. M. Wheeler, in his brief memoir on Thomson (*Freethinker*, Feb. 10, 1889), recalls how he was amazed at Thomson's knowledge of Buddhism, a subject on which Wheeler had been doing research in Thomson's last years. The extent of Thomson's knowledge in the 1850's is unknown.

[6] See Bertram Dobell's notes in *The Poetical Works of James Thomson (B.V.)* (2 vols.; London, 1895), II, 442–443.

[7] In a manuscript copy of the poem, Thomson stated that these two stanzas were written in 1855, two years before the rest of the poem, and were later worked in even though they did not "fit in precisely" —a comment applicable to a good many aspects of Thomson's world picture in these years.

[8] "A Few Words about Burns," *Investigator* (April 1, 1859), reprinted in *Poems, Essays, and Fragments.*

[9] "Shelley's Religious Opinions," *National Reformer* (Aug. 25, 1860), reprinted in *Biographical and Critical Studies*, pp. 283–289. This was a letter to the editor, but a few months later Thomson published a long essay on Shelley in which he defended both his Manichean doctrine ("Let those who scoff so liberally at this, account for the existence of evil, and a devil created by an omnipotent,

all-holy God") and his idealism ("Let those who so stolidly sneer at this, expound by what possibility spirit and matter can influence each other without one attribute in common; or let them demonstrate the existence of matter apart from our perception; or let them show, if there be but one existing substance, that it is such as we should call matter rather than spirit").

[10] In 1858–1859 Thomson had also contributed three articles and a poem to Bradlaugh's short-lived periodical, the *London Investigator.* Between August 25, 1860, and his arrival in London in November, 1862, his *National Reformer* contributions had been "A Letter Addressed to the Editor, on Shelley's Religious Opinions" (Aug. 25, 1860); "Scrap Book Leaves" (Sept. 1, 22, 1860); "Shelley" (Dec. 22, 1860); "The Dead Year" (Jan. 6, 1861); and a review of Emerson's *The Conduct of Life* (March 9, 16, 1861).

[11] "The Meaning of History, by F. Harrison," *National Reformer* (Jan. 3, 1863). "Bysshe Vanolis" was first used in the *London Investigator.* Although it is the most famous of Thomson's pseudonyms, it was far from being the only one he used; his work also appears under the signatures "Crepusculus," "X," "Sigvat," "J. S. T.," "T. J.," and "J. T." The full name appears only in the "respectable" journals in which he published in his last years.

[12] Bradlaugh had a superb library which, when sold after his death in 1891, contained some 7,000 volumes and 3,000 blue books, plus unbound pamphlets. Thomson, who could never afford to collect books, did most of his research at the British Museum, but a few of his personal volumes turned up at the Bradlaugh sale, notably Schlegel's *Philosophy of Life* and *Philosophy of History,* which he had received in 1851. Marginalia are, however, unimportant, and the pages in the last half of the *History* have not even been cut. Bertram Dobell purchased the two books, and they were presented to the Bodleian Library along with seventeen other books that Dobell said had been Thomson's. Heine's *Buch der Lieder* contains most of Thomson's translations in the margins, but with the exception of these translations there is nothing of interest in the way of marginalia, and the volumes themselves reveal nothing significant about Thomson's reading.

[13] The first edition, edited by Bradlaugh and Joseph Barker, a "convert" from Christianity who later returned to the Church, appeared on April 14, 1860. The coeditors disagreed violently on virtually every phase of secularism, and, after a year in which the paper was literally split in half (Barker being responsible for the first four pages, and Bradlaugh, for the second), the dispute ended with a vote of the stockholders giving Bradlaugh complete control. In January, 1862, G. J. Holyoake became joint editor, but this arrangement also resulted in disagreement. On March 8 Bradlaugh resigned, only to be elected again on March 29, 1862, to sole editorship. After this, with the exception of a period from March 28, 1863, through April 29, 1866, when health forced him to relinquish the editorship to John Watts, Bradlaugh retained complete control of the paper until his death in January, 1891. During the fifteen years of Thomson's connection with it, other leading contributors, in addition to Bradlaugh,

included Austin and G. J. Holyoake, John and Charles Watts, William Maccall, J. P. Adams, and, later, G. W. Foote and Annie Besant.

[14] *National Reformer* (Feb. 28, 1863).

[15] Salt (1898 ed.), p. 42, quotes a letter from Thomson to his friend James Potterton in which it seems that Thomson considered the *National Reformer* to be almost a joke. The letter, dated October 11, 1860, reads: "You old matter-of-fact! Of course I sent that ditty to Bradlaugh as a chaff, and called it the 'Reformer's Hymn'!"

[16] *National Reformer* (Nov. 15, 1862), reprinted in *Satires and Profanities.*

[17] *National Reformer* (Dec. 13, 1862).

[18] When "A Lady of Sorrow" was finally published in the *National Reformer* (in eight consecutive installments, July 14 to September 1, 1867), Thomson prefixed a short introduction explaining that he had received the manuscript from his friend Vane. This passage reveals Thomson's belief at the time the phantasy was completed in 1864.

[19] "Sayings of Sigvat," *National Reformer* (Oct. 14, 1866), reprinted in *Essays and Phantasies.*

[20] The theory of evolution made a tremendous impression upon Thomson, and, from at least 1865 on, his work is filled with allusions to it. That the fascination actually grew with the years is indicated by the fact that when preparing "The City" for publication in 1880, the only important change made from the 1874 published version was the addition of stanza 10 in Section XIV:

> We finish thus; and all our wretched race
> Shall finish with its cycle, and give place
> To other beings, with their own time-doom:
> Infinite aeons ere our kind began;
> Infinite aeons after the last man
> Has joined the mammoth in earth's tomb and womb.

In 1874, in fact, Thomson wrote in his essay on Mill (apparently forgetting about his Harrison review) that "the theory of Natural Selection, of Evolution . . . appeared to me the only true doctrine of the development of Nature, years before it had been formulated, vindicated, and so splendidly illustrated by our leading contemporary philosophers."

[21] This passage is the climax, and main message, of "A Lady of Sorrow."

[22] Thomson was first attracted to Blake by one poem he read in Garth Wilkinson's *The Human Body and Its Connexion with Man,* but did not become familiar with Blake's work until Alexander Gilchrist's two-volume edition came out in 1863, the reproductions of Blake's drawings attracting Thomson as much as the poetry. I suspect that the inspiration for "Night," for instance, with its man crying out to an unanswering universe, came from two of the small woodcuts from the *Gates of Paradise* series (no. 9, "I Want! I Want!" and no. 10, "Help! Help!") which were reproduced in Gilchrist. The first engraving in the volume also seems to have inspired another Thomson poem of this period, the 1863 allegory, "The Three That Shall Be One," for the opening lines are almost a verbal illustration of Blake's famous drawing "Glad Day."

[23] *National Reformer* (July 30, 1865). The Mill passage was also found in *ibid.*, July 9, 1865, as Mill, who was running for Parliament at the time, had attracted a good deal of attention among the National Reformers.

[24] As a general rule, free-thought editors found poetry a great nuisance, and, except for Thomson's poems, only those of J. M. Peacock appeared with any regularity in the *National Reformer*. By 1866 Bradlaugh was pleading that no one send him either "rhymes or poetry," as "each piece we refuse we deeply offend one contributor; each piece we insert we irritate another dozen, whose effusions have not the same good fortune." He never, however, went so far as one free-thought editor (George Standring), who noted (in his *Republican Chronicle*, March, 1883) that "we offer the usual wastepaper price for poetry, if in quantities of not less than one hundred weight. Poets should write on stout paper, as buttermen prefer that to the thin article."

[25] *National Reformer* (Sept. 24, 1865), reprinted in *Satires and Profanities*.

[26] Thomson's translation, taken from his biographical study of Heine which appeared in the *Secularist* (Jan. 8–Feb. 12, 1876). Equally relevant is Heine's statement from his "mattress grave": "If I could even get out on crutches, do you know whither I would go? Straight to church. Most decidedly to church. Where else should one go with crutches? Faith, if I could walk out without crutches, I should prefer to stroll along the lively boulevards, or to the Jardin Mabille."

[27] Thomson had, in fact, been outraged by evangelical enthusiasm even during his Christian years, perhaps in reaction to his childhood experiences with Irvingites. The first poem he ever published (in the *Investigator*, Feb., 1858) was a satire on "Mr. Save-His-Soul-Alive, O!"

[28] Published in London in 1865. Thomson, however, based his article (in the *National Reformer*, Dec. 10, 1865) on a report printed in the *Scotsman* (Nov. 4, 1865).

[29] "The Story of a Famous Old Firm" (later titled "Story of a Famous Old Jewish Firm") first appeared in the *National Reformer* Christmas issue for 1865. It was republished in pamphlet form in 1876 and again in 1883, and was reprinted in *Satires and Profanities*. "Christmas Eve in the Upper Circles," which first appeared in the *National Reformer* (Jan. 7, 1866), also appears in *Satires and Profanities*.

[30] Bodleian Library MS, Don. f. 8, entry dated Dec. 29, 1865.

[31] *National Reformer* (March 18, 1866), reprinted in *Satires and Profanities*.

[32] Dobell suggested that Thomson was introduced to Leopardi through an essay Gladstone published in the *Quarterly Review* (March, 1850), and that he began to study him "perhaps in 1864—or thereabouts." I am convinced he did not hear of Leopardi until reading an anonymous article in *Blackwood's* (Oct. 1865), for this article, unlike Gladstone's, stressed those aspects of Leopardi's work which would have attracted Thomson, and also recommended him as an excellent person to read should one want to learn Italian. On October 9, 1865, Thomson recorded in his diary, "began the Italian,"

and on October 29 a *National Reformer* essay of Thomson's contained his first mention of Leopardi in print, including Leopardi in a list of great poets. In a November 12 essay the Italian was again mentioned, Thomson erroneously stating that "Leopardi devoted himself in despair to scholarship and poetry, because physical infirmity excluded him from active life," an impression he could easily have gained from the *Blackwood's* article, but not possibly from Gladstone or from the one other article on Leopardi which had been published up to that time (*Fraser's Magazine,* Dec., 1848), as both of these made it clear that Leopardi had been an active scholar before his health broke down. Thomson did not follow through with his Italian studies in 1865, but a diary entry of August 23, 1866, reads: "began the Italian for the second time—having forgotten what little I learnt last year." By March, 1867, he was able to translate four paragraphs from Pietro Colletta's *History of Naples* for a *National Reformer* article, and I suspect it was by this date, or within a few months of it, that Thomson was reading Leopardi; passages from Leopardi (not translated) were placed as an epigraph to "The Naked Goddess" (completed 1867, published June 23, 1867) and as an epilogue to Section I of "A Lady of Sorrow" which, although completed in 1862, was not published until July 14, 1867. The 1867 "Indolence" contains the first translated passage from Leopardi, and the first complete translation of a dialogue appeared in the *National Reformer* on November 3, 1867.

[33] Only two pieces appear to have been written during these years, although both were important: the long narrative poem "Weddah and Om-el-Bonain," and at least part of the essay, "Proposals for the Speedy Extinction of Evil and Misery."

[34] Lyman A. Cotten, whose "Leopardi and 'The City of Dreadful Night'" (*Studies in Philology,* [July, 1945], 675–689) treats the problem thoroughly, comes to the same conclusion: Thomson "did not go to Leopardi to borrow ideas in the creation of a philosophic attitude or to learn a language in which to express it: what he found in Leopardi was what the wanderers of his City found in the statue of Melencolia, 'renewed assurance and confirmation of the old despair.'" Henri Peyre, in his article "Les Sources du Pessimisme de Thomson" (*Review Anglo-Américaine,* II [Dec., 1924]), also agrees that Thomson had attained his own pessimism before reading Leopardi.

[35] "Liberty and Necessity," *National Reformer* (May 20, 1866), reprinted in *Essays and Phantasies.* See also Thomson's note to "Speedy Extinction" as published in *ibid.*, p. 77.

[36] *Poems, Essays, and Fragments,* p. 262. A fragment dated 1873.

[37] *Ibid.*, p. 263. A fragment dated 1873.

[38] In my article, "The Two Cities of Dreadful Night," *PMLA,* LXXVII (Dec., 1962), I have treated the matter of chronology in Thomson's masterpiece. The sections written in 1870, in order of composition, were II, XVIII, XX, I, V, XI, VII, IV, X, VI, and III.

[39] It quite definitely, however, does not refer to Matilda Weller, as nothing in the myth would suggest that the relationship with

Thomson, whatever it might have been, concluded through being "stabbed by its own worshipped pair."

[40] George M. Harper, "Blake's *Nebuchadnezzar* in 'The City of Dreadful Night,'" *Studies in Philology,* L (Jan., 1953), 68–80.

[41] This statement is probably the clearest in all Thomson's poetry as to his position on the matter of free will and determinism. By this time he seems to have decided that free will was, as he wrote in his "Speedy Extinction" essay, an "absurdity." While holding his "live life" philosophy, he had definitely taken the opposite view, emphatically so in the 1866 "Liberty and Necessity," but with the completion of "The City" he considered "Necessity alone Supreme." Perhaps, however, the most interesting document of all in relation to the problem is an early (1858) fragmentary narrative poem which was, I feel, to have been his own "Aurora Leigh." Although Thomson was still very much a Christian at the time he wrote it, and although the narrative is clearly intended to be dramatic, the opening lines reveal that he was at least very much aware of the problem. We might suppose them to have been written by Hardy himself:

> The dice to play this dubious game of life
> Are forced into our hands—and we must play—
> But chance still rules the fortune of the strife.
>
> We throw and throw—and throw our skill away
> If this blind chance keep stolidly unjust,
> And destiny finds not a mite to pay
>
> Our winnings, while our losses pay we must,
> Although with loaded dice be cheated still
> Although we stake Heaven's life against earth's dust,
>
> And myriad gains make good no loss's ill—
> Yet some among us play it first and last
> With too keen earnestness, as if our skill
>
> Could rule the issue of a single cast,
> And count on six instead of empty nought.

[42] The Hunt allusion in "The City" has not been previously suggested. Thomson probably considered Hunt to be the greatest artist of the age (see "The Poet, High Art, Genius" and "Pilgrimage to St. Nicotine," where "The Scapegoat" receives particular mention), and thus it seems highly probable that the "wild sea-shore" with its cliffs and "league-broad strand" may have been partly inspired by the desolate wastes surrounding "The Scapegoat." The same day on which he began writing this desert sequence in Section IV, he also wrote Section VII of the poem, in which he mentions that wandering through the City, he had "caught breathings acrid as with Dead Sea foam." As to the Browning influence, in an essay written as early as 1862 Thomson had praised "Childe Roland" as "a series of pictures very powerful, weird and Rembrandt-like, elevated above grotesqueness by the stern heroic fortitude of the Childe."

[43] "How the Bible Warns against Authorship," *National Reformer* (Aug. 21, 1870), reprinted in *Poems, Essays, and Fragments.*

[44] *Poems, Essays, and Fragments,* p. 263. Epigram dated 1874.

[45] "Mill on Religion," *National Reformer* (Nov. 8, 1874).

[46] *The Secular Song and Hymn Book,* ed. Annie Besant (London, 1876). Thomson's review appeared in the *Secularist* (April 8, 1876).

[47] "Secularism and the Bible," *Secularist* (Jan. 1, 1876).

[48] Beginning in 1875, and continuing through its final issue in January, 1881, Thomson wrote most of his essays for *Cope's Tobacco Plant.*

CHAPTER 3.

[1] Reference is made to the "B.V. Memorial," a mural tablet presenting a three-quarter face medallion of Thomson, in "B. E.'s" introduction to Leek Bijou Freethought Reprint No. VI (1883), a selection of Thomson's prose and poetry. Bradlaugh's statement occurs in a letter, apparently to J. W. Barrs, dated November 12, 1882 (Bodleian Library MS, Don. d. 109/2).

[2] Other free-thought periodicals to which Thomson contributed were *Secular Review, Secular Review and Secularist, Republican Chronicle,* and *London Investigator.* The work in *Progress,* however, consisted entirely of posthumous publications, the first issue (with Foote as editor) appearing six months after Thomson's death.

[3] The signature "X" was first used in 1870 in a *National Reformer* column titled "Jottings." Originally, "B.V." was used only for non-secularist material, "X" probably designating articles Thomson was doing at Bradlaugh's request. Between 1871 and 1874 only four essays (reviews of Long's *Marcus Aurelius Antoninus* and Rossetti's Shelley edition, a translation from Goethe, and "Proposals for the Speedy Extinction of Evil and Misery") were published under "B.V." After 1874, although Thomson continued to use "X" extensively, the choice appears to have been based more on quality than on content, "B.V." being used, in general, for his better work.

[4] *Investigator* (Feb. 1, 1859), reprinted in *Poems, Essays, and Fragments.*

[5] A reference to Garibaldi in "The Dead Year" is the only notable exception.

[6] *National Reformer* (April 29, 1866). The *National Reformer* was, in fact, the first free-thought periodical to show any interest at all in politics. Robert Cooper's *London Investigator,* on which Bradlaugh served his apprenticeship as a free-thought editor, had insisted: "*Our mission is anti-theological.* We are *really* Secular; that is, *not* religious. Science is our only providence, and morality our only creed. Politics we leave to other hands. The people have many able champions in that department of progress. In our view, *the* obstacle to freedom and civilization is *Supernaturalism.*"

[7] "L'Ancien Régime," written in 1867, is probably Thomson's strongest indictment of monarchy from this period. That Thomson was not fully convinced as to the desirability of a democracy, however, is indicated by a notebook jotting dated February 9, 1867

(British Museum MS, Add. 38535): "Men are so unfit for governing and so demoralised with power, that the fewer who have to do with governing, the better. Men are so fit to be governed, so improved by subjection, that the more who are simply governed, the better."

[8] In "Mr. Kingsley's Convertites" (*National Reformer*, Sept. 24, 1865), Thomson stated that *Elements of Social Science* preached "the Gospel of the body and this life . . . with more thoroughness, knowledge, and ability than any other English work I have met so far." The comment on the Hyde Park riots also occurred in the *National Reformer* (July 29, 1866); it was the only comment of this nature which Thomson wrote during these years, no doubt in a flurry of excitement over the riots in which Bradlaugh was, of course, involved. Bradlaugh's remarks in the same issue were considerably stronger: "The people of England are challenged by Lord Derby, Mr. Disraeli, Mr. Walpole, and Sir Richard Mayne. Let the challenge be accepted; let us meet in our hundreds of thousands. We are strong enough and cool enough to compel them to retire defeated from the struggle they invoke. 'We are many, they are few.' "

[9] This attitude was, for the most part, true throughout Thomson's entire life, but particularly during the 1860's. In a February, 1867, essay, "The 'Saturday Review' on 'Mr. Bright's Edition of Mr. Bright,' " he noted: "As I am no politician, care nothing for Reform and about as much for Mr. Bright, I brought a most rare and valuable impartiality to the study of this particular review."

[10] During these years, 1865–1867, Thomson wrote at least a dozen poems dealing with the working classes as they "live life" ("Sunday up the River" is the best known), but only "Low Life," which alludes to drab working conditions in a seamstress shop, attempts any sort of social comment. As regards his reluctance to become involved in the immediate scene, the short poem, "Mr. Maccall at Cleveland Hall," is of interest. In it Thomson is supposedly reporting a lecture that treats "the Conflict of Opinions in the Present Day," but all the time his attention is on a pretty girl sitting in the front of the auditorium.

[11] Thomson's early verse made frequent reference to prostitution, and there is no doubt that he considered Lust to be the most deadly of the seven deadly sins. In the 1855 verses suggested by Arnold's "Grande Chartreuse," the main reason men needed a guide was that they had become "unmanned" through spending their youth in "foul and sensual slavery." In the 1856 "Tasso to Leonora," life was defiled by "filth of lust" which men would not understand is "self-pollution." In the 1857 "Festival of Life," life is described as a lewd dance, and in "The Doom of a City," also written in 1857, Thomson actually feared that the fire that had rained on Sodom was about to descend on England because the flaring streets each night were filled with "thousands of harlots abroad," meeting with the "other thousand" who had "made them first and who keep them harlots yet."

[12] Section VII of "Sunday at Hampstead" contains a description of life on Hampstead Heath 30,000 years ago, the typical housewife feeding an eagle or stroking "with careless hand a lion's mane." But,

in a broader sense, Thomson also felt, as a pantheist, that nature and man were intimately united through matter. In "A Lady of Sorrow" he wrote: "Let no atom in the world be proud; it is now in the heart of a hero, it may soon be in a serpent's fang. Let no atom in the world be ashamed; it is now in the refuse of a dunghill, it may soon be in the loveliest leaf of a rose."

[13] The key essays all appeared in the *National Reformer:* "Bumble, Bumbledom, Bumbleism" (Oct. 29, Nov. 5, 1865); "Per Contra: The Poet, High Art, Genius" (Nov. 12, 19, 1865); "An Evening with Spenser" (Nov. 26, 1865); "Open Secret Societies" (Feb. 18, 25, March 4, 1866); "Sympathy" (Oct. 28, Nov. 18, 25, 1866); "The Swinburne Controversy" (Dec. 23, 1866). With the exception of "The Swinburne Controversy" (reprinted in *Satires and Profanities*), all the essays were selected by Thomson for the 1881 *Essays and Phantasies.*

[14] Thomson's essay on Bumbleism preceded Arnold's *Culture and Anarchy* by some four years; it preceded "Culture and Its Enemies," as published in *Cornhill,* by almost two years. The idea for Bumble, however, came from Arnold's comments on Philistines in his *Cornhill* essay on Heine, although Thomson rejected the term "Philistine" because he felt it had a continental connotation which was not applicable to the English scene. He also noted that Arnold was not the first to use the term in English, citing two examples of earlier usage (see *Essays and Phantasies,* pp. 104–107).

[15] Thomson quotes Byron, "Many are poets who have never penned / Their inspiration—and perchance the best," then adds that he considers Byron's reasons for this to be "stuff and nonsense": "They do not *pen* their inspiration simply because they are able throughout and equably to *live* it; so far from repressing the deity within, they express it every day and hour and moment in their most ordinary words and deeds, an infinitely better kind of expression than that which is found in spasmodic poems of a dozen or two astonishing fyttes." Thomson was, of course, also familiar with Carlyle's "The Hero as Poet," where Carlyle states that whether the poet (the man who possesses the "seeing eye") writes poetry or prose, or writes at all, depends on accidents.

[16] The essay, although written in 1867, was not published until 1876 in the *Secularist.* Apparently Thomson intended it to be a much longer essay, including a classification of the "energetic" along with the "indolent," but he lost interest in the project and did not pick it up again until under pressure for material. This delay was not uncommon; his other essay on the theme of indolence, "A National Reformer in the Dog Days," was begun in 1869 but not published until 1874.

[17] *National Reformer* (April 21, 1867), dated 1866, reprinted in *Essays and Phantasies.* The title is taken from a couplet ("Whene'er I take my walks abroad / How many poor I see") which, within the essay, Thomson twice attempts to place: "Is it Shakespeare or Mr. Tupper, is it Shelley or Dr. Isaac Watts?" It was, in fact, Watts, whose poem, "Praise for Mercies, Spiritual and Temporal; or the Song of the Rich Man's Child," which begins,

Whene'er I take my walks abroad
How many poor I see;
What shall I render to my God
For all his gifts to me?

was reprinted in the *National Reformer* seven years earlier (Aug. 25, 1860), and was followed by an unsigned parody, "Per Contra: The Song of the Beggar Boy":

Whene'er I take my walks abroad
How many fops I see,
Who taunt me that a great just God
Cares more for them than me.

I suspect that the latter was Thomson's work, and that it may be the "Reformer's Hymn" he once mentioned in a letter to James Potterton (see n. 15, chap. 2).

[18] "Sympathy," *National Reformer* (Oct. 28, Nov. 18, 25, 1866), reprinted in *Essays and Phantasies.*

[19] "Open Secret Societies," *National Reformer* (March 4, 1866), dated 1865, reprinted in *Essays and Phantasies.*

[20] "Sayings of Sigvat," *National Reformer* (Sept. 30, Oct. 14, 1866), reprinted in *Essays and Phantasies.* The "Sayings" were epigrams which Thomson had written over the years. They were not dated, and some were probably written earlier than 1866, although this particular comment seems to have been written just before publication, for it not only corresponds with his views at that time, but occurs near the end of the series. In a much earlier article, the 1860 "Shelley's Religious Opinions," Thomson had also suggested that Nature "is no saint," but at that time he felt that she was "thoroughly just and independent in her own way."

[21] The lines taken for the epigraph are (Bickersteth's translation):

. . . in mysterious dance
Immortal feet shook the wild-ridged fells
And tangled wood (which now the winds have made
Their desolate den).

This passage is, of course, appropriate to Thomson's poem, for his naked goddess also deserts the human world. At the end of the "Naked Goddess," however, hope has not been abandoned, and the "Sacred Fire divine" still burns in the hearts of the children who have learned to "live." On the other hand, Leopardi, in concluding his poem, pleaded with Nature to have pity and to kindle the "ancient fire" within his soul:

. . . if thou indeed dost live,
And if there dwell in heaven,
Or on the radiant earth or azure main
A single being that, though it pity not,
At least will notice, Man's inhuman lot.

[22] *Essays, Dialogues and Thoughts of Giacomo Leopardi* (1905), pp. 49, 95, 208.

[23] *National Reformer* (in nine installments, Aug. 27–Nov. 12, 1871), reprinted in *Essays and Phantasies.*

[24] "Jottings," *National Reformer* (Aug. 2, 1874).

[25] "Paul-Louis Courier," *National Reformer* (July 31, 1870).

[26] "France Declares War against Prussia," *National Reformer* (July 24, 1870). At the start of the war, Thomson severely condemned France as the aggressor, but shrewdly predicted that it would be a war of surprises, feeling that the Germans had a better army and superior chiefs and council. He was convinced that, whoever won, the unity of Germany would be accelerated, and felt that the time was not very distant "when France will be glad to have in the centre of Europe, between herself and Russia, a solid German Fatherland peopled by forty or fifty millions of Germans, a people on the whole as honest, industrious, frugal, peaceful, kindly, brave, and intelligent, as the nineteenth century can show anywhere in the world." Six months later, when the tide of sentiment had turned, Thomson had no comment to make, although in the same issue of the *National Reformer* in which Bradlaugh came out in support of republican France, Thomson introduced Goethe's *West-östlicher Divan* to his readers. His later writings make no further reference to the war.

[27] "Despotism Tempered by Dynamite" was one of four occasional poems Thomson sold to the *Weekly Dispatch* in the last months of his life, referring to them in a letter to Dobell (Henry S. Salt, *The Life of James Thomson ("B.V.")* [rev. ed.; London, 1914], p. 131) as "little skits." His reminiscences of the Carlist War, which might be expected to contain interesting comments on government, are of little value; although he felt sympathy for the "valiant and honest people" on the Royalist side, he was glad that their cause did not prevail.

[28] "In the Valley of Humiliation," *Liberal* (Jan., 1879).

[29] "Walt Whitman," *National Reformer* (Sept. 6, 1874).

[30] "The 'Standard' on the Whigs and the Church," *Secularist* (May 27, 1876).

[31] "Jottings," *National Reformer* (Jan. 31, 1875).

[32] "In the Valley of Humiliation."

[33] The *Liberal* article of January, 1879, treats these objections thoroughly, but it was mainly the "Eastern Question" that interested Thomson. He sided with Gladstone, for the most part, feeling that the only sane solution was "the establishment by Concord of the Great Powers, and especially of England and Russia, of a chain of autonomous or self-ruling states, tributary to Turkey, from the Black Sea to the Adriatic" (*Secularist,* Sept. 16, 1876). In December, when reviewing Swinburne's "Note of an English Republican," Thomson still felt that cooperation with Russia was the best means of controlling her selfish interests (*ibid.,* Dec. 30, 1876). By April, 1877, his attacks on Disraeli and the Tories were underway; he felt that, "Activated by an insane jealousy and suspicion of Russia," they had made Russia the sole power to whom eastern Europe could turn (*Secular Review,* April 22, 1877).

[34] "Open Secret Societies." Thomson had some right to speak with confidence on the Crimean War, for in 1857, when stationed in Dublin, he was attached as army schoolmaster to the 55th Foot directly upon their return from the Crimea. In the essay he noted: "I have known pretty well some of the men who rode and rode well in the Balaclava Light Cavalry Charge; some brave fellows, and some

good fellows not specially brave; but I do not remember a hero amongst them."

[35] Had Thomson lived another decade, it is possible that he would have been attracted to socialism. He never directly alluded to socialism in his writings, and, at least in 1876, he probably agreed with Foote's belief that neither communism nor socialism is "fitted for the wants of human beings, at any rate in the present era" (*Secularist*, Jan. 1, 1876). Nevertheless, in the eighties and nineties a good deal of secularist activity was directed into socialist channels, and in 1881, in his address to the Leicester Secular Society, Thomson wrote:

Down with our dead walls!—let us all enjoy
Our neighbours' industry without alloy;
The bloom and odours of their fruits and flowers
Which are so like and yet so unlike ours;
The singing of the birds among their trees:
Their glancing butterflies and honey-bees;
And sharing thus the pleasures of the whole,
Tend that which is within our own control
More cheerfully, more earnestly, lest weeds
Disgracing ours, taint theirs with wafted seeds;
And let us cherish kindly interchange
Of help and produce in our social range.

Granting the vagueness of the passage, and recognizing that Thomson may have had nothing more than "sympathy" and human fellowship in mind, we still find here a suggestion of socialism which is lacking in his earlier writing. During the 1870's Thomson did almost all his research and writing at the British Museum, and undoubtedly became acquainted with some of the other regular workers there. Included in a short list of names and addresses in his 1880 diary is the name "Karl Marx." Unfortunately, I can find no further reference to their acquaintance.

[36] "Walt Whitman," *National Reformer* (Aug. 30, 1874).

[37] "The 'Standard' on the Whigs and the Church."

[38] "The Incidence and Increase of Taxation," *Secular Review* (May 13, 1877).

[39] "The London School Board Elections," *Secularist* (Sept. 30, 1876). Thomson's "Jottings" of 1874–1875 contain numerous references to education, including a note supporting the establishment of public free libraries. Even as early as 1864, when he made a brief and unsuccessful attempt to write editorials for the *Daily Telegraph*, the one article we can definitely attribute to Thomson was "Middle Class Education."

[40] All these comments occur in the essay "On Suicide," in *Poems, Essays, and Fragments*, pp. 248–252.

[41] *Secularist* (Feb. 17, 1877), reprinted in *Essays and Phantasies*. It is probably significant, as regards my suggestion that this essay climaxes his views on man's relations to man, that Thomson placed it as the final essay in the only volume of prose published in his lifetime.

[42] By the end of 1877, in fact, Thomson was not on speaking terms with either Foote or Bradlaugh, and, although his closest friends were still freethinkers, the only writing he did for the secularists consisted

of the Disraeli article in the January, 1879, *Liberal,* and the address at the opening of the Leicester Secular Hall in 1881.

[43] The "happy" poems of the 1860's must, therefore, be seen as an expression of joy resulting directly from the loss of God; we give a very false picture of Thomson's nature if, in order to prove that he was not always a "gloomy" man, we set passages from these poems beside passages written in the early years when he was despairing over God, or in later years when he was despairing over man, the impression being that he was some sort of rubber ball bouncing idiotically between intense joy and intense gloom.

[44] "Mill on Religion," *National Reformer* (Nov. 8, 1874).

[45] "Heinrich Heine," *Secularist* (Jan. 8–Feb. 12, 1876).

Chapter 4.

[1] Henry S. Salt, *The Life of James Thomson ("B.V.")* (rev. ed.; London, 1914), pp. 6–7.

[2] The two earliest, both love poems, are dated 1852. There are also a few lyrics and sonnets, and a drinking song. The 1855 poem inspired by Arnold's "Grande Chartreuse" is the earliest serious statement in verse, but insofar as it was a prayer, it was personal rather than didactic.

[3] "Shelley," *National Reformer* (Dec. 22, 1860), reprinted in *Shelley, a Poem; Poems, Essays, and Fragments;* and *Biographical and Critical Studies.*

[4] In addition to the two early poems, "A Happy Poet" and "The Lord of the Castle of Indolence," both of which were in part inspired by the eighteenth-century James Thomson's "Castle of Indolence," Thomson wrote, in 1865, "On the Terrace at Richmond," a poem in which he discusses his namesake as having been his great-great-grandfather, Thomson being heir to the Castle of Indolence.

[5] Singing hymns of the Lord did not, of course, imply that the poet was restricted to religious verses, and the idea of singing all he "feels and knows" is reflected in the wide range of subject matter Thomson used in the late fifties: light love poems ("Arch Archery"), romantic ballads ("The Dreamer"), drinking songs ("The Jolly Veterans"), occasional poems ("To a Pianiste"), memorial verses ("E. B. B."), and even, in disgust with Tennyson's, "A Real Vision of Sin." But, in spite of poetic theory and the importance of inspiration, Thomson was experimenting with a great variety of verse forms—ottava rima, rhyme royal, Spenserian stanza, ballad stanza, triplets, hexameters, and, in "To Our Ladies of Death," the seven-line stanza that he took from Browning's "Guardian Angel" and was to use again for the odd-numbered sections of "The City."

[6] From the 1860 sonnet, "Why Are Your Songs All Wild and Bitter Sad."

[7] In the spring of 1862 Thomson wrote the six sonnets to the Barneses, a sonnet later published as Section X of "Sunday up the River," and two short unpublished poems under the title "Havre-des-pas." In 1863 he wrote the unpublished narrative poem, "A Slight Mistake"; "A Polish Insurgent," inspired by his working for the

Polish Committee that summer; and "The Three That Shall Be One," earliest of the poems inspired by Blake.

[8] In the process of revising his old views, Thomson did, however, find time to take poetic stock and see what he could salvage from old fragments written while he had been "God-possessed." In 1864, then, as a "self-possessed" poet, he completed three long poems: "Ronald and Helen" (begun in 1859 and largely completed in 1861), "Sunday up the River" (which combines fragments, including a translation from Heine, from as far back as 1852), and "Vane's Story" (which, insofar as it relates to the 1858–1859 Dead Girl–Angel poems, was probably conceived at least as early as 1862, when "The Angel" section of "A Lady of Sorrow" was written).

[9] "The Poet, High Art, Genius," *National Reformer* (Nov. 12, 19, 1865), reprinted in *Essays and Phantasies.*

[10] When Thomson told Foote, "I write what I have seen" (see n. 4, chap. 1), he was no doubt referring to his observational expeditions. The titles of many of these "live life" poems also indicate that they were written "on location": "Aquatics (Kew)," "Low Life: As Overheard in the Train," "Polycrates on Waterloo Bridge," "Richmond Hill," "On the Terrace at Richmond," "The Star and Garter," "Shameless: Kew Gardens," and "Sunday at Hampstead."

[11] Leopardi and Novalis were also given as examples of men who were forced into writing poetry through privation; those who considered authorship subservient to other ends of life included More, Raleigh, Bacon, Selden, Vane, the two Sidneys, Bunyan, Swift, Defoe, Johnson, and Scott.

[12] The only poems we can definitely ascribe to this period are the April 17, 1866, "Mr. Maccall at Cleveland Hall," and the June 8, 1866, "Don Giovanni at Covent Garden"—both short occasional poems apparently conceived as "pleasant relaxation," a hobby to carry Thomson through dull hours.

[13] "A Strange Book," *Liberal* (Sept.–Dec., 1879), reprinted in *Biographical and Critical Studies.*

[14] "Walt Whitman," *National Reformer* (July 26–Sept. 6, 1874), reprinted in *Walt Whitman* and in *Poems, Essays, and Fragments.*

[15] The notebook entry appears in Bodleian Library MS, Don. f. 10. The Browning paper was published in *Browning Society's Transactions,* Part I (1882), reprinted in *Biographical and Critical Studies.*

[16] In addition to the four poems I have termed "significant," Thomson also wrote a few epigrams, the address to the Leicester Secular Society, and three "tobacco poems." Two of these were the Cope's "Christmas Cards," satiric drawings for which Thomson wrote explanatory verses, and the third was a short piece humorously commenting on an antitobacco poem that had been written by an Anna Linden and published in a San Francisco paper. Thomson noted when publishing his piece that it was written "by order" of the editor, and it sounds like it:

> O Anna Linden! How could you,
> You dear Pacific beauty,
> Make war upon us like a shrew
> And think such war a duty?

There were also three short poems probably written "by order" of Thomson's secularist friends ("Creeds and Men," "Bill Jones on Prayer," and "Our Congratulations on the Recovery of His Royal Highness"), and a twenty-four-line song, "The Nightingale Was Not Yet Heard," written in February, 1877, and published at once in the *Secularist*. It was inspired by Fitzgerald's "Omar Khayyám," although Foote, in his *National Reformer* article on Thomson (April 21, 1889), said it was the result of a sleepless night, adding the mysterious comment: "I had and have a private opinion as to some circumstances of the composition."

[17] This fact has not been previously noted. "Insomnia" was definitely written between February 23 and March 8, 1882 (Bodleian Library MS, Don. d. 108), and the four poems to Harriet Barrs were also new work written during Thomson's stay at Forest Edge. "Richard Forest's Midsummer Night," although dated December, 1881, seems to have been originally conceived as a companion piece to "Sunday up the River" (an early manuscript version of which is titled "A Midsummer's Day Dream"), for not only is it written in the same style with a similar viewpoint, but an early Thomson notebook (B.M. MS, Add. 38535) lists a poem under the title "A Summer's Night" as one either completed in or planned for 1868. The same list contains a title "Dialogue with Muse," which I suspect referred to the poem Thomson completed in 1882 and titled "The Poet and His Muse"; on the final manuscript he had written "not true now," indicating that the poem had been started, and perhaps completed, at an earlier date. Even "A Voice from the Nile," dated November, 1881, seems to have been conceived and worked on as much as ten years earlier. Bodleian Library MS, Don. c. 73, a notebook from the early 1870's, contains careful notes in preparation for the poem, the opening line of which had been written at least as early as 1873 (B.M. MS, Add. 38532); and Foote, in his 1889 article, said that he once visited Thomson in 1874 and found him with a big book on Egypt, writing the opening lines of the poem. Finally, then, the poem, "O Antique Fables," dated January 5, 1882, in one manuscript, appears in another dated December 8, 1871, which leads me to suspect that the other two poems of these final years ("He Heard Her Sing"—again very much in the "live life" period in theme and style—and "A Stranger") were similarly conceived or in part written long before Thomson's supposed final surge of poetic powers.

[18] Salt, p. 131.

[19] As the great majority of these were written either for freethinkers or tobacco smokers, there were obviously a few selections that Thomson would not otherwise have chosen had he been publishing in a purely literary journal. He had complete freedom in selecting these works, no matter what the periodical involved (it was, in fact, one of his conditions for working as a staff writer), so most of the items may therefore be considered accurately to reflect his interests.

[20] These two essays appeared in the *Investigator* (Dec., 1858; April, 1859). Both are reprinted in *Poems, Essays, and Fragments.*

[21] The short note that Thomson published on Wordsworth ("Scrap Book Leaves," *National Reformer*, Sept. 1, 22, 1860) might also be

mentioned here as "criticism," for he explained Wordsworth's line, "The light that never was on sea or land / The consecration and the poet's dream," as meaning that the poet, apparently in communion with the infinite and the eternal, has a vision that a "spiritual life, which is Love and Truth, burns and throbs" through the universe.

[22] *Jersey Independent* (Feb. 20, 1862). This important essay has not previously been noted by Thomson's critics, and apparently not even Bertram Dobell (who, with J. M. Wheeler, compiled a careful bibliography of all Thomson's writings) was aware of its existence.

[23] The essay, however, clearly falls within Thomson's early Christian phase. Although it contains this new note of admiration for flesh-and-blood reality, the idea of soul mates is strongly emphasized (Browning's love "is so intense and all-absorbing, that when its pure fire has wholly consumed this world and life it flings out its electric flames into the infinite future, thrilling along the endless life-line of the immortal married souls"), as is the idea of Christianity, for Thomson felt that few realize the importance of the Brownings "in upholding the sway of Christianity over the minds of young and thoughtful persons who turn with contempt from the abounding trash of tracts, . . . scarcely meet with a minister liberal and wise enough to command their intellectual esteem, . . . know that modern erudition has beaten down and undermined many of what were once considered main bulwarks and buttresses of the Church, and above all, ponder frequently on the fact that not a few of those living writers whom they most revere—men like Carlyle and Emerson, Francis Newman and Froude—have found the Christian formula too strait to cover the whole of now-known truth." That Thomson was still holding Christian views is even more strikingly revealed in the fact that just two weeks after this essay appeared, he published, in the same paper, his first translations from Heine, apologizing for the "scornfully and bitterly heterodox" subject matter, in spite of which the poems were admired for "spontaneity, subtle melody, and rare suggestiveness"—again the idea of an "inspired" singer.

[24] "The Poems of William Blake," *National Reformer* (Jan.–Feb., 1866), reprinted in *Shelley, a Poem; Poems, Essays, and Fragments;* and *Biographical and Critical Studies.* The essay was written in 1864, two years before publication (see *Biographical and Critical Studies,* p. 321).

[25] As to the pantheism behind Thomson's "live life" poetry, it is worth noting that he felt that Blake "sees, and is continually rapturous with seeing, everywhere correspondence, kindred, identity, not only in the things and creatures of earth, but in all things and creatures and beings of hell and earth and heaven, up to the one father (or interiorly to the one soul) of all." This, of course, was the later Blake, "William Blake the Second," who had become a child again in his "mystical simplicity."

[26] In addition to the Romantics, Thomson also commented on a few of the Victorian poets, measuring them for "simplicity." Tennyson had no more of it than Byron had; Mrs. Browning (who was rapidly losing favor) had much of it, but never succeeded in giving it fair

expression as her style was "rugged with pedantry" and she was often "intoxicated" with her own vehemence. Robert Browning, however, "a really great thinker, a true and splendid genius, has this simplicity in abundant measure."

[27] Bodleian Library MS, Don. e. 48.

[28] In the 1866 "Philosophy."

[29] "An Evening with Spenser," *National Reformer* (Nov. 26, 1865), reprinted in *Essays and Phantasies.* Although this particular comment was written almost a decade before the period in question, there is no reason to suspect that Thomson ever changed his views on the Elizabethans.

[30] "A National Reformer in the Dog Days," *National Reformer* (July 12, 19, 1874), reprinted in *Essays and Phantasies.* Milton's religious beliefs were not alone responsible for this attitude. Thomson had high regard for both George Herbert and Jeremy Taylor, and Milton's works were included in a short list of "great works of our literature" (along with Shakespeare, Burns, Fielding, Sterne, Scott, and Carlyle) which he recommended that new converts to free thought should study ("On the Duty of Converts to Freethought," *Secularist,* Sept. 23, 1876).

[31] A review of John Forster's *The Life of Jonathan Swift,* Vol. I, in the *Secularist* (May 20, 1876), reprinted in *Essays and Phantasies.* Swift probably exerted a stronger influence on Thomson's prose satires than anyone else, particularly in "Speedy Extinction," "A Commission of Inquiry as to Complaints against Royalty," and "Religion in the Rocky Mountains."

[32] "Walt Whitman," *National Reformer* (Aug. 30, 1874). It was, however, in Section XVIII of "The City" that Thomson most emphatically shut the door on Blake, or at least on his interpretation of Blake.

[33] After the 1864 essay on Blake, Thomson scarcely mentioned the Romantics. Although Dobell was able to compile a small volume of Thomson's writing on Shelley, the only pieces written after 1861 were two book reviews and the notes on "Prometheus Unbound," which had been compiled mainly for Rossetti.

[34] In reviewing Christina Rossetti's poems (*Secularist,* March 25, 1876), Thomson wrote: "I lack words tender and exquisite enough to praise them." Foote, in his 1884 article, claimed that Thomson told him Swinburne possessed the "finest lyrical faculty since Shelley." "Omar" was not discovered until 1876, and made a tremendous impression on Thomson; Flaws (Bodleian Library MS, Don. d. 109) mentioned how "B.V. and I talked Khayyam plentifully, and with poor P. B. Marston, sometimes into the small hours" (see also Salt, p. 124).

[35] There are numerous incidental references to Tennyson throughout Thomson's writings. Passages quoted here (from the 1864 essay on Blake and an 1876 essay in the *Secularist*) are typical.

[36] Even as early as 1865, in the essays on Bumbleism, Thomson mentioned Browning as the only "living artistic genius . . . exercising influence and commanding homage of which a lofty-minded and strong-minded man could justly be proud."

[37] This was particularly true of De Quincey and, to a lesser extent, of Lamb; although both were greatly admired in the late fifties and sixties, neither received mention in the seventies.

[38] The Huxley comments occur in Thomson's two reviews of Huxley's *Hume* (*Liberal*, March, 1879; *Cope's Tobacco Plant*, June, 1879). Mill's *Three Essays on Religion* was reviewed in the *National Reformer* in eight installments (Nov.–Dec., 1874), and the Newman passage occurs in the essay "On the Worth of Metaphysical Systems" (*Secularist*, May 13, 1876). I suspect one of the reasons for Carlyle's being considered with less enthusiasm in the seventies was that Carlyle, unlike George Eliot, had never replied when Thomson sent him a copy of "The City."

[39] Review of Forster's *Swift*. Thomson was particularly upset by Macaulay's portrait of Swift: "This is really very fine in the way of the dreadful, my rhetorical Lord; but if we could only have, to hang beside it, Swift's portrait of *you!*"

[40] "The 'Daily News,'" *National Reformer* (Nov. 1, 1874), reprinted in *Satires and Profanities;* "Mr. Matthew Arnold on the Church of England," *Secularist* (April 8, 1876). The attitude toward Arnold is somewhat surprising, for Thomson obviously followed Arnold's career closely and was influenced by him in the Bumbleism essays and, very likely, in many of his critical views. Although Arnold's position on the Church and the Bible, and his essay on Shelley, surely did not endear him to Thomson, I suspect that Thomson's attitude was in large part due to his dislike of university graduates in general, and of Oxford men in particular. When reviewing a book by a university scholar, he could seldom resist making comments such as the following (in his review of Mark Pattison's *Milton*): "Mr. Pattison, though a good writer as well as a good scholar, is not altogether free from a certain laxity of style common to women in general and university men in particular."

[41] Thomson attempted writing fiction as early as 1854, a one-page fragment still remaining from what was apparently intended to be a novel. Three later attempts, all artistic failures, are: "Sarpolus of Mardon," an oriental tale of which only a fragment remains (published posthumously in *Progress*, 1887); the 1863 "Seen Thrice: A London Study," which Thomson allowed Foote to print in the *Secularist* (July 8, 15, 1876); and an untitled fragment of a short story about a pianist (named Leopardi) who possessed "the power" (published posthumously in the *National Reformer*, June 7, 14, 1891).

[42] Review of *Richard Feverel* (the 1878 one-volume edition), in *Cope's Tobacco Plant* (May, 1879). Reviews of *Beauchamp's Career* also appeared in *Cope's* (June, 1876) and in the *Secularist* (June 3, 1876). All three were reprinted in a private press edition, *James Thomson (B.V.) on George Meredith* (1909).

[43] George Eliot was not, however, considered Meredith's equal in "subtlety of intellect." Thomson also felt her to be Meredith's inferior in "the faculty of conceiving and describing vigorous or agonistic action," since "in the fateful crises her leading characters are apt to drift" (review of *Beauchamp's Career* in the *Secularist*). It would seem, however, that Thomson's enthusiasm for George Eliot waned somewhat in the last years; although he faithfully attended her fu-

neral and, shortly afterward, obtained agreement from Reeves and Turner to publish his critical study of her work, he never followed through with the project, and abandoned it after a few months.

[44] Bulwer-Lytton was insulted to such an extent that after Thomson's death a rumor circulated that he had been Bulwer-Lytton's illegitimate son. I can find no evidence to support such an idea, and suspect that the rumor developed partly because very little was known about Thomson when he died in 1882, and partly because it was during those years that Lady Lytton's *Blighted Life* and Louisa Devey's two studies appeared. There are, however, some undeniably mysterious, and fascinating, circumstances connected with the rumor: Thomson was born nine months after the Lyttons had their famous quarrel after returning from Italy; there is no adequate explanation why Thomson, in May, 1870, should have abruptly stopped work on "The City" to write his vicious satire on Bulwer-Lytton ("A Supplement to the Inferno," from which the above quotations are taken); why, having written it, he should never have published it; and why, most important, he had felt that 1869 was such a "terrible year" that he was forced to burn all his papers and letters. William Sharpe, who was present when Thomson died, was the first to mention the rumor in print, noting, in his review of Salt's *Life,* that there was considerable uncertainty on several points in Thomson's life, particularly as to "the floating rumour which attributes Thomson's paternity elsewhere than to the obscure sea-captain of whom we have such contradictory accounts." Bulwer-Lytton's name was not mentioned, but Salt, when revising his biography in 1898, added a footnote denying the rumor in which he stated that Bulwer-Lytton was the "elsewhere" Sharpe had in mind. The RPA Collection has a letter from Thomson's brother to Salt, dated November 3, 1898, which says: "We are perfectly satisfied with the very fair remarks you have made upon the point in question in the recent issue of my brother's Life, and are quite content now to let the matter rest." One of those apparently satisfied was Helen Birkmyre, whose mysterious letter to Salt has already been quoted (see n. 38, chap. 1). There are, indeed, contradictory reports about Thomson's parents, so perhaps, after all, the rumor is not so absurd as all later critics and biographers have considered it to be.

[45] Review of *Beauchamp's Career* in the *Secularist* (June 3, 1876).

[46] Review of Trollope's *Thackeray* in *Cope's Tobacco Plant* (July, 1880).

[47] Review of Forster's *Swift* in the *Secularist* (May 20, 1876).

[48] "Jottings," *National Reformer* (Feb. 7, 1875).

[49] The attraction actually seems to have begun earlier than the seventies. In the essay on Bumbleism (1865), in a list of great authors one might expect to find in a scholar's library, only five of the fourteen mentioned were Englishmen (Shakespeare, Swift, Burns, Shelley, Carlyle).

[50] In the *National Reformer* essay on Whitman. Thomson first read both Whitman and Melville when he visited America in 1873. Melville fascinated him, but he felt he was "sometimes strangely unequal to his better self, and has lavished much strength in desultory doings."

[51] Review of *La Tentation de Saint Antoine* in the *Secularist* (Sept.

30–Nov. 4, 1876). This review, in five installments, was largely a condensed translation of the novel. Thomson was also familiar with and greatly respected the work of Gautier and Baudelaire, translating passages from each (on hasheesh eating) for the tobacco readers.

[52] One of the earliest articles on Thomson was titled "Why James Thomson Did Not Kill Himself" (*Spectator*, March 23, 1889).

[53] "Sayings of Sigvat," *National Reformer* (Sept. 30, Oct. 14, 1866), reprinted in *Essays and Phantasies.*

[54] See chapter 2 for my discussion of this symbol in "The City." Thomson used the symbol as early as 1858 in "Sarpolus of Mardon": in front of the tomb "was couched a Mammoth-Sphynx upon whose countenance gazed steadfastly a mightier angel, leaning upon his naked sword, his wings folded in marble patience."

[55] As the poem now ends, strong men turn to "Melencolia" "to drink new strength of iron endurance," but originally Thomson had written that they turn to her "to drink new strength of stern defiance" (Morgan Library MS of Thomson's final copy of the poem).

Bibliography

I. Works of James Thomson

A. Books and Pamphlets, Listed in Order of Publication

The Story of a Famous Old Jewish Firm. London, 1876.
A Commission of Inquiry on Royalty, Etc. London, 1876.
The Devil in the Church of England and The One Thing Needful. London, 1876.
The City of Dreadful Night and Other Poems. London, 1880.
Vane's Story, Weddah and Om-el-Bonain, and Other Poems. London, 1881.
Address on the Opening of the New Hall of the Leicester Secular Society. N.p., n.d.
Essays and Phantasies. London, 1881.
The Story of a Famous Old Jewish Firm and Other Pieces in Prose and Rime. Imprinted for B. E. and W. L. S., 1883.
A Voice from the Nile and Other Poems. London, 1884.
Satires and Profanities. London, 1884.
Shelley, a Poem; with Other Writings Relating to Shelley, by the Late James Thomson ('B.V.'): to which is Added an Essay on The Poems of William Blake, by the same author. Printed for private circulation by Charles Whittingham and Co. London: Chiswick Press, 1884.
Selections from Original Contributions by James Thomson to "Cope's Tobacco Plant." London, 1889.
Poems, Essays, and Fragments. London, 1892.
The Poetical Works of James Thomson (B.V.), ed. Bertram Dobell. London, 1895. 2 vols.
Biographical and Critical Studies, ed. Bertram Dobell. London, 1896.
Essays, Dialogues and Thoughts of Giacomo Leopardi, ed. Bertram Dobell. London: New Universal Library, 1905.

James Thomson ("B.V.") on George Meredith. London: privately printed, 1909.
Walt Whitman: The Man and the Poet, ed. Bertram Dobell. London, 1910.

B. Prose Contributions to Periodicals

The following entries are listed in order of publication. Unsigned articles of doubtful authorship are not included. Most of the articles were written within a few weeks of their appearance, but in those instances where it is known that composition preceded publication by a year or more, a notation occurs to that effect. If the article has been republished, the volume or volumes in which it appears are noted in parentheses at the end of the entry, the following abbreviations being employed for this purpose:

EP *Essays and Phantasies*
SP *Satires and Profanities*
PEF *Poems, Essays, and Fragments*
BCS *Biographical and Critical Studies*
S *Shelley, a Poem*
GM *James Thomson ("B.V.") on George Meredith*
WW *Walt Whitman: The Man and the Poet*
L *Essays, Dialogues and Thoughts of Giacomo Leopardi*

"Notes on Emerson," *Investigator* (Dec. 1, 1858) (PEF).
"The King's Friends," *Investigator* (Feb. 1, 1859) (PEF).
"A Few Words about Burns," *Investigator* (April 1, 1859) (PEF).
"A Letter Addressed to the Editor, on Shelley's Religious Opinions," *National Reformer* (Aug. 25, 1860) (S, BCS).
"Scrap Book Leaves," *National Reformer* (Sept. 1, 22, 1860).
"Shelley," *National Reformer* (Dec. 22, 1860) (S, PEF, BCS).
"The Conduct of Life, by Emerson," a review, *National Reformer* (March 9, 16, 1861).
"Robert Browning's 'Men and Women,'" *Jersey Independent* (Feb. 20, 1862).
"The Established Church," *National Reformer* (Nov. 15, 1862) (SP).
"The Life of Moses, by J. Lotsky," a review, *National Reformer* (Dec. 13, 1862).
"The Meaning of History, by F. Harrison," a review, *National Reformer* (Jan. 3, 1863).
"The 'Saturday Review' on Dr. Newman," *Daily Telegraph* (July 1, 1864).
"Middle Class Education," *Daily Telegraph* (July 19, 1864).

"Poems and Songs, by J. M. Peacock," a review, *National Reformer* (Nov. 19, 1864).
"The Athanasian Creed," *National Reformer* (Jan. 1, 1865) (SP).
"The Almighty Devil," *National Reformer* (July 30, 1865).
"Mr. Kingsley's Convertites," *National Reformer* (Sept. 24, 1865) (SP).
"Bumble, Bumbledom, Bumbleism," *National Reformer* (Oct. 29, Nov. 5, 1865) (EP).
"Per Contra: The Poet, High Art, Genius," *National Reformer* (Nov. 12, 19, 1865) (EP).
"An Evening with Spenser," *National Reformer* (Nov. 26, 1865) (EP).
"Mr. Gladstone's Edinburgh Address," *National Reformer* (Dec. 10, 1865).
"The Story of a Famous Old Firm," *National Reformer* (Dec. 24, 31, 1865) (SP).
"Christmas Eve in the Upper Circles," *National Reformer* (Jan. 7, 1866) (SP).
"The Poems of William Blake," *National Reformer* (Jan. 14, 21, 28, Feb. 4, 1866), written in 1864 (S, PEF, BCS).
"Open Secret Societies," *National Reformer* (Feb. 18, 25, March 4, 1866) (EP).
"A Coincidence," *National Reformer* (March 11, 1866).
"Jesus: As God; as a Man," *National Reformer* (March 18, 1866) (SP).
"Liberty and Necessity," *National Reformer* (May 20, 1866) (EP).
"The Hyde Park Meeting," *National Reformer* (July 29, 1866).
"The One Thing Needful," *National Reformer* (Aug. 5, 1866) (SP).
"Sayings of Sigvat," *National Reformer* (Sept. 30, Oct. 14, 1866) (EP).
"A Word for Xantippe," *National Reformer* (Oct 21, 1866) (EP).
"Sympathy," *National Reformer* (Oct. 28, Nov. 18, 25, 1866) (EP).
"The Swinburne Controversy," *National Reformer* (Dec. 23, 1866) (SP).
"The 'Saturday Review' on 'Mr. Bright's Edition of Mr. Bright,'" *National Reformer* (Feb. 3, 1867) (PEF).
"Giordano Bruno," *National Reformer* (Feb. 10, 24, March 3, 1867).
"A Walk Abroad," *National Reformer* (April 21, 1867), written 1866 (EP).

"The 'Saturday Review' and the 'National Reformer,'" *National Reformer* (April 28, May 5, 1867) (SP).
"A Lady of Sorrow," *National Reformer* (July 14, 21, 28, Aug. 4, 11, 18, 25, Sept. 1, 1867), written 1862, 1864 (EP).
"The Pilgrim and the Shrine, and Its Critics," *National Reformer* (Aug. 29, 1869).
"Leopardi," *National Reformer* (Oct. 3, 10, 17, Nov. 7, 21, 28, Dec. 12, 1869; Jan. 2, 9, 16, Feb. 6, 1870) (L).
"France Declares War against Prussia," *National Reformer* (July 24, 1870).
"Paul-Louis Courier," *National Reformer* (July 31, Aug. 7, 14, 1870).
"How the Bible Warns against Authorship," *National Reformer* (Aug. 21, 1870) (PEF).
"Jottings on the Franco-Prussian War," *National Reformer* (Sept. 4, 1870).
"A Commission of Inquiry as to Complaints against Royalty," *National Reformer* (Sept. 18, 1870) (SP).
"Marcus Aurelius Antoninus," *National Reformer* (Oct 23, 30, Nov. 6, 1870).
"The Assassination of Paul-Louis Courier," *National Reformer* (Oct. 30, 1870).
"Cowper's Task (New Version)," *National Reformer* (Nov. 13, 1870).
"Hints for Freethought Novels," *National Reformer* (Nov. 20, 1870).
"A Bible Lesson on Monarchy," *National Reformer* (Nov. 27, 1870) (SP).
"Feuerbach's Essence of Christianity," *National Reformer* (Dec. 4, 1870).
"Infidelity in the United States," *National Reformer* (Dec. 11, 1870).
"With the Christian World," *National Reformer* (Dec. 18, 1870).
"International Socialism in Spain," *National Reformer* (Jan. 1, 1871).
"The Divan of Goethe," *National Reformer* (Jan. 22, 1871) (PEF).
"Strange News for the Secularists," *National Reformer* (Jan. 22, 1871).
"Atheism in Spain," *National Reformer* (Feb. 5, 1871).
"Anastasius," *National Reformer* (Feb. 12, 19, 1871).
"Association for Intercessory Prayer," *National Reformer* (Feb. 26, 1871).
"Moxon's Cheap Edition of Shelley's Poems," a review, *National Reformer* (March 12, 1871) (S).

"Insults to the Church in Spain," *National Reformer* (April 2, 1871).
"Another Spanish Atheistic Periodical," *National Reformer* (April 30, 1871).
"Proposals for the Speedy Extinction of Evil and Misery," *National Reformer* (Aug. 27, Sept. 3, 10, 17, 24, Oct. 8, 22, Nov. 5, 12, 1871), written 1868, 1871 (EP).
"Notes on Religious Matters," *National Secular Society's Almanac* (1872).
"Religion in the Rocky Mountains," *National Reformer* (March 30, April 13, 1873) (SP).
"Reports on the Carlist Revolution," *New York World* (Aug. 12, 15, 30, Sept. 16, 22, 1873).
"Funeral of Mr. Austin Holyoake," *National Reformer* (April 26, 1874).
"Jottings," *National Reformer* (July 5–Sept. 27, Oct. 25–Dec. 20, 1874; Jan. 24–March 14, April 4, 25, May 2, 1875).
"A National Reformer in the Dog Days," *National Reformer* (July 12, 19, 1874), written 1869 (EP).
"Walt Whitman," *National Reformer* (July 26, Aug. 2, 9, 16, 23, 30, Sept. 6, 1874) (PEF, W).
"Uhland in English," a review, *National Reformer* (Sept. 13, 20, 1874).
"Bishop Alford on Professor Tyndall," *National Reformer* (Sept. 27, 1874).
"Extra-Experimental Beliefs," *National Reformer* (Oct. 11, 1874).
"Jesus Christ, Our Great Exemplar," *National Reformer* (Oct. 25, 1874).
"The 'Daily News,'" *National Reformer* (Nov. 1, 1874) (SP).
"Mill on Religion," a review, *National Reformer* (Nov. 8, 15, 22, 29, Dec. 6, 13, 20, 27, 1874).
"Freethought in India," *National Reformer* (Jan. 24, 1875).
"Henri Beyle (De Stendhal)," *National Reformer* (Jan. 31, Feb. 7, 14, 1875).
"Raffaele Sonzogno," *National Reformer* (Feb. 28, 1875).
"Great Christ Is Dead," *National Reformer* (March 14, 1875) (SP).
"The Sankey Hymns," a review, *National Reformer* (April 25, 1875).
"Never Forsake the Ship and Other Poems, by Finola," a review, *National Reformer* (May 2, 1875).
"Mr. Moody's Addresses," *National Reformer* (May 16, 1875).
"A Popular Sermon," *National Reformer* (May 23, 1875).
"Some May Meeting Figures," *National Reformer* (May 30, 1875).

"Some May Meeting Speeches," *National Reformer* (June 6, 1875).
"Debate between Mr. Charles Watts and Mr. Z. B. Woffendale," *National Reformer* (June 13, 20, 1875).
"The Past Session," *Republican Chronicle* (Sept., 1875).
"Stray Whiffs, from an Old Smoker," *Cope's Tobacco Plant* (Sept., 1875).
"A French Novel: *Un Homme Sérieux*, by Charles de Bernard," a review, *Cope's Tobacco Plant* (Dec., 1875).
"Some Anecdotes of Rabelais," *National Secular Society's Almanac* (1876).
"The Fair of St. Sylvester," *Cope's Tobacco Plant* (Jan., 1876) (EP).
"Reverberations, by W. M. W. Call," a review, *Secularist* (Jan. 1, 1876).
"Secularism and the Bible," *Secularist* (Jan. 1, 1876).
"Whitman and Swinburne," *Secularist* (Jan. 8, 1876).
"Heinrich Heine," *Secularist* (Jan. 8, 15, 22, 29, Feb. 5, 12, 1876).
"Saint Amant," *Cope's Tobacco Plant* (Feb., March, April, 1876) (BCS).
"Among the Christians," *Secularist* (Feb. 5, May 6, Aug. 26, 1876; Jan. 13, 1877).
"Arthur Schopenhauer, by H. Zimmern," a review, *Secularist* (Feb. 19, 26, March 11, 1876).
"The Devil in the Church of England," *Secularist* (Feb. 26, March 4, 1876) (SP).
"Carlist Reminiscences," *Secularist* (March 11, 18, 25, April 1, 1876).
"Goblin Market, The Prince's Progress, and Other Poems, by Christina Rossetti," a review, *Secularist* (March 25, 1876).
"The Life of Jonathan Swift, by John Forster," a review, *Cope's Tobacco Plant* (April, 1876).
"Heinrich Heine, by William Stigand," a review, *Cope's Tobacco Plant* (April, 1876).
"A Great Modern Astrologer," *Secularist* (April 1, 1876).
"Dr. Kenealy in a New Character," *Secularist* (April 8, 1876).
"Mr. Matthew Arnold on the Church of England," *Secularist* (April 8, 1876).
"The Secular Song and Hymn Book, edited by Annie Besant," a review, *Secularist* (April 8, 1876).
"Correspondence," *Secularist* (April 22, May 13, Sept. 16, 1876).
" 'The Bugbears of Infidelity' at Perth," *Secularist* (May 6, 1876).
"On the Worth of Metaphysical Systems," *Secularist* (May 13, 1876) (EP).

"The Burial Question in the House of Lords," *Secularist* (May 20, 1876).
"The Life of Jonathan Swift, by John Forster," a review, *Secularist* (May 20, 1876) (EP).
"The 'Standard' on the Whigs and the Church," *Secularist* (May 27, 1876).
"William Godwin, by C. Kegan Paul," a review, *Cope's Tobacco Plant* (June, 1876).
"Beauchamp's Career, by George Meredith," a review, *Cope's Tobacco Plant* (June, 1876) (GM).
"Rabelais," *Cope's Tobacco Plant* (June, July, Aug., Oct., 1876) (BCS).
"Beauchamp's Career, by George Meredith," a review, *Secularist* (June 3, 1876) (EP, GM).
"A Few Words on the System of Spinoza," *Secularist* (June 10, 1876) (EP).
"The Leeds Conferences," *Secularist* (June 17, 1876).
"William Godwin, by C. Kegan Paul," a review, *Secularist* (June 24, July 1, 8, 1876).
"Seen Thrice: A London Study," *Secularist* (July 8, 15, 1876), written 1863.
"The Bishop of London's Fund," *Secularist* (July 15, 1876).
"Mr. Foote at the London Hall of Science," *Secularist* (July 15, 1876).
"Christian Evidences, Popular and Critical," *Secularist* (July 22, 29, 1876).
"Indolence: A Moral Essay," *Secularist* (July 22, 29, Aug. 5, 1876), written 1867 (EP).
"The Resurrection and Ascension of Jesus," *Secularist* (Aug. 5, 1876) (SP).
"Some Muslim Laws and Beliefs," *Secularist* (Aug. 12, 19, 1876) (SP).
"Sayings of Sigvat," *Secularist* (Aug. 19, 1876).
"Stray Thoughts," *Secularist* (Aug. 26, 1876).
"The 'Christian World' and the 'Secularist' Again," *Secularist* (Sept. 9, 1876) (SP).
"Pacchiarotto, by Robert Browning," a review, *Secularist* (Sept. 9, 1876) (BCS).
"Conversions, Sudden and Gradual," *Secularist* (Sept. 16, 1876).
"The Eastern Question," *Secularist* (Sept. 16, 1876).
"On the Duty of Converts to Freethought," *Secularist* (Sept. 23, 1876).
"The London School Board Elections," *Secularist* (Sept. 30, 1876).
"The 'Cornhill Magazine' on Leopardi," *Secularist* (Sept. 30, 1876).

"La Tentation de Saint Antoine, par Gustave Flaubert," a review, *Secularist* (Sept. 30, Oct. 7, 21, 28, Nov. 4, 1876).
"The Primate on the Church and the World," *Secularist* (Oct. 7, 1876) (SP).
"The 'Daily News' on Materialism," *Secularist* (Oct. 7, 1876).
"Ben Jonson," *Cope's Tobacco Plant* (Nov., Dec., 1876; Jan., Feb., March, May, June, Aug., Sept., Oct., Nov., Dec., 1877; Jan., March, 1878) (BCS).
"Spiritism in the Police Court," *Secularist* (Nov. 11, 1876) (SP).
"The Huddersfield Prosecution of a 'Medium,'" *Secularist* (Nov. 18, 1876).
"The London School Board Elections," *Secularist* (Dec. 9, 1876).
"An Inspired Critic on Shelley," *Secularist* (Dec. 9, 1876) (S).
"Note of an English Republican on the Muscovite Crusade, by A. C. Swinburne," a review, *Secularist* (Dec. 30, 1876).
"Our Obstructions," *Secularist* (Jan. 6, 1877) (SP).
"The Works of Francis Rabelais," a review, *Secularist* (Jan. 13, 1877).
"In Our Forest of the Past," *Secularist* (Feb. 17, 1877) (EP)
"Principal Tulloch on Personal Immortality," *Secularist* (Feb. 24, 1877) (SP).
"Rubáiyát of Omar Khayyám," a review, *Cope's Tobacco Plant* (March, 1877).
"Professor Martineau and the Reverend H. H. Dobney on Prayer," *Secularist* (March 3, 1877).
"Jottings," *Secular Review* (March 4, 1877).
"The Bi-centenary of Spinoza, M. Renan's Address," *Secularist* (March 10, 1877).
"The Discourses of Epictetus," a review, *Cope's Tobacco Plant* (April, 1877).
"A History of English Thought in the Eighteenth Century, by Leslie Stephen," a review, *Cope's Tobacco Plant* (April, 1877).
"The Discourses of Epictetus," a review, *Secularist* (April 14, 21, May 5, 12, 1877).
"Clerical Modesty," *Secular Review* (April 15, 1877).
"The Eastern Crisis," *Secular Review* (April 22, 1877).
"The Incidence of Taxation," *Secular Review* (April 29, 1877).
[38] "The Incidence and Increase of Taxation," *Secular Review* (May 13, 1877).
"Trois Contes, par Gustave Flaubert," a review, *Secular Review and Secularist* (July 7, 21, 1877).
"The Complete Poetical Works of Percy Bysshe Shelley," a review, *Cope's Tobacco Plant* (April, 1878) (S).
"John Wilson and the Noctes Ambrosianae," *Cope's Tobacco Plant* (April, 1878; May, 1879) (BCS).

"Tobacco Smuggling in the Last Generation," *Cope's Tobacco Plant* (May, June, July, Aug., Sept., Oct., Nov., 1878).
"The Tobacco Duties," *Cope's Tobacco Plant* (Dec., 1878; Jan., March, 1879).
"In the Valley of Humiliation," *Liberal* (Jan., 1879).
" 'Social Notes' on Tobacco," *Cope's Tobacco Plant* (Jan., 1879).
"Tobacco at the Opera," *Cope's Tobacco Plant* (Feb., 1879).
"Professor Huxley on Hume," a review, *Liberal* (March, 1879).
"Tobacco Legislation in the Three Kingdoms," *Cope's Tobacco Plant* (March, April, Sept., Nov., Dec., 1879; Jan., March, April, May, June, Aug., Sept., Nov., 1880).
"An Old New Book," a review (of George Meredith's *Ordeal of Richard Feverel*), *Cope's Tobacco Plant* (May, 1879) (GM).
"Hume, by T. H. Huxley," a review, *Cope's Tobacco Plant* (June, 1879).
"Gibbon, by J. C. Morison," a review, *Cope's Tobacco Plant* (June, 1879).
"Samuel Johnson, by Leslie Stephen," a review, *Cope's Tobacco Plant* (June, 1879).
"Goldsmith, by William Black," a review, *Cope's Tobacco Plant* (July, 1879).
"Daniel DeFoe, by William Minto," a review, *Cope's Tobacco Plant* (Aug., 1879).
"James Hogg, the Ettrick Shepherd," *Cope's Tobacco Plant* (Aug., Sept., Oct., 1879) (BCS).
"Robert Burns, by Principal Shairp," a review, *Cope's Tobacco Plant* (Sept., 1879).
"Sir Walter Scott, by R. H. Hutton," a review, *Cope's Tobacco Plant* (Sept., 1879).
"A Strange Book," a review (of Garth Wilkinson's *Improvisations from the Spirit*), *Liberal* (Sept., Oct., Nov., Dec., 1879) (BCS).
"Cope's Mixture," *Cope's Tobacco Plant* (Dec., 1879; Jan., Feb., April, May, 1880).
"George Meredith's New Work," a review (of *The Egoist*), *Cope's Tobacco Plant* (Jan., 1880) (GM).
"Spenser, by R. W. Church," a review, *Cope's Tobacco Plant* (Jan., 1880).
"Shelley, by J. A. Symonds," a review, *Cope's Tobacco Plant* (Feb., 1880) (BCS, S).
"Walt Whitman," *Cope's Tobacco Plant* (May, June, July, Aug., Sept., Oct., Nov., Dec., 1880) (WW).
"Burke, by John Morley," a review, *Cope's Tobacco Plant* (June, 1880).

"Thackeray, by Anthony Trollope," a review, *Cope's Tobacco Plant* (July, 1880).
"Milton, by Mark Pattison," a review, *Cope's Tobacco Plant* (Aug., 1880).
"Notes on the Structure of Shelley's 'Prometheus Unbound,'" *Athenaeum* (Sept. 17, 24, Oct. 8, Nov. 5, 19, 1881) (S).
"The Ring and the Book," *Gentleman's Magazine* (Dec., 1881) (BCS).
"Notes on the Genius of Robert Browning," *Browning Society's Transactions,* Part I (1882) (BCS).
"A Note on Shelley," *Progress* (Feb., 1884), written 1878 (S).
"Sarpolus of Mardon," *Progress* (Feb., March, April, May, June, 1887), written 1858.
"Selections from the Manuscript Books of 'B.V.'" *National Reformer* (April 19, May 3, 10, 17, 24, June 7, 14, 1891) (PEF).

C. Poetry

Owing to the nature of this study, Thomson's poetry is listed in order of date of composition. The date that precedes the title is the one that appears on Thomson's manuscript copy of the poem, except for the few instances where poems are undated and I have assigned the logical date, followed by a question mark. The title of each poem is followed by place and date of its earliest publication, or, if the poem is unpublished, by its location in the manuscript collections. Unless otherwise noted, all the published poems appear in the two-volume *The Poetical Works of James Thomson (B.V.)*, edited by Bertram Dobell.

1852

1852. "Love's Dawn," *Tait's Edinburgh Magazine* (Oct., 1858), as Part I of "Four Stages in a Life."
October 15, 1852. "To ———," unpublished, Bodleian Library MS, Don. e. 37.

1853

1853. "Love Song," *Poems, Essays, and Fragments* (1892), not included in *Poetical Works.*
1853. "A Proem," *A Voice from the Nile and Other Poems* (1884).

1854

1854. "Song," unpublished, Bodleian Library MS, Don. e. 37.

June, 1854. "Parting," *Tait's Edinburgh Magazine* (Oct., 1858), as Part III of "Four Stages in a Life."

1855

1855. "Far-far away, my 'Sister' Dear," unpublished, Bodleian Library MS, Don. e. 37.

1855. "The Approach to St. Paul's," first published in Anne Ridler, ed., *Poems and Some Letters of James Thomson* (1963).

July, 1855. "Suggested by Matthew Arnold's 'Stanzas from the Grande Chartreuse,'" *A Voice from the Nile and Other Poems* (1884).

September 4, 1855. "The Dreamer," *A Voice from the Nile and Other Poems* (1884).

1856

November, 1856. "Tasso to Leonora," *Tait's Edinburgh Magazine* (May, 1859).

1857

January 10, 1857. "Marriage," *Tait's Edinburgh Magazine* (Oct., 1858), as Part II of "Four Stages in a Life."

January, 1857. "Bertram to the Most Noble and Beautiful Lady Geraldine," *Tait's Edinburgh Magazine* (Nov., 1859).

February, 1857. "A Festival of Life," *Tait's Edinburgh Magazine* (April, 1859).

1857. "The Doom of a City: A Fantasia," *A Voice from the Nile and Other Poems* (1884).

1857. "Withered Leaves," *Tait's Edinburgh Magazine* (July, 1859).

1857. "The Purple Flower of the Heather," *Tait's Edinburgh Magazine* (Jan., 1860).

1857. "A Chant," *A Voice from the Nile and Other Poems* (1884).

1857. "The Jolly Veterans," *Tait's Edinburgh Magazine* (Aug., 1859).

1857. "A Capstan Chorus," *Tait's Edinburgh Magazine* (Aug., 1859).

November 16, 1857. Untitled 80-line humorous poem on drinking, unpublished, Bodleian Library MS, Don. e. 37.

November, 1857 (completed April 3, 1859). "A Happy Poet," *Tait's Edinburgh Magazine* (Dec., 1859).

November 23, 1857. "Twenty-third Birthday," first published in Ridler, *Poems and Some Letters of James Thomson* (1963).

1857(?). "Mr. Save-His-Soul-Alive, O!" *Investigator* (Feb., 1858), not included in *Poetical Works.*

1858

January 10, 1858. Untitled fragment of a narrative poem influenced by "Aurora Leigh," unpublished, Bodleian Library MS, Don. d. 108.
1858. "Siren's Song," *Progress* (March, 1886).
1858. "A Requiem," *National Reformer* (Sept. 1, 1867).
1858. "The Cypress and the Roses," *Tait's Edinburgh Magazine* (June, 1859).
1858. "A Winter's Night," *Tait's Edinburgh Magazine* (Jan., 1860).
1858. "The Fadeless Bower," *Tait's Edinburgh Magazine* (July, 1858).
June 6, 1858. "At Death's Door," *Tait's Edinburgh Magazine* (Oct., 1858), as Part IV of "Four Stages in a Life."
August 5, 1858. "Heresy" (title later changed to "A Recusant"), *National Reformer* (Nov. 22, 1862).

1859

1859. "The Lord of the Castle of Indolence," *Tait's Edinburgh Magazine* (March, 1860).
1859. "Robert Burns," *Investigator* (April, 1859), as part of the essay, "A Few Words about Burns."
March, 1859. "To a Pianiste," *Tait's Edinburgh Magazine* (Nov., 1859).
March 4, 1859. "A Real Vision of Sin," *Progress* (Nov., 1884).
September 23, 1859. "An Old Dream," *Tait's Edinburgh Magazine* (June, 1860).
November 2, 1859. "A Sergeant's Mess Song," *Cope's Tobacco Plant* (Nov., 1880).
November, 1859. "The Deliverer," *Fortnightly Review* (Nov., 1881).
November 21, 1859. "Mater Tenebrarum," *Vane's Story, Weddah and Om-el-Bonain, and Other Poems* (1881).
1859(?). "Sonnet" ("Through foulest fogs of my own sluggish soul"), *Poems, Essays, and Fragments* (1892).

1860

March, 1860. "Arch Archery," *London Society* (March, 1863).
May 29, 1860 (stanzas 1–16); December 8, 1860 (stanzas 17–32). "To Our Ladies of Death," *National Reformer* (Feb. 28, 1863).

September 24, 1860. "Meeting Again," *Liberal* (June, 1879).

November 30, 1860. "The Dead Year," *National Reformer* (Jan. 6, 1861).

December 16, 1860. "Two Sonnets," *Vane's Story, Weddah and Om-el-Bonain, and Other Poems* (1881).

1861

1861. "E. B. B.," *National Reformer* (Nov. 29, 1862).

September 7, November 11, 1861. "Shelley," *Shelley, a Poem* (1884).

Xmas 1861 (some sections written earlier; poem not completed until July, 1864). "Ronald and Helen," sections only published in *Secularist* (Jan., 1876), *Liberal* (Jan., July, 1879), and *Progress* (Nov., 1885); complete poem not published until included in *Poetical Works* (1895).

1862

January 12, 15, 1862. "Havre-des-pas," two 8-line poems, unpublished, Bodleian Library MS, Don. d. 108.

March 25–April 10, 1862. "To Joseph and Alice Barnes," first published in Dobell's memoir in *Poetical Works* (1895).

April 15, 1862. "To ———," published as Section X of "Sunday up the River," *Fraser's Magazine* (Oct., 1869).

1863

July, 1863. "A Slight Mistake," unpublished narrative, Bodleian Library MS, Don. e. 37.

1863. "A Polish Insurgent," *National Reformer* (March 18, 1866).

October 21, 1863. "From the Midst of the Fire I Fling," epigraph to "A Lady of Sorrow," *National Reformer* (July 14, 1867).

November 30, 1863. "The Three That Shall Be One," *Secularist* (June 3, 1876).

1864

February, 1864. "Versification of Thomas Cooper's Argument," *National Reformer* (Feb. 13, 1864).

February 11, 1864. "Desolate" (title later changed to "Night"), *National Reformer* (Aug. 25, 1867).

February 29, 1864. "The Fire That Filled My Heart of Old," *Vane's Story, Weddah and Om-el-Bonain, and Other Poems* (1881).

1864. "Garibaldi Revisiting England," *Vane's Story, Weddah and Om-el-Bonain, and Other Poems* (1881).

1864. "Vane's Story," *National Reformer* (May 13, 27, June 3, 10, 1866).

1864(?). Three epigrams: "On a Broken Pipe," *Cope's Tobacco Plant* (Sept., 1875); "Iphigenia à la Mode," *Poems, Essays, and Fragments* (1892); "On George Herbert's Poems," *Poetical Works* (1895).

1865

1865. "Allace! That Samyn Sweit Face!" *Vane's Story, Weddah and Om-el-Bonain, and Other Poems* (1881).

March 11, 1865. "William Blake," *National Reformer* (Feb. 4, 1866).

March 14, 1865. "Virtue and Vice," *National Reformer* (Dec. 17, 1865).

March–April, 1865 (several sections were apparently written earlier). "Sunday up the River: An Idyll," *Fraser's Magazine* (Oct., 1869).

April 3, 1865. "Aquatics (Kew)," *Progress* (Nov., 1887).

April 3, 1865. "Low Life: As Overheard in the Train," *Secularist* (Aug. 19, 1876).

April 7, 1865. "Polycrates on Waterloo Bridge," *National Reformer* (Oct. 14, 1866).

April 19, 1865. "Richmond Hill," unpublished narrative poem, Bodleian Library MS, Don. e. 41.

April, 1865 (several sections were probably written in 1863). "Sunday at Hampstead," *National Reformer* (July 15, 22, 1866).

April–May, 1865. "The Star and Garter," two unpublished poems under the same title, Bodleian Library MS, Don. e. 41.

May 28, 1865. "On the Terrace at Richmond," first published in Ridler, *Poems and Some Letters of James Thomson* (1963).

May 28, 1865. "Once in a Saintly Passion," first published in Dobell's memoir in *Poetical Works* (1895).

1865 (before June). "Art," *National Reformer* (Feb. 17, 1867).

1865. "Shameless: Kew Gardens," *Secularist* (Aug. 12, 1876).

October 7, 1865. "In the Train," unpublished, Bodleian Library MS, Don. e. 41.

1865. "Love's Logic" (a 3-line epigram), *Poems, Essays, and Fragments* (1892).

1866

April 17, 1866. "Mr. Maccall at Cleveland Hall," *Poems, Essays, and Fragments* (1892).

June 8, 1866. "Don Giovanni at Covent Garden," *Secularist* (May 20, 1876).

September 5, 1866. "Life's Hebe," *National Reformer* (Jan. 13, 1867).

December 1, 1866. "Day," *National Reformer* (Aug. 25, 1867).

December 6, 1866. "Philosophy," *National Reformer* (Jan. 20, 1867).

December 19, 1866–March 31, 1867. "The Naked Goddess," *National Reformer* (June 23, 1867).

1866. "A Timely Prayer" (a 4-line epigram), *National Reformer* (March 18, 1866).

1866. "Who Killed Moses?" (an 8-line epigram), *National Reformer* (July 15, 1866).

1866. "Suggested from Southampton" (a 4-line epigram), *National Reformer* (Sept. 2, 1866).

1866. "Versicles" (three short epigrams), *National Reformer* (Nov. 25, 1866).

1866(?). "Better the Love of a Woman You Love" (a 4-line epigram), unpublished, British Museum MS, Add. 38535.

1867

January 28, 1867. "Most of Your Poetry Is Now Dyspeptic" (a 4-line epigram), unpublished, Bodleian Library MS, Don. e. 48.

1867. "Europe's Rouge et Noir" (a 5-line epigram), *National Reformer* (Nov. 24, 1867).

1867. "The Pan-Anglican Synod," *National Reformer* (Oct. 13, 1867), not included in *Poetical Works,* but republished in *Poems, Essays, and Fragments* (1892).

1867. "L'Ancien Régime; or, The Good Old Rule," *National Reformer* (July 7, 1867).

December 15, 1867. "Two Lovers," *National Reformer* (Jan. 5, 1868).

December 29, 1867–February 23, 1868. "In the Room," *National Reformer* (May 19, 1872).

1868

January 13, 1868. "A Song of Sighing," *National Reformer* (April 28, 1872).

June 27, 1868–April 4, 1869. "Weddah and Om-el-Bonain," *National Reformer* (Nov. 19, Dec. 3, 24, 1871; Jan. 21, 28, 1872).

December, 1868. "L'Envoy," *Poems, Essays, and Fragments* (1892).

1869

February 14, 1869. "'Lilah, Alice, Hypatia," *Poems, Essays, and Fragments* (1892).

March 25, 1869. "I've Done My Best" (a 4-line epigram), unpublished, British Museum MS, Add. 38535.

1870

January 16, 1870. "A Graveyard" (a 4-line epigram, later titled "In a Christian Churchyard"), *National Reformer* (May 7, 1871).

January 16–October 23, 1870. Sections II, XVIII, XX, I, V, XI, VII, IV, X, VI, and III of "The City of Dreadful Night," *National Reformer* (March 22, April 12, 26, May 17, 1874).

May 18, 1870. "Supplement to the Inferno," *Progress* (Feb., 1885).

1871

1871. Six short epigrams ("In Exitu Israel," "Change for a Bad Napoleon," "Poor Indeed," "The Successors Who Do Not Succeed," "Bless Thee! Thou Art Translated," "We Croak"), *National Reformer* (March 19, April 9, 16, 23, May 7, 1871).

1872

January, 1872. "Pathetic Epitaph" (an 8-line epigram), *National Reformer* (Jan. 28, 1872).

January, 1872. "Our Congratulations on the Recovery of His Royal Highness," *National Reformer* (Jan. 28, 1872).

1873

May–October 29, 1873. Sections VIII, XIX, IX, proem, XII, XIV, XVII, XV, XIII, XVI, and XXI of "The City of Dreadful Night," *National Reformer* (March 22, April 12, 26, May 17, 1874). An early, undated draft of Section XXI, titled "The 'Melencolia' of Albrecht Dürer," is published in Ridler, *Poems and Some Letters of James Thomson* (1963).

1874–1876

No poetry was written in 1874–1876.

1877

February, 1877. "Song: The Nightingale Was Not Yet Heard," *Secularist* (Feb. 17, 1877).

1877. "The Pilgrimage to Saint Nicotine of the Holy Herb," *Cope's Tobacco Plant* ("Christmas Card" issued with the Feb., 1878, issue); prologue only included in *Poetical Works* (1895).

1878

January, 1878. "To Anna Linden" (contained in an article titled "You Love Tobacco Better"), *Cope's Tobacco Plant* (Jan., 1878), not included in *Poetical Works.*

1878. "Creeds and Men," *Poems, Essays, and Fragments* (1892).

September 16–18, 1878. "I Had a Love," first published (as "Lines, 1878") in Ridler, *Poems and Some Letters of James Thomson* (1963).

1878. "The Pursuit of Diva Nicotine," *Cope's Tobacco Plant* ("Christmas Card" issued with the Feb., 1879, issue), not included in *Poetical Works.*

1879

No poetry was written in 1879.

1880

November 1, 1880. "Bill Jones on Prayer," *Progress* (Aug., 1884).

1881

March, 1881. "Address on the Opening of the New Hall of the Leicester Secular Society, March 6, 1881," printed copies distributed at time of opening.

November, 1881. "A Voice from the Nile," *Fortnightly Review* (July, 1882).

November 23, 1881. "To H. A. B.—On My Forty-seventh Birthday," first published in *Poetical Works* (1895).

December, 1881. "Richard Forest's Midsummer Night," *A Voice from the Nile and Other Poems* (1884).

1882

January 5, 1882. "Proem: O Antique Fables," *Fortnightly Review* (Feb., 1892). Bodleian Library MS, Don. d. 108, contains an early draft of four stanzas of this poem, dated August 12, 1871.

January 15, 1882. "At Belvoir," *A Voice from the Nile and Other Poems* (1884).

January, 1882. "The Sleeper," *Cornhill Magazine* (March, 1882).

1882. "Modern Penelope," *A Voice from the Nile and Other Poems* (1884).

February, 1882. "The Poet and His Muse," *A Voice from the Nile and Other Poems* (1884).

February, 1882. "He Heard Her Sing," *A Voice from the Nile and Other Poems* (1884).

February 23–March 8, 1882. "Insomnia," *A Voice from the Nile and Other Poems* (1884).

March, 1882. "A Stranger," *A Voice from the Nile and Other Poems* (1884).

March, 1882. "Law v. Gospel," *Weekly Dispatch* (March 26, 1882).

March, 1882. "The Old Story and the New Storey," *Weekly Dispatch* (April 2, 1882).

April, 1882. "The Closure," *Weekly Dispatch* (April 30, 1882), not included in *Poetical Works.*

May, 1882. "Despotism Tempered by Dynamite," *Weekly Dispatch* (June 4, 1882).

D. Translations, Listed in Order of Publication

"Songs from Heine" (from Heine's *Buch der Lieder*), *Jersey Independent* (March 7, 1862). Thomson continued to translate poems from this volume throughout his life, often publishing the same poem twice after slight revision. Other "Songs from Heine" appear in the *National Reformer* (Dec. 6, 20, 27, 1862; Feb. 5, 1865; Feb. 11, 1866; Feb. 3, 1867; July 12, 19, Aug. 23, 1891), the *Secularist* (Jan. 29, Feb. 5, 12, 19, 26, March 4, 11, April 29, May 12, June 24, Aug. 5, Sept. 9, 30, Oct. 14, Nov. 4, 1876), and *Progress* (Dec., 1883; Jan., March, May, 1884). Most of the translations appear in Volume I of *Poetical Works* (1895).

"The Good God" (from Béranger), *National Reformer* (July 11, 1864).

"The Death of the Devil" (from Béranger), *National Reformer* (March 26, 1865).

"The Origin of Evil" (from Heine's *De l'Allemagne*), *National Reformer* (Feb. 11, 1866).

"Goethe's Israel in the Wilderness" (from Goethe's *West-östlicher Divan*), *National Reformer* (June 17, 24, July 1, 8, 1866).

"An Auto-da-fe" (from Pietro Colletta, *History of Naples*), *National Reformer* (March 10, 1867).

"Heine on Kant" (from Heine's *De l'Allemagne*), *National Reformer* (May 19, 1867).

"Heine on Spinoza" (from Heine's *De l'Allemagne*), *National Reformer* (May 26, June 2, 1867).

"Heine on an Illustrious Exile, with Something about Whales" (from Heine's *De l'Allemagne*), *National Reformer* (June 9, 16, 1867).

"Copernicus: A Dialogue" (from Leopardi), *National Reformer* (Nov. 3, 10, 1867).

"Dialogue between a Natural Philosopher and a Metaphysician" (from Leopardi), *National Reformer* (Dec. 1, 1867).
"Dialogue of Timander and Eleander" (from Leopardi), *National Reformer* (Dec. 8, 15, 1867).
"Dialogue between Nature and the Soul" (from Leopardi), *National Reformer* (Dec. 29, 1867).
"Dialogue of Christopher Columbus and Peter Gutierrez" (from Leopardi), *National Reformer* (Jan. 5, 1868).
"Dialogue between Frederic Ruysch and His Mummies" (from Leopardi), *National Reformer* (Jan. 26, 1868).
"Dialogue between Tristan and a Friend" (from Leopardi), *National Reformer* (Feb. 9, 16, 1868).
"Dialogue between a Vendor of Almanacs and a Passer-by" (from Leopardi), *National Reformer* (March 15, 1868).
"In Praise of Birds" (from Leopardi), *National Reformer* (March 22, 1868).
"Dialogue of Plotinus and Porphyry" (from Leopardi), *National Reformer* (April 5, 12, 1868).
"Comparison of the Last Words of Brutus the Younger, and Theophrastus" (from Leopardi), *National Reformer* (May 3, 17, 1868).
"Selections from the Thoughts of Leopardi" (from Leopardi), *National Reformer* (May 31, June 7, 1868).
"Prometheus" (from Goethe), *National Reformer* (July 31, 1870).
"How Heine Forewarned France" (from Heine's *De l'Allemagne*), *National Reformer* (Sept. 11, 1870).
"Paul-Louis Courier on the Land Question" (from Courier), *National Reformer* (Oct. 9, 1870).
"Paul-Louis Courier on the Character of the People" (from Courier), *National Reformer* (Oct. 16, 1870).
"The Divan of Goethe" (eight poems translated from Goethe's *West-östlicher Divan*), *National Reformer* (Jan. 22, 1871).
"Cross Lines from Goethe" (from Goethe's epigrams), *National Reformer* (April 23, 1871).
"Charles Baudelaire on Hasheesh" (condensed translation of chapters 3, 4, and 5 of Baudelaire's *Les Paradis Artificiels*), *Cope's Tobacco Plant* (Oct., 1875).
"Théophile Gautier as Hasheesh-Eater" (condensed translation of two Gautier articles, "Les Club des Haschichins" and "La Pipe d'Opium"), *Cope's Tobacco Plant* (Nov., 1875).
"Renan's Memories of His Childhood" (from Renan's "Souvenirs d'Enfance" in *Revue des Deux Mondes*, 1876), *Secularist* (April 15, 1876).
"Religion in Japan" (condensed translation of George Bousquet's article, "La Religion au Japan," in *Revue des Deux Mondes*, 1876), *Secularist* (April 22, 1876).

E. Manuscript Material

Bodleian Library MSS, Don. c. 73, d. 104–110, e. 36–50, f. 8–24, g. 1–7. This extensive collection was compiled by Thomson's literary executor and close friend, Bertram Dobell, and includes early drafts and fair copies of virtually all of Thomson's poetry, except for "The City"; copies of translations from Leopardi, Thomson's phantasies, and miscellaneous prose fragments, including unfinished essays on George Eliot and Browning; notebooks and memorandum books from the 1860's and the 1870's which contain epigrams, observations, personal notations, fragments of verses composed by Thomson throughout his career, and Thomson's copies, in his own hand, of poems by Blake, Heine, the Brownings, and so on; letters from Thomson to W. M. Rossetti, Bertram Dobell, J. W. Barrs, and other friends; miscellaneous correspondence between Thomson's friends during the last year of his life, and all of Dobell's correspondence from the years in which he was preparing his editions of Thomson's works; Thomson's journals and account books kept during his trips to America and to Spain; and Thomson's diaries for the years 1874 and 1876–1881.

British Museum MSS, Add. 38532–38535. Four volumes, including two early drafts of "The City," a final copy of "Weddah," and proofs for "Sunday up the River," with J. A. Froude's comments and Thomson's corrections. Two small memorandum books contain miscellaneous notations and drafts and fragments of various poems, in pencil, from the 1860's.

J. Pierpont Morgan Library MS, copy of "The City." Two small memorandum books containing Thomson's final copy of the poem, with minor corrections and additions made just prior to its publication, and dates of composition for each stanza.

Rationalist Press Association, Ltd., London, holds material collected during the years 1886–1903 by Henry S. Salt, when he was writing his biography of Thomson. This RPA Collection includes letters to Salt from friends and relatives of Thomson's, and notes of Salt's interviews with various friends of Thomson's who knew him intimately at one period of his life.

II. Biographical, Critical, and General

"Academy Portraits," *Academy*, LV (Dec. 3, 1898), 383.

Altick, Richard D. "*Cope's Tobacco Plant:* An Episode in Victorian Journalism," *Papers of the Bibliographical Society of America*, XL, no. 4 (1951), 333–350.

Antheunis, Louis. "James Thomson," *Revue Générale,* LXXIX (1904), 838–858.

"B. E." Introduction to *The Story of a Famous Old Jewish Firm and Other Pieces in Prose and Rime.* Leek Bijou Freethought Reprint No. VI. 1883.

Benton, Joel. "A New English Poet," *Appleton's Journal,* X (May, 1881), 468–471.

Birchmeier-Nussbaumer, Annette Katherina. *Weltbild eines Pessimisten: Die Struktur der konkreten Vorstellungswelt von James Thomson (B.V.).* Zurich, 1957.

Black, G. A. "James Thomson: His Translation of Heine," *Modern Language Review,* XXXI (Jan., 1936), 48–54.

Blunden, Edmund. Introduction to *The City of Dreadful Night and Other Poems.* London, 1932.

Bonner, Hypatia Bradlaugh. *Charles Bradlaugh: A Record of His Life and Work.* London, 1895. 2 vols.

———. "Childish Recollections of James Thomson ("B.V.")," *Our Corner,* VIII (Aug., 1886), 65–74.

———. "Letters of James Thomson ("B.V.")," *Our Corner,* VIII (Sept., 1886), 150–156.

[Bradlaugh, Charles.] "Reviews," *National Reformer,* XLIV (Nov. 9, 1884).

Briton, S. "A Great Poet's Prose," *Progress,* IV (Dec., 1884), 250–253.

"Bysshe Vanolis," *Times Literary Supplement,* June 9, 1932, p. 422.

Cavazza, E. Introduction to *The City of Dreadful Night.* Portland, Me.: Thomas Mosher, 1892.

Cazamian, Louis. *Etudes de Psychologie Littéraire.* Paris, 1913.

Chapman, Edward Mortimer. *English Literature in Account with Religion, 1800–1900.* Boston and New York, 1910.

Chauvet, Paul. *Sept Essais de Littérature Anglaise.* Paris, 1931.

Church, Richard. "Pale Melancholy," *Spectator,* CXLI (Oct., 1928), 479–480.

"City of Dreadful Night, The" (anon. rev.), *Academy,* V (June 6, 1874), 632.

"City of Dreadful Night, The" (anon. rev.), *Athenaeum* (May 1, 1880), pp. 560–562.

Cotten, Lyman A. "Leopardi and 'The City of Dreadful Night,'" *Studies in Philology,* XLII (July, 1945), 675–689.

———. "The Prose Writings of James Thomson ("B.V.")." Unpublished Ph.D. dissertation, Yale University, 1941.

Dahl, Curtis. "The Victorian Wasteland," *College English,* XVI (March, 1955), 341–347.
DeCamp, David. "Thomson's 'The City of Dreadful Night,'" *Explicator,* VII (Feb., 1949).
Dobell, Bertram. Introduction to *Essays, Dialogues and Thoughts of Giacomo Leopardi.* London, 1905.
———. Introduction to *Walt Whitman: The Man and the Poet.* London, 1910.
———. *The Laureate of Pessimism.* London, 1910.
———. Memoir in *The Poetical Works of James Thomson (B.V.).* London, 1895. 2 vols.
———. Memoir in *A Voice from the Nile and Other Poems.* London, 1884.
———. Preface to *The City of Dreadful Night and Other Poems.* London, 1899.
———. Preface to *Shelley, a Poem; with Other Writings Relating to Shelley, by the Late James Thomson* ('*B.V.*'). London, 1884.
Dobell, Bertram, and J. M. Wheeler. Bibliography in *The City of Dreadful Night.* Portland, Me., 1892.
Drinkwater, John. "The Poetry of the 'Seventies," in *The Eighteen-Seventies.* Cambridge, Eng., 1929.
Evans, B. Ifor. *English Poetry in the Later Nineteenth Century.* London, 1933.
Fairchild, Hoxie N. *Religious Trends in English Poetry.* Vol. IV. New York, 1957.
Flaws, Gordon G. "James Thomson: A Study," *Secular Review* (June 24, July 1, 1882).
Foakes, R. A. *The Romantic Assertion.* New Haven, 1958.
Foote, G. W. "James Thomson," *National Reformer,* LIII (March 31, April 7, 14, 21, 1889), 198, 213, 228, 250.
———. Preface to *Satires and Profanities.* London, 1884.
[Foote, G. W.] "James Thomson: The Man," *Progress,* III (April, 1884), 250–254.
———. "James Thomson: The Poet," *Progress,* III (June, 1884), 367–373.
Forsyth, R. A. "Evolutionism and the Pessimism of James Thomson (B.V.)," *Essays in Criticism,* XII (April, 1962), 148–166.
G., A. *James Thomson: Biographical and Bibliographical Sketch.* New York, 1893.
Gerould, G. H. Introduction to *Poems of James Thomson "B.V."* New York, 1927.
Harper, George M. "Blake's *Nebuchadnezzar* in 'The City of Dreadful Night,'" *Studies in Philology,* L (Jan., 1953), 68–80.

Harris, Frank. "James Thomson: An Unknown Immortal," *Contemporary Portraits: Second Series*. New York, 1919.

Hearn, Lafcadio. "Pessimists and Their Kindred," in *Interpretations of Literature*. New York, 1927. 2 vols.

Heath-Stubbs, John. *The Darkling Plain*. London, 1950.

"Heine on Crutches" (anon. rev.), *National Observer*, IX (1893), 343–344.

Hillier, Arthur Cecil. "James Thomson," *Dublin University Review* (Dec., 1885), pp. 351–365.

Hoffman, Harold. "An Angel in the City of Dreadful Night," *Sewanee Review*, XXXII (July, 1924), 317–335.

Hoyt, Arthur S. *The Spiritual Message of Modern English Poetry*. New York, 1924.

Hueffer, Ford Madox. *Memories and Impressions: A Study in Atmospheres*. New York and London, 1911.

Leatham, James. *James Thomson (B.V.): The Laureate of Pessimism*. Cottingham, Yorks., n.d.

LeRoy, Gaylord C. *Perplexed Prophets*. Philadelphia, 1953.

Letters of George Meredith. Collected and edited by his son. New York, 1912. 2 vols.

Lewin, Walter. Introduction to *Selections from Original Contributions by James Thomson to "Cope's Tobacco Plant."* Liverpool, 1889.

Little, James Stanley. "B.V.," *Literary World*, XLVII (1893), 124.

Maccall, William. *A Nirvana Trilogy: Three Essays on the Career and the Literary Labours of James Thomson*. London, 1886.

McGann, Jerome J. "James Thomson (B.V.): The Woven Hymns of Night and Day," *Studies in English Literature*, III (Autumn, 1963), 493–507.

Marks, Jeannette. "Disaster and Poetry: A Study of James Thomson (B.V.)," *North American Review*, CCXII (July, 1920), 93–109.

———. *Genius and Disaster*. London, 1928.

Marston, Philip Bourke. "The City of Dreadful Night and Other Poems," *Modern Thought* (May, 1881), pp. 105–108.

———. Introduction to Thomson's poetry in *The English Poets*. Ed. T. H. Ward. New York, 1885.

———. Obituary notice, *Athenaeum* (June, 1882).

Meeker, J. Edward. *The Life and Poetry of James Thomson (B.V.)*. New Haven, 1917.

Meester, Marie E. de. "Oriental Influences in the English Literature of the Nineteenth Century," *Anglistische Forschungen* (1915), pp. 67–70.

More, Paul E. "James Thomson ("B.V.")," *Nation,* LXXXV (Dec., 1907), 583–586.
———. *Shelburne Essays.* Series 5. New York, 1908.
"Necessitarian Poet, A" (anon. rev.), *Spectator,* XLVII (June 20, 1874), 780–782.
Neuburg, Victor. "James Thomson (B.V.)," *Freethinker,* LIV (Nov. 18, 25, Dec. 2, 1934), 723–725, 741–742, 762–763.
———. "James Thomson: Journalist," *Rationalist Annual* (1953), pp. 54–58.
Noel, Roden. Introduction to Thomson selections in *The Poets and the Poetry of the Century.* Ed. A. H. Miles. London, 1892.
Olivero, Federico. "Un Sequace del Leopardi: James Thomson," *Revista d'Italia,* XXV, no. 3 (1922), 403–414.
Peyre, Henri. "Les Sources du Pessimisme de Thomson," *Revue Anglo-Américaine,* II (Dec., 1924; Feb., 1925), 152–156, 217–231.
"Poet of To-day, A" (anon. rev.), *To-Day,* I (July, 1883), 311–319.
Power, William. *Robert Burns and Other Essays and Sketches.* London and Glasgow, 1926.
Powys, Llewelyn. "A Tragedy of Genius," *Freeman,* V (Sept., 1922), 609–611.
Quennell, Peter. "A Victorian Pessimist," *New Statesman and Nation,* IV (Aug., 1932), 235–236.
Reyburn, Marjorie L. "James Thomson in Central City," *University of Colorado Studies,* Series B, Studies in the Humanities, I, no. 2 (June, 1940), 183–203.
Ridler, Anne, ed. *Poems and Some Letters of James Thomson.* London: Centaur Press, 1963.
Robertson, J. M. Preface to *Poems, Essays, and Fragments.* London, 1892.
[Robertson, J. M.] "B.V.," *National Reformer,* LXI (Jan. 15, 1893), 41–42.
Rod, Edouard. *Marceaux Choisis des Littérature Étrangères.* Paris, 1899.
Ross, W. Stewart. "A Last Interview with a Man of Genius: James Thomson ("B.V.")," *Agnostic Journal* (April, 1889). Reprinted in *Roses and Rue.* London, 1890.
Rossetti, William M. *Some Reminiscences of William Michael Rossetti.* London, 1906. 2 vols.
Saintsbury, George. "The City of Dreadful Night," *Academy,* XVII (June, 1880), 432.
———. *A History of Nineteenth Century Literature.* New York, 1899.

———. "Vane's Story," *Academy*, XIX (Feb., 1881), 92–93.
Salt, Henry S. *Company I Have Kept*. London, 1930.
———. *The Life of James Thomson ("B.V.")*. London, 1889. Rev. eds.: London, 1898; London, 1914.
———. "The Poet of Pessimism," *Humane Review*, IX (1908), 141–147.
———. Preface to *The City of Dreadful Night and Other Poems*. London, 1932.
———. *Seventy Years among Savages*. New York, 1921.
———. "Some Extracts from James Thomson's Notebooks," *Scottish Art Review*, II (Aug., 1889), 91–93.
———. "Thomson and Thompson," *Rationalist Annual* (1929), pp. 56–60.
———. "The Works of James Thomson ("B.V.")," *Gentleman's Magazine*, XXXVI (June, 1886), 593–610. Reprinted in *Literary Sketches*. London, 1888.
Schaefer, William D. "The Two Cities of Dreadful Night," *PMLA*, LXXVII (Dec., 1962), 609–615.
Schiller, F. C. S. *Must Philosophers Disagree?* London, 1934.
Sharp, William. Introduction to Philip Bourke Marston, *For a Song's Sake, and Other Stories*. London, 1887. Reprinted in *Papers Critical and Reminiscent*. New York, 1921.
———. "The Life of James Thomson," *Academy*, XXXV (April, 1889), 247.
Simcox, G. A. "A New Poet," *Fortnightly Review*, XXXIV (July, 1880), 31–41.
Stedman, Edmund C. "Twelve Years of British Song," *Century Magazine*, XXXIV (Oct., 1887), 909–910.
Symonds, John Addington. Letters to unknown correspondent published in Horatio F. Brown, *Biography of John A. Symonds*. New York, 1895.
[Symons, Arthur.] "James Thomson," *Saturday Review*, LXXIX (Feb., 1895), 215. Reprinted in *Studies in Two Literatures*. London, 1897.
Three Rossettis. Unpublished letters to and from Dante Gabriel, Christina, and William Rossetti. Cambridge, Mass., 1937.
"Truth of Midnight, The," *Nation*, VII (May, 1910), 271–272.
Vachot, Charles. "James Thomson et l'Amérique," *Revue de Littérature Comparée*, XXII (Oct.–Dec., 1948), 487–507.
———. "James Thomson et l'Orient," *Revue de Littérature Comparée*, XXVII (1953), 287–300.
"Vision of the Unseen, The" (anon. rev.), *Nation*, LXXXV (Dec., 1907), 535.
Walker, Hugh. *The Literature of the Victorian Era*. Cambridge, Eng., 1910.

Walker, Imogene. *James Thomson (B.V.): A Critical Study.* Ithaca, 1950.

Wallis, N. Hardy. "James Thomson and His 'City of Dreadful Night,'" in *Essays by Diverse Hands,* ed. Right Hon. Earl of Lytton, XIV (1935), 137–165.

Weissel, Josefine. "James Thomson der Jüngere: Sein Leben und Seine Werke," *Wiener Beiträge zur Englischen Philologie,* XXIV (1906).

Welby, T. E. *Back Numbers.* London, 1929.

———. *The Victorian Romantics, 1850–1870.* London, 1929.

Wheeler, J. M. "James Thomson," *Freethinker* (Feb. 10, 1889).

"Why James Thomson Did Not Kill Himself" (anon. rev.), *Spectator,* XLII (March 23, 1889), 394–395.

Wolff, William. "James Thomson, B.V.: A Study in Poetic Melancholy," *Poetry Review,* XXVIII (1937), 275–281.

Woodbridge, Benjamin M. "Poets and Pessimism: Vigny, Housman et Alii," *Romanic Review,* XXXV (Feb., 1944), 43–51.

———. "A Strange Visitor in 'The City of Dreadful Night,'" *Dial,* LIX (Dec., 1915), 603–604.

Woods, Margaret L. "Poets of the 'Eighties," in *The Eighteen Eighties.* Cambridge, Eng., 1930.

Worcester, David. "James Thomson the Second: Studies in the Life and Poetry of 'B.V.'" Unpublished Ph.D. dissertation, Harvard University, 1933.

Wright, T. R. "Life of James Thomson (B.V.)," *Literary Guide and Rationalist Review* (April, May, 1889).

Wyndham, Horace. "James Thomson, Duke of York's Boy and Poet," *The Regiment: An Illustrated Military Journal for Everybody,* XXIV (Oct. 19, 1907), 367.

Zabel, Morton D. "James Thomson," *Poetry,* XXXII (July, 1928), 229–233.

———. "Two Versions of the Nineteenth Century," *Poetry,* XLIV (Aug., 1934), 270–276.

Index

Schaefer, William D.

James Thomson.